W9-CCI-510

THEOLOGICAL INVESTIGATIONS

Volume XVIII

THEOLOGICAL INVESTIGATIONS

THEOLOGICAL INVESTIGATIONS

VOLUME XVIII
GOD AND REVELATION

by
KARL RAHNER

Translated by Edward Quinn

CROSSROAD · NEW YORK

1983
The Crossroad Publishing Company
575 Lexington Avenue, New York, N.Y. 10022

A translation of the first four sections of
SCHRIFTEN ZUR THEOLOGIE, XIII
© Copyright 1978 by Benziger Verlag
Zürich Einsiedeln Köln

This translation © Darton, Longman & Todd Ltd. 1983

All rights reserved. No part of this book may be reproduced,
stored in a retrieval system, or transmitted, in any form
or by any means, electronic, mechanical, photocopying,
recording or otherwise, without the written permission of
The Crossroad Publishing Company.

Library of Congress Catalog Card Number: 61-8189
ISBN: 0-8245-0571-9
Printed in the United States of America

CONTENTS

PART ONE

Theological Hermeneutics

1

YESTERDAY'S HISTORY OF DOGMA AND THEOLOGY FOR TOMORROW

The author of the following reflections from the field of systematic theology is not at all sure if he is right to assume that he is raising what to some extent is a new question or whether it only seems to be new because of his inadequate knowledge of the relevant literature. Even then however he could take comfort in the thought that many others might also lack this sort of knowledge and consequently that his reflections could be useful to them.

To anticipate formally the basic question to be considered, it may be stated as follows: From the period of Catholic modernism—that is, roughly speaking, from the beginning of the present century— reflection has been largely concentrated on the nature of the development of dogma as such. It was not a question only of describing in a historical sequence the history of particular dogmas (this had been done from the time of Petavius [d. 1652], with increasing interest of course and with continually improved methods), but mainly of examining the more general problem of the nature of development of dogma as such and as a whole and of the limits to this development. In this connection various theories were put forward, all of which aimed on the one hand at upholding the permanent identity of the Christian faith and on the other hand at recognizing without embarrassment the undeniable fact that the Church's faith and dogma have had a history, and at seeing these two realities as compatible, at reconciling the identity of faith and its actual history. It is no part of our task here to set out these different theories of the development of dogma, which tended mainly toward an increasingly relaxed acceptance of the true historicity of dogmas, in order to avoid seeing this history of dogma simply (as happened at first) as a logically conclusive explication of what had always been said, simply restating the old truth in new words. What is important here however seems to be the hitherto too little or perhaps not at all considered feature of the theology of development of dogma, that it has been too retrospective within the field of Catholic theology: in other words this theory of the history of dogma made too little effort to develop out of its historical observations methodical and hermeneutical principles which could and should be applied to open questions of a current or future development of dogma.

In the first half of the twentieth century there were historians of dogma (we may recall, for example, great historians of theology such as Martin Grabmann or A. Landgraf) who tacitly or expressly favoured the opinion that (apart from marginal areas like Mariology) the history of dogma had more or less reached its close, that— admittedly after a very long process of development—dogmas had now been given their definitive formulations, and consequently that theological science (apart from passing on its final achievements in systematic theology) could continue to work as an academic study almost in principle merely as a retrospective survey of the history of dogma. Certain papal doctrinal statements too (as recently as those of Pius XII) on the Catholic understanding of the development of dogma give the impression of admitting a history of dogma for former times, but of regarding the results now attained (especially with reference to the terminology involved) as unsurpassable, not in need of any further interpretation and no longer open to any real modification in the future.

It is however really obvious that the history of dogma (in the widest sense of the term) continues and must continue. The task of transposing Christian faith into modern horizons of understanding is not one which the Church and its theology have yet adequately fulfilled, although this does not mean that the task has not been appreciated at all or is not yet being slowly taken in hand. But there is still a vast amount to be done in regard to this task, which has existed from the time of the Enlightenment. The history of dogma therefore continues and must continue. But then the question arises whether it might not be possible to derive from what has happened hitherto in the history of dogma and the history of theology insights and principles (of the most varied kinds), the knowledge and application of which could be useful and perhaps indispensable for current and future history of dogma.

It seems obvious that a question of this kind must in principle be answered in the affirmative. But has there been sufficient reflection on these experiences in the course of the history of dogma and on the insights and principles drawn from them for the progress of this history? Are these insights and principles available to the history of dogma at the present time, when new controversies and new confrontations between the magisterium and academic theology are emerging, when 'new' interpretations of the old dogma are being put forward? Are they stated clearly enough to be able to determine this theological development, to allow it perhaps to run its course more peacefully and rapidly, to help to avoid unnecessary conflicts between the magisterium and modern theology, between 'conservative' and 'progressive' Catholics?

Whether this is an old question or a new one is in fact irrelevant. But if we observe or are involved in those concrete events in the Church today which can be subsumed under the notion of development of dogma, we shall not be able to say that the answer to the question is so clear as to make an adequate impact on the course of these events on all sides in theological controversies. Otherwise, would it have been possible, in the schemata prepared by the commission of the Second Vatican Council before the latter's opening, to put forward as definable truths propositions which twenty years later can scarcely count on a majority among the theologians in the world or among the ordinary believers: propositions, for instance, like those on monogenism or on the limbo of infants? Otherwise, how are we to explain the widespread discontent of many theologians (and especially of moral theologians) in regard to declarations of the magisterium after the last council, theologians who have the greatest respect for the Church's teaching authority and its intentions but who also have the impression that in these declarations too little account is taken of the historicity and historical relativity involved in former statements of the magisterium? Too much of what was said in the past is merely 'repeated'; statements are made with too little open contact with the modern human sciences or even with contemporary theology.

The following reflections will be concerned with these insights and principles. And it is a question here only of quite simple, really obvious insights and principles, not of profound and difficult hermeneutical theories in the light of which the present course of the history of dogma and theology would, as far as possible, have to be guided. A deeply probing theory of hermeneutical principles of this kind for the further course of the history of dogma is not possible here, if only because this sort of thing would presuppose an exact and definite theory of development of dogma as a whole, which of course does not exist in any generally accepted form and certainly could not be worked out here. The insights and principles to be put forward here are derived—as will become apparent—from the straightforward observation of events of the history of dogma up to the present time. These will simply be mentioned. At the same time there will be no attempt to work out a system even of these insights and principles; they will merely be placed one after another in a somewhat arbitrary sequence, since a 'system' of such principles and its substantiation is of course also impossible here. The principles will be illustrated and authenticated by brief allusions to particular occurrences in the history of dogma. At the same time there is no need to offer historical documentation for these examples from the previous history of dogma, since they are well known and the documentation of the historical sources is easily accessible for anyone who is interested in it.

With these occurrences from the previous history of dogma (together with the history of theology) it is not of decisive importance for us here whether it is a question of the history of a dogma in the strict sense of the term or merely one of the history of a doctrine put forward by the magisterium as indeed 'authentic' but with minimal binding force. There is no need to explain the special reasons why in the present context this distinction, important as it is in itself, can be neglected with reference to our examples, which are themselves presented unsystematically. But what is important in regard to these examples is the fact that in many if not all of them this development led to 'new' dogmas or to 'new' doctrines presented as authentic by the magisterium. This means that the hermeneutical principle implicitly involved in such a doctrinal development (if the implications can be clearly shown) are tacitly recognized as legitimate by the magisterium itself; not only the new teaching, but also the way that led to it (by and large), is recognized by the magisterium as legitimate and thus as applicable at least in principle to other cases to the extent to which the magisterium accepts this 'new' doctrine as its own and puts it forward as binding. What exactly is meant by this will be seen from the examples with which we are attempting to illustrate and authenticate the insights and principles to be put forward for a still continuing and future history of dogma and theology. With these reservations and demarcations of our theme we may now attempt to come directly to the essential problem.

I

In the future also the history of dogma will be beset with friction, accompanied by struggles, conflicts, denunciations. All this happened so often in the past that we cannot expect things to be different in the future, even though the human style of these bitter controversies as a driving force of history today and (it is to be hoped) in the future is assuming by and large more humane and more tolerant forms.

In the past the Church's official declarations and determinations of obligatory teaching generally presented the matter as if the true doctrine had 'actually' always been clear and obvious even before these official determinations, as if the opponents of these teachings had been stupid and malicious and as if the doctrine concerned—being obvious and comprehensibly explained directly in Scripture or in earlier tradition—had been questioned and disputed only out of malicious impiety. Countless examples of this could be cited, but we shall spare ourselves the trouble of enumerating them here. This denunciation of opponents as stupid and malicious was (it might almost be said, from the New Testament onward) the style that declarations of the Church's magisterium formerly simply took for granted, which today seems to have been abandoned.

But, as opposed to this interpretation of history, it is obvious that, after achieving the result of a particular teaching, this history itself continued in the midst of many difficulties, obscurities, and frictions that cannot be blamed unilaterally on stupid and malicious heretics, but are involved in the very nature of the case and amount to the toll exacted by the historicity of human knowledge, even in the dimension of faith. As new questions emerge in a way that cannot be blamed simply on the malice or human presumption and pride of theologians, it cannot be maintained that everything is actually clear from the outset or that an answer is immediately available for every question. This way of thinking is possible only in the light of a theory of development of dogma that sees the latter as a purely logical explication of what was already present and the concrete occasions of an historical character for such a logical explication as purely external stimuli, without which the explication could still have taken place in principle. But such a theory of the development of dogma fails to appreciate the historicity of truth itself and will scarcely be seriously maintained today.

The average theologian today may simply take it for granted that the Council of Chalcedon was right and that it interpreted the Council of Ephesus correctly. But what difficulties, obscurities, and terminological confusion had in reality to be overcome in the couple of decades between the two councils and how great were the difficulties afterwards which well-meaning defenders of a Cyrillic Christology of Ephesus felt after Chalcedon (actually up to the present time) in pursuing this path as the right and necessary one?

If the history of dogma and the history of theology went on in the past only in the midst of friction and bitter struggle, we cannot simply expect to be spared this sort of thing today and tomorrow. There has been, if for once we may be so rash as to use the term, a change of emphasis in the Church's awareness of the truth. Where the stress was formerly laid on the objective dignity of truth as such (which was also assumed only too readily to be clearly evident in itself or in its fundamental theological presuppositions and to be accessible to every intelligence [cf., for example, DS 3009, 3013]), there is now a recognition and respect for the dignity of the subjective conscience in regard to truth, which can never be eliminated and which found its distinctive confirmation, again after considerable conflict, at the Second Vatican Council. It is to be hoped that this respect for conscience will determine more than formerly the style of such controversies (including the very practical consequences which must be thought out more carefully than they have been hitherto). The result will be that a questioning of this change of emphasis can never be explained again as formerly almost solely by stupidity or malice and that it will be impossible to declare the questioner a 'subjective' heretic.

II

In the future also the history of dogma can continue with consider-able revision of former (authentic) declarations of the Church's mag-isterium. The situation is not, as is frequently implied in textbooks of the history of dogma, that the history of dogma and theology runs only from what is less to what is more clear, from global to more articulate statements, that it is merely a beautiful and undisturbed 'unfolding' of the original substance of faith.

While the development of dogma in the strictest sense may run definitely and, in the last resort, on a 'single track'—in other words, an actually attained and absolute assent of the Church's sense of faith is not revisable (as 'erroneous') retrospectively (although this process which led to an absolute assent of faith remains open to the future)—that is not to say that a development of faith and theology has taken place and will take place in the future only in the sense of a frictionless explication. On the contrary, this development is very often also marked by wrong decisions on the part of the magiste-rium, wrong decisions which add a further element of friction to that which is necessarily always involved in the historicity of truth, dis-turbing the course of historical development and making it humanly more difficult and more bitter.

Again, all this is obvious if we look back, but not readily noticed by the Church's magisterium in the present course of history. In practice, the magisterium not infrequently acts as if its authentic but basically revisable (and therefore possibly erroneous) doctrinal statements were factors to be respected for ever. Consequently these doctrinal statements then refer to earlier examples, even though the latter as such are not absolutely binding, that is, strictly speaking, they prove only that the earlier teaching was the same as the present and therefore scarcely give a greater weight to the new statement than it would possess without such a quotation; this is evident today since, after learning from the history of dogma of the temporally long duration of an authentic teaching, as distinct from former times we shall not attach so much importance to proving its objective correctness. (We may recall for instance the approval of torture and of the burning of heretics from Innocent IV, against Nicholas I [DS 648], up to Leo X [DS 1483] or the prohibition of usury even in times when it certainly could no longer be justified by the existing economic structure.)

At the present time also it is scarcely possible to find a declaration of the Church's magisterium in which the universal principles of any normal fundamental theology even of the most orthodox kind in regard to the degrees of binding force of such declarations are provided expressly and openly together with the particular declaration in question. Even today, for dubious ('educational') reasons, the impression is given in such authentic declarations that they are obviously not open to revision and that they could not possibly turn out later to be mistaken and to place an obstacle on the path that the history of faith and theology will actually follow in the future. But there are and there will continue to be such obstacles, since the Church's magisterium can err and often has erred in its authentic declarations, and this is obviously possible also in future.

It is scarcely necessary here to cite further examples from history of these wrong decisions. For the fact itself was quite frankly acknowledged in a letter by the German episcopate. Nor is this the place to consider how precisely the respect due to such doctrinal statements can be combined with the necessity and permissibility of allowing for the possibility of error in these declarations. In this connection it need only be said quite frankly and without prejudice that this question was not given a sufficiently clear answer even in *Lumen Gentium* at the Second Vatican Council, since it is not explained (no. 25) how the recognition of the 'supreme magisterium' and the 'sincere adherence' demanded for merely authentic doctrinal declarations of this magisterium can co-exist with a critique of these statements which may be the right and even the duty of theologians.

III

Even truths that are absolutely binding dogmatically can be stated and handed down with ideas actually held at the time, with conceptual models and accepted modes of understanding, which are transmitted inseparably and as a matter of course with the essential statement and later turn out to be entirely without binding force or even to be false.

It can and must rightly be said (as we mentioned above) that the history of dogma properly speaking moves along a single track and cannot be revised retrospectively in such a way that a defined proposition could later be declared to be absolutely erroneous; nor could this happen even if the kind of explication of faith used in this connection cannot be established conclusively in a purely logical argument from more fundamental data of faith. None of this however excludes the possibility that in the transmission and expression of dogmas properly speaking there may be inseparably mingled ideas, interpretations, etc., which are not part of the binding content of the article of faith concerned but which have not been explicitly separated from this article at a particular epoch in history by traditional theology or even by the Church's magisterium, and for historical reasons cannot be separated up to a certain point in time. There may be such amalgams (if we may use this admittedly problematic expression) even with dogmas properly so called.

Not every idea then that was actually but without further reflection brought to bear at a particular time on the elucidation of the meaning of an article of faith is in principle really an indissoluble part of this article itself. This must be clearly understood today in regard to the future history of dogma and realistically taken into account in interpreting the teaching of Vatican I in particular that a dogma must continue to be upheld for ever in the 'sense' it had at its first proclamation. There are amalgams of this kind; in view of the historicity of truth they are simply unavoidable; they will remain (even though in such a way that the elimination of one such amalgam means that another takes its place).

If, for instance, it is shown historically that the Fathers of Trent in their teaching on transsubstantiation unanimously assumed as a matter of course a particular meaning of the 'substance' of bread and wine, this is far from saying that this notion of substance, actually held at Trent and not excluded from what was really meant in a dogmatic sense, still remains binding today for the interpretation of transsubstantiation. If Augustine regarded a directly paternal procreation and the libido involved in it as the necessary vehicle for the transmission of original sin (with the result that, even up to recent times, the very fact that Jesus had no earthly father was seen as a reason why he was free from original sin) and explained original sin in this way as Catholic dogma, this is far from saying that we should or even could consider *this* understanding of original sin today as dogma. If Pius XII (and after him the preparatory commission of the

Second Vatican Council) still thought that monogenism is an indispensable and unrenounceable (even directly definable as dogma) element of the Catholic doctrine of original sin, we may nevertheless hold a different opinion today and, while upholding the doctrine of original sin and its essential meaning, eliminate a monogenistic interpretation of this doctrine as an historically conditioned amalgam, even though the theology of former times and the magisterium never thought and could not have thought of this possibility. Pius XII declared that it is part of the Catholic faith (DS 3896) that the human soul is directly created by God. But, as could easily be proved historically, in this statement (correct in itself) he had in mind a conceptual model which is not shared today by many theologians (with their theory of the self-transcendence—even as essential—of the living person), and Pius XII did not think of such a possibility of distinguishing between what is really meant in the dogma and the conceptual model that can be eliminated from it.

If today, as a matter of course, we stick to the teaching that Jesus 'founded' the Church and instituted seven sacraments, we shall see, in the light of historical studies, a number of things differently in these statements and eliminate interpretations accepted at first without reflection, even though the possibility of these distinctions was not appreciated in former times. In the traditional doctrine of inspiration could we not distinguish between a kind of 'authorship' of God as part of salvation history, which can truly be predicated of God, and a literary 'authorship' that must not be predicated of him, and thus eliminate from this doctrine of God as the author of Scripture amalgams which can be made intelligible today only with difficulty? Otherwise we must qualify the statement that God is the 'author' of Scripture in a literary sense with so many reservations about its purely 'analogical' meaning that any understanding of Scriptural inspiration is made more difficult instead of being facilitated.

In the light of the history of faith and the history of ideas, perhaps the most significant and almost terrifying example of an historical development of dogma as understood here can be seen in both the unity and the distinction between the imminent expectation on the part of the historical pre-Easter Jesus and what the Church today thinks is really meant in this imminent expectation. While our faith remains the same also in regard to this question, the distinction became evident only in a long process which can be seen at work already in the New Testament itself but even today is not completely closed and yet is legitimate. Of course many other examples could be produced of such amalgams in a dogma and of their elimination from that dogma in its obligatory sense. But those mentioned will be sufficient.

Such a process of elimination must of course make simultaneously clear that the sameness of the dogma in the old sense is assured and the effort to do this must not be regarded in principle as dubious, as a feeble and cowardly compromise between holding on verbally to a traditional doctrine and its formulations on the one hand and a new perception on the other which, if expressed honestly, would presumably be bound to exclude the previous teaching as erroneous. This is not the situation. But neither must the proof of the preservation of a doctrine under old and new, mutually diverse conceptual models, interpretations, etc., be handled in such a way as if it had to be shown with historical certainty that this distinction had been clearly seen even in earlier times and the old interpretation understood even then as no more than an interpretation.

It is of course obvious that such processes of distinguishing will continue also in future, without there being any need to prophesy which of them will crop up today or soon. It is really obvious that the processes of elimination will go on only in the midst of friction and struggle. For what is involved is precisely the question (at first obscure) of whether something is part of what is really meant or merely an historically conditioned interpretation of the latter, belonging to a particular period and able to be eliminated at a later period. It not infrequently happens that the Church's sense of faith (as the sum total of historically conditioned convictions of the faithful and also of the teachers in the Church) has to get accustomed psychologically only slowly and with difficulty to the knowledge that the elimination of such an amalgam and the new interpretation formulated in the light of new horizons of understanding really maintain the dogma intact. If this is true, the magisterium and theology must at times allow patiently for shorter or longer periods during which the justification or nonjustification of this sort of elimination remains uncertain, when a decision for one side or the other cannot be quickly and impatiently enforced (periods which must be endured with patience and confidence). (We may recall, for instance, new interpretations of the doctrine of transsubstantiation or the question of the precise sense in which a pre-existence of the Logos present for us in Jesus is to be understood.)

All this of course presupposes a religious education of the faithful, to prevent them from assuming that these periods of some uncertainty always and in every case represent a threat to the actual substance of faith and ought to be brought to an end as quickly as possible by a decree of the Church's magisterium. It also presupposes that in a period of this kind the theologians, too, will not proclaim their new interpretations too apodictically and 'infallibly'. Such periods formerly could in a sense be taken for granted simply because a slow tempo was imposed purely as a result of the sociological and technological preconditions of theological dialogue; today we would have to create deliberately the pauses for reflection that are necessary for the magisterium and theology. In many cases the magisterium ought not to try to reach a quick decision, but should stimulate and gently accompany such a process of reflection.

We may be permitted to extend these reflections with the aid of some further considerations, even though the latter perhaps reach a little beyond our essential theme. For the sake of brevity we shall refrain from illustrating them with examples. If however a concrete case is required for the elucidation of these further considerations, we may recall the above-mentioned example of Jesus' imminent expectation. We shall continue to make use here of the term 'amalgam', even though we are aware that what it means is objectively very complex and would, and perhaps should, be much more precisely stated and differentiated epistemologically and hermeneutically; but that is not possible here. We are starting out from the phenomenon already observed, that a particular truth was stated at a particular epoch only together with such an amalgam, that it could not then have been stated differently at all (since at that period a different conceptual model or anything of the kind was simply not concretely available as an amalgam), and that the objectively possible distinction between the truth as it was actually meant and the amalgam could not by any means be explicitly perceived.

We distinguish now between the question (1) how a statement of this kind as a unity of what is really meant and its amalgam is to be evaluated against the background of the historical period in which it emerged, and the question (2) how it is to be assessed (in its unity between what is meant and its amalgam) at the present time when this distinction is explicitly perceived and the opportunity exists in principle of possibly excluding the amalgam itself as false or perhaps false or as dispensable and replaceable by a different conceptual model.

The first question is meaningful with reference to the evaluation of the statement as made at that time only if this evaluation is made in the light of the present time. For, without this present point of reference, the question cannot be raised at all. Seen in the light of that time (even though it belongs to that time) the problem simply does not exist. Are we to say that the statement was 'erroneous' also at that time (even though this can only now be perceived), since it was in fact made in a unity with an (*ex supposito*) erroneous amalgam, since the possible distinction between what (according to our present-day judgment) was really meant and the amalgam itself was not explicitly considered, and since moreover purely historically it is not certain that the amalgam itself was not then expressed with the same absolute assent with which what was really meant as the content of faith was affirmed? We think that such a statement in the situation of its own historical period cannot be qualified as erroneous or, if it is so qualified, such linguistic usage should be expressly noted: that is, attention should be drawn to the fact that the qualification of error itself in reality withdraws the statement in question from its own original historical situation. For a statement that cannot in a particular historical period express what is supposed to be true otherwise than in the light of a particular conceptual model, etc. ('amalgam'), may not be qualified as erroneous, since in that historical situation it is the only possible way of expressing the truth that is really meant. Anyone who made such a statement at that time was speaking the truth at that time. It must also be remembered that a 'present-day' distinction between what is really meant and the amalgam is not made in such a way that now what is really meant is stated 'in chemical purity', for its own sake alone, but this statement is again made in the light of different and still historically conditioned conceptual models; which does not of course mean that the models and horizons of understanding involved in this exchange must simply be regarded as absolutely equal in value and equally good among themselves.

We come to the second question. If and in so far as such a statement is transferred into a different situation of understanding, if nevertheless it is considered as a unity of what is meant and its amalgam, if in this transposition into a new situation of understanding the amalgam is seen explicitly as false or as not binding or as replaceable, then of course the statement involved (in its unity with the amalgam) can be qualified as 'erroneous'. But then it really is not today in any sense the statement that was formerly made. It was not erroneous, but it has become erroneous, because it is now made in the light of horizons of understanding which were by no means those involved in its original form of expression.

All that we have been saying here refers objectively and methodically to specifically religious statements. We have no intention of making any statement of universal hermeneutical significance. Nor are we going to consider the problem of an elimination of such amalgams which might lead eventually to the elimination of what is 'really' meant, a process of elimination leading eventually to the destruction of any real meaning of a religious statement, ultimately depriving it of all meaning. On this it need only be said that a religious statement in the last resort points not to what is drained of meaning, but to the ineffable mystery that we call God, and it is this reference alone which makes a statement a religious one. In other words, these processes of elimination are basically continually recurring events pointing to that mystery and must occur over and over again in the history of abiding religious truth, since this liberating and hopeful approach to the mystery of God must take place in the light of continually new historical situations of truth.

IV

In this history of dogma, in its further course and in its presentation, there must always be a recourse to a more fundamental global approach to faith, from which, if often only with very little reflection, a particular theological doctrinal statement emerges, a statement to be examined and tested in the light of the past history of dogma and theology and of possible future developments; this recourse to the actual point of origin of a particular statement can also provide a criterion for the correct understanding of the statement and for a possible and perhaps necessary elimination of traditional interpretations from it.

In the light of its nature and according to the evidence of an actual *history* of dogma, the Church's dogma, in the form of its individual statements and articulations, can be understood and expressed today less than ever as a purely additive sum total of individual propositions, each of these being presented as based themselves on individual statements of Scripture or of former declarations of the magisterium. Each individual statement must be presented in its coherence with the faith as one and whole and with the original and unitive centre of the reality of faith. Otherwise the teaching of Vatican II on the 'hierarchy of truths' amounts to idle talk or a feeble excuse.

The original one and unitive event of the definitive, eschatological revelation in Christianity is not something made up subsequently (not even subjectively) by adding together a sum total of individual statements to be simply accepted, seen as communicated separately by God as and when he chose to do so. It is the one event of God's most authentic self-communication, occurring everywhere in the world and in history in the Holy Spirit offered to every human being; as such it has itself the character of revelation of the truth and finds in Jesus crucified and risen its complete historical tangibility and eschatological irreversibility. (This description of the most fundamental event of revelation is not meant to be taken as the only possible or even as the only adequate characterization; but there is in fact and in content such a basic substance of the most fundamental event of revelation in the light of which individual articles of faith can and must be both positively and critically understood, even though conversely this most fundamental event of revelation itself must be grasped over and over again through the individual events of revelation and through the individual statements objectifying these events: that is, there is a mutual interdependence—a 'circle'—between these two factors.)

This recourse to the most fundamental event of revelation is often necessary and legitimate also with reference even to individual statements of the New Testament and is in fact used (more or less deliberately) in order to define more precisely in the light of the analogy of faith the actual meaning or the real status of individual

statements of Scripture. This of course is not to say that this fundamental event of salvation history, grace, and revelation, together
with its eschatological irreversibility in Christ, is not also attested
expressly and thematically already in Scripture itself. A recourse of
this kind is particularly necessary in order to make clear (possibly
with the aid of distinctions) the meaning and limits of later declarations of the Church's magisterium. This continually fresh recourse
to the original and unifying centre of faith (which is always active in
the history of dogma even though it may often occur metahistorically and cannot be shown historically to be very clearly involved in
individual cases in the course of the past history of dogma) certainly
does not mean at all (as already pointed out) that development of
dogma (that is, the explicitation of the original and global experience
of revelation) follows anything but a one-track course into individual
statements; on the contrary, it can be shown to be quite compatible
with the fact that an explicitation of this kind, if and when it has led
to an individual, particular statement, can no longer be revised retrospectively in the sense that the statement in question might later
be declared to be erroneous. Nor could it be so described even if
such an explicitation of faith, which took place at an earlier stage,
cannot be reconstructed and shown rationally to be conclusive in a
purely logical argument.

This understanding of the development of dogma in the Catholic
sense however does not exclude but in fact includes the necessity of
a further question about the original understanding of faith. Otherwise the systematic theologian, for instance, would need to practice
only Denzinger theology and could spare himself the trouble of doing biblical theology or might even regard the latter as no more than
historical curiosity. (May it perhaps be suggested, to take one example, that the Credo of the People of God of Paul VI on the whole
follows too closely the style of a Denzinger theology—that is, states
too positivistically the Christian faith, making too little attempt to
derive it from what we understand here as the basic substance of the
event of revelation and thus makes it more difficult for people today
to assimilate the meaning and status of the individual articles of
faith?)

If, for example, we want to know what the doctrine of the sacramental character is supposed to mean today and in what sense it is
binding for us, it is not sufficient to appeal merely to Augustine's

teaching or merely to collect and interpret and systematize the later declarations of the magisterium; we must also ask how Augustine came to know all this four hundred years after the Gospel; we must ask what was the point of origin (up to a point, to be inferred only metahistorically) of this doctrine of the sacramental character; what the character implies and what it does not imply; consequently in what sense the traditional teaching is really dogmatically binding, how much of it is interpretation and free theological speculation: a question which can certainly be addressed also to declarations of the Church's magisterium, while answers to it must be worked out in the light of declarations still to be made by the magisterium. There are also many other questions which must be regarded today as open in sacramental theology and which have no prospect of finding a real and convincing answer, if we appeal only to 'Denzinger' or other explicit declarations of the magisterium in the past. On the one hand we must form a truly historically convincing idea of the meaning of the statement that (or how?) the sacraments have their origin from Jesus ('instituted' by him) and on the other hand we must consider what is the connection of the individual sacraments with the nature of the Church as 'basic sacrament' of salvation. Only in this way can we hope at the present time to find a plain answer, for example, to the question of who can be a recipient of the sacrament of holy orders (a woman?), what sacramental signs may perhaps be sufficient in extraordinary cases, how the one sacrament of holy orders may possibly be differentiated into individual sacramental functions (differing in character and grade), etc.

The further questions, of which we are thinking here and which may certainly serve as a critical criterion in regard to the traditional understanding of a theological statement, appear generally in traditional textbook theology under the heading of 'reasons of convenience'. But this way of categorizing them only tends to conceal the actual nature of this recourse and prevents a correct appraisal of the process of development of a dogma and of its continually new reconstruction in the light of the most authentic original centre of the event of revelation.

At least one example of what is meant here may be mentioned. In the Apostolic Constitution *Munificentissimus Deus* in 1950, on the bodily assumption of Mary into definitive salvation, there is first of all a long historical survey of testimonies from the theology and piety of the past to this dogmatic statement. Taken by themselves, these testimonies may perhaps be considered unsatisfactory, since they appeared at so great a distance in time from the New Testament and the primitive Church and may perhaps show that the later Church held this view but cannot make the doctrine absolutely convincing as a truth binding in faith. But then the constitution (DS 3900–3901) uses also what we have described here as a 'recourse' behind an individual statement to a more fundamental and global understanding of faith. We are not discussing here whether this recourse in the present constitution is satisfying in every respect (there is no appeal, for instance, to general eschatology; the body-soul unity of the human person is not always and everywhere made sufficiently effective). But the constitution nevertheless looks to the global and original understanding of faith as one and whole that the Church has of Mary and her function in salvation history and in that light justifies the statement there defined.

Even if it is not directed to the originally one revelation, but to a fundamental particular reality of faith dependent on the former and at the same time related to the theological statement in question, such a recourse is not simply to be depreciated as based on reasons of convenience produced subsequently to support an already established statement. For if it is decided with adequate historical certainty that this dogma cannot seriously be understood as a statement explicitly and formally taught from apostolic times, this recourse is in principle the real source of the statement, whether the explication of the latter from that source (as in the constitution above-mentioned) is sufficiently clear and comprehensive) or whether in this connection (theologically speaking) a great deal is left to be desired.

Such a recourse (to return to our general reflections) is not necessarily and always a recourse to what has always been more clearly and explicitly formulated; the recourse can certainly be from an explicit statement already present (in Scripture or tradition) in the Church's awareness of faith to a global but more fundamental reality lying behind it, a reality which itself becomes clearer and more explicit in this recourse but which thus in its comprehensive unity becomes more clearly evident as indispensable to the Church's awareness of faith than the very statement from which the appeal was made in the first place.

The recourse to this originating reality of faith, either already explicitly present or only more clearly reflected in itself, is wholly suitable to provide a critical criterion for determining the exact meaning and the limitations of a theological statement, even though the latter has itself been established dogmatically as binding.

How, for example, is the question to be decided (if it should turn out to be unavoidable) whether a material identity of the risen body with the glorified body is implied in the dogma of the resurrection of the body (as very many theologians have maintained, even as a dogma, up to very recent times) if there is no recourse behind the individual dogmatic statement about the resurrection of the body to a more fundamental conviction of faith in regard to the abiding unity (even in salvation history) of the human being as body and soul and to the basic conviction of that person's definitive coming to be with God, even though recourse to such a basic conviction would mean that the latter was all the more clearly formulated? How are we to grasp properly today what is really meant by transsubstantiation without such a recourse to a more fundamental, more global understanding of the eucharist? How are we to avoid today an always latent tritheism (which, despite all verbal orthodoxy, appears illogically but actually to affect our explanations of the doctrine of the Trinity) and to interpret correctly the dogmatically binding teaching on the 'immanent' Trinity, unless we continually and repeatedly reflect on its actual point of origin for us, on the doctrine of the Trinity of God in the economy of salvation? How can we make historically credible today the doctrine of the institution of all the sacraments by Jesus Christ, if we do not have recourse to the doctrine of the Church as the primordial sacrament originating in Christ, of the Church as the abiding presence of God's irreversible self-promise made historically tangible in its word? Recourses of this kind of course do no more than reconstruct as well as possible the ways in which the Church's sense of faith extends from its global and fundamental knowledge to particular statements and forms of expression which have already appeared in the course of the history of faith and which from that standpoint alone acquire their formal binding force as matters of faith; they are not however merely pious arguments based on subsequently discovered reasons of convenience, but the way in which we can and must today genuinely achieve an understanding of faith. They provide also a critical criterion which however must in principle respect the authority of the

Church's magisterium, but which may question purely authentic interpretations of a dogma when they hand on the latter together with uneliminated amalgams.

All that has been said is still very vague; it could be formulated and substantiated more precisely only in a comprehensive and multidimensional theory of the development of dogma. But what has been said seems anyway to provide an understanding which results from the previous history of dogma and consequently is of considerable importance for the further course of the history of dogma and theology, which in future must not go on almost entirely without reflection but, in the light of earlier history, can and should be more explicitly aware of the principles by which its course is governed, even though it will still be far from coming under an autonomous and adequate control by people in the Church or even by the Church's authorities.

It would therefore be desirable also for the Church's magisterium in its pronouncements not merely to appeal to its formal authority or to recall former individual statements which themselves contained explicitly the teaching now to be put forward, nor simply to quote individual statements of Scripture which are perhaps not so unambiguous exegetically as is often assumed in these doctrinal pronouncements, but here, too, to show that there has been that recourse of which we spoke to the original centre of faith. Today the magisterium should not simply say or tacitly assume that this is purely a task for theologians. The magisterium must not merely take for granted its formal authority (which cannot be denied to it), but must make an effort really to gain the assent of believers to its teachings. Moreover a recourse of this kind seems more or less indispensable today, particularly since the formal authority of the magisterium is not an absolutely fundamental datum of faith, but itself as such and particularly in its effectiveness rests on this original basic substance of faith, which for the faith of the individual is prior to his acknowledgment of the magisterium.

V

The rules of biblical hermeneutics, which have slowly entered from the time of the Enlightenment into the Church's reflex awareness and after a long and difficult development have by now been explicitly or tacitly recognized also by the magisterium, must be seen and acknowledged also (*mutatis mutandis,* of course) as rules of interpretation for the later teachings of the magisterium.

Considered objectively, this statement may perhaps seem to be no more than a different way of expressing what has already been said. But it is useful to look once more at the interpretation of declarations of the magisterium (which lead also to the further interpretation of the history of dogma) from the standpoint of the experiences which the exegete and the theologian have had with Scripture texts, especially from the time of the Enlightenment. For the fact cannot seriously be disputed that in both cases the same questions are involved at least wholly in principle and in the last resort, particularly since biblical theology is largely the description of what happened by way of history of dogma in the Old and also in the New Testament, a history of dogma which certainly exists even in the New Testament and without which the true meaning of many individual statements of Scripture cannot be discovered, neither with reference to the extent to which these statements in their true sense are binding in faith nor with reference to what cannot be so regarded.

On the other hand however the hermeneutics of biblical statements seems to have reached a stage of exact and discriminating reflection beyond that of the hermeneutics of later statements of the magisterium, so that the former could be useful and exemplary for the latter, even though this exploitability has scarcely yet been taken in hand and from the nature of the case must certainly be treated with caution. Here indeed there lies an important task of theological hermeneutics with reference to declarations of the Church's magisterium which has not yet been properly faced. For the exegete and biblical theologian today it is, for instance, quite obvious that the real meaning as far as it is binding in faith of a biblical statement can be discovered only by a precise and discriminating inquiry into the literary genre of that statement. Is there also an explicit and considered theory in the theological hermeneutics of Catholic theology of the different literary genres of a theological statement on the part of the magisterium? Why should there not be something of this kind?

Is it *a priori* certain that this sort of thing cannot exist, perhaps because of a greater uniformity of literary stylization of these declarations of the magisterium? Are there not also, for example, in papal encyclicals a kind of language of piety, doxological statements, etc., with a literary genre that must be considered if the meaning and scope and binding force of these statements are to be precisely determined? Is it possible to discover in pronouncements of the Church (for example, in the social encyclicals from the time of Leo XIII) a literary genre which might be described as that of 'directives' (which certainly exist in Scripture), representing an historically conditioned synthesis between an abiding principle and an imperative or counsel which involve the application of the principle to a particular situation and is not meant at all to be valid for ever and in all situations, without this literary genre really present in such statements being explicitly distinguished from a statement intended to perennially valid? What is meant, for example, when it is said (DS 3917) that Mary's abundance of grace at the very first moment of her existence excelled that of all the saints? Without disputing a statement of this kind, we may have the impression that it does not belong to the literary genre of a plainly objective dogmatic statement.

Is there perhaps a literary genre in which the legitimacy of a practice of the Church is defended for the present time (and really no more than that), although at first sight this statement is put forward in the style of a perpetually valid essential statement? Does the teaching of Trent, for instance, on the justification and benefits of indulgences imply that indulgences will continue to be granted in the form of the medieval practice of indulgences for all future times? Does this teaching of Trent amount to a promise that in the Church's practice indulgences will be explicitly 'gained' even in the distant future? From the standpoint represented here ought not also the declarations of the Council of Trent on the indissolubility of Christian marriage to be considered again more urgently, if the literary genre of the rejection of divorce in the New Testament is defined in its meaning and scope? If the biblical statements on the possibility of a final perdition (existentially of course to be taken absolutely seriously) are to be interpreted as 'threatening speeches', could not statements of the magisterium on this theme also be interpreted in the same way, even though at first they sound doctrinally like those simply about facts known for certain in advance?

Speaking more generally, if on the one hand statements of the magisterium seem merely to pass on biblical statements and thus merely to refer back to the latter for their own more precise meaning and its limits and if on the other hand today we determine and define more closely exegetically the meaning of these biblical statements (for example, with reference to the position of women in relation to men in Paul's writings) in so far as they are binding in faith, can we not also transfer this restrictive determination to later declarations of the magisterium? Is not this the way in which modern theology works with reference, for example, to monogenism? In the light of the precise definition of the literary genre of the statements concerned it finds in the Bible that there is nothing about monogenism that is binding in faith and consequently interprets the declarations of the magisterium (for instance, in the fifth session of the Council of Treat) based on these biblical statements in the same way.

Here however questions are involved which, since they are unanswered, cannot yet even be clearly formulated or distinguished. The enormous difficulties which Catholic biblical hermeneutics had to face but which have now been largely overcome, with results that are recognized (at least tacitly) by the magisterium, should be a warning not to regard a similarly exact hermeneutics of statements of the magisterium as impracticable merely because it will come up against great difficulties.

VI

Declarations of the magisterium (even in the form of definitions and thus also dogmas) contained occasionally in the past and will also contain in the future an element of linguistic usage for the common statement of truths in the Church: a linguistic usage which on the one hand is not simply the necessary and sole possible way of stating what is meant, but can be considerably different and even apparently the very opposite, and which on the other hand in such a statement of the magisterium is not expressly identified as linguistic usage (which in principle and as such could be different and thus up to a point is freely adopted).

What is meant here is not only that in such statements of the magisterium new terms appear which were not used hitherto and which were introduced into the Church's official language only in a slow historical process. It is true that this alone implies an established usage, in so far as later proclamation and theology can no longer simply ignore such terminology of the statements making use of it. But more than this is meant when we speak of 'linguistic usage'. For when such terms have been accepted and are used in the declarations of the magisterium the impression may be gained that they are the only possible terms and that these alone will be legitimate in the future; that (from now on) what is meant can be expressed only in this way; that these terms are adequate at least for the expression of the objective meaning in the sense that a statement making use of them brings out what is meant in a way that cannot be improved and as exhaustively as possible. Nor is this impression removed by the fact that every theologian of course knows that these terms have to be explained again—and this in fact is an important part of the business of theology—and that obviously different expressions and terms have to be used in these explanations; in other words, a further process of explanation of this kind is in principle never finished. Even after all this is considered, the impression may persist that these further explanations in reality continually lead us back necessarily to the term explained and are adequately summarized and safeguarded in that term and consequently that the linguistic usage cannot be detached from the objective statement. But this impression is wrong, at any rate in many cases.

Let us consider a single example from the history of dogma. As distinct from the theology of the Eastern Church, Western theology from Augustine up to the present time has been committed to the use of the term 'original sin'. Declarations of theology and the magisterium on original sin give the impression that what is really meant cannot be expressed without using the term 'sin', that the latter is irreplaceable, and therefore that there is no question here of a linguistic usage in the sense explained. For some centuries at least theology has become increasingly clearly aware that the term 'sin' in the teaching on original sin is used only 'analogously', since it means primarily subjective, personal sin and the state of the actual sinner resulting from this. But in such an analogy it is clear that the two analogates differ in every respect from one another as much as they agree with one another. If this is true, it might be just as well to avoid a common term for the two analogates (in order not to obscure or overlook the difference) as it is to bring out the resemblance by seeing them together under a common but analogous term.

In our case this means that, as far as 'linguistic usage' goes, without having to deny or conceal what is meant by 'original sin', the term might have been avoided or prohibited, in order not to obscure its very profound difference from personal sin: that is, on the assumption that a different and certainly possible way would have been found of expressing what is described in Western theology and the teaching of the Church's magisterium, with considerable danger of misunderstanding, as original sin. Here obviously we have an example of linguistic usage in the sense explained, for on the other hand it cannot be denied that even a modern theology may not simply disregard the term 'original sin', however much its task today must be to bring out the purely analogous use of the term as compared with that of personal sin.

These linguistic usages may even be revised and changed also by the magisterium itself. If today we were to keep to the usage of the Council of Orange, we would have to say in the language of Augustine that every act of a person who is not justified is a 'sin'. But this is the very thing that seems to be forbidden to us by the usage which Pius V adopted against Baius. It is also possible for several mutually inconsistent usages to be present side by side in declarations of the Church's magisterium. It may perhaps be said that the terms 'hypostasis' and 'person' are used in the same sense in official teaching on the Trinity (at least if we prescind from the element of rationality and freedom in the notion of person). But this in no way alters the fact that the two terms in their origin and further history can be made compatible with each other only with difficulty; in other words, we have here a dual and not a single linguistic usage. If we have to allow for such linguistic usages, which are not simply required solely by the nature of what is to be expressed but which up to a point are freely chosen in the light of the development of ideas, this means for the future history of dogma that we may well expect to find this aspect of linguistic usage present in existing statements of the magisterium, even if it has not hitherto been explicitly recognized as such. It would however take us too long to suggest possible examples of this sort of thing here.

It is also possible for a process tending toward a definition based on a linguistic usage to come to a halt and eventually to be broken off. In the fifties of the present century there was a considerable movement toward defining the position of the blessed Virgin as 'mediatrix'. Today this movement seems to have slackened and to have no prospects in the foreseeable future. Despite descriptions of Mary in papal encyclicals as 'mediatrix' and 'co-redemptrix', we now hesitate to use the one term (even analogously) to describe the function of Jesus Christ in salvation history and that of the most blessed Virgin (which bears only the most remote resemblance to that of Christ) since it seems obvious that the use of such a term, even if its analogous character is subsequently stressed, obscures the radical difference that exists between the two 'mediatorships'. Here then the policy in regard to linguistic usage seems to be following a trend opposite to that which we observed in the use of the term 'original sin', where the dubious character of the analogous term was accepted without much embarrassment. Might not the discovery of purely 'verbal' heresies, which really amount to a 'schismatic' rejection of a linguistic usage on the part of the Church's magisterium, be part of a history of dogma in the future as well as of an ecumenical theology?

VII

Despite appearances to the contrary, the fact that one 'party' in a theological dispute is admitted to be right does not mean that the other 'party' (as it actually existed historically) was purely and simply wrong.

This observation may sound like a truism; humanly speaking however it is very important when a controversy is still raging or immediately after it has come to an end (provisionally or 'definitively') as a result of a decision of the magisterium. The point of this observation is that the 'victor' in such a dispute may not triumph over the 'vanquished', nor need the latter think that he has utterly lost the battle. He need not assume this even if he cannot really say himself how his essential 'concern' can still be basically assured even after the decision has gone against him.

It is right to assume of course that the complete negation of a positively affirmative statement of the magisterium (disregarding for the moment its theological qualification) must be false. But in a concrete dispute in theological history contentious theological statements are not opposed to one another as purely contradictory and consequently the confirmation of one statement by the magisterium is far from implying an absolute rejection of the other statement opposed to it in the course of the controversy. The latter may well include concerns, elements of truth which are not present in the officially approved statement, but which can be right and significant and can have a future even if the other party with its frequent triumphant shouting will not admit this, even indeed when the losing party at the very moment of condemnation cannot itself clearly see what can be rescued of its basic concern.

Was everything false, for instance, that Pelagius and Julian of Eclanum had to say against the apparently completely victorious Augustine, or have they not later been proved right in many respects in the course of a slow development up to the present time, when the doctrine of limbo, for instance, seems to have been abandoned and the Augustinian doctrine of original sin has been quite considerably modified? And has not all this led to the introduction of greater precision into Augustine's doctrine of sin and justification, through a clearer distinction between nature and grace which was not known to Augustine and which goes a long way toward the rehabilitation of his opponents? In other words, was Pelagius actually a heretic objectively, in regard to the matter of the dispute as such, or only in the interpretation (understandable humanly speaking and in the light of the historical situation) of Augustine, who could not in fact understand Pelagius in any other way and therefore attacked him as a heretic and successfully established his own linguistic usage in the Church? Was monophysitism in some churches in the East after Chalcedon of an objective or purely verbal character, in a sense more 'schismatic' than heretical, since its supporters felt unable to follow the linguistic usage of Chalcedon? Is it absolutely certain that the doctrine of justification (and sanctification), as commonly understood and regarded as binding in the Protestant churches, is quite clearly opposed to the teaching of the Council of Trent on justification? Did Bossuet turn out to be absolutely right against Fénelon? After the severe condemnation of modernism (under Pius X), how much of its aspirations and the problems it raised slowly came to be accepted subsequently in Catholic theology and biblical studies, and how often in fact did this happen contrary to the official rejection of individual propositions of the modernists by the Church's magisterium?

Decisions of the Church's magisterium, too, even in the form of definitions, never incorporate the entire and complete truth in all aspects and in all dimensions of the reality of faith; even after the settlement of a controversy, history goes on, so that the 'victors' in the conflict must be modest and circumspect and the 'vanquished' can always hope for a better understanding of their real concern (and also of a great deal of what they have explicitly said) on the part of the institutional Church in the future.

VIII

The history of dogma and theology remains history: that is, in the last resort unpredictable and not under the control of human beings or of the Church's authority.

No matter how much the history of dogma (together with the history of theology) can be seen as an 'organic' process of explication of the real basic substance of revelation (and it is thus possible to attempt retrospectively to make this process intelligible as 'logical' sequence), it remains nevertheless in the last resort a history of freedom to be accepted in its indissoluble facticity as gift and as burden. This must be so if only because there is an indissoluble relationship of mutual dependence between the history of dogma and theology on the one hand and the universal history of ideas, of civilisation and even economics, on the other; but this history is and remains precisely history and cannot even subsequently be logically deduced. In the Christian view it is true that the history of faith and dogma is under the guidance of the Holy Spirit and certainly has its supreme entelechy in that Spirit; but the Spirit is effective in this history because he is also the secret and, for us in the last resort before the end of history, the inscrutable innermost principle of history as such. That is why it is not possible to make unambiguous and secure prognoses for the future history of dogma and faith.

In view of the 'single line' course of this history, we are certainly bound to assume that truths once grasped with an explicit and absolute assent of faith in the Church cannot simply be 'forgotten' again, since the Church's ever present sense of faith remains the same only by retaining also the memory of its own history. But this tells us little in regard to the future about the existential and consequently theological status which such a truth will retain concretely in the Church's sense of faith and in its practice. This is particularly true for theological statements and views with a lesser degree of binding force.

Such shifts in the existential and theoretical status of truths can easily be observed in the past. How long did it take, for instance, for the ecclesiology accepted under the influence of Bellarmine in the sixteenth century to be changed again, after a recourse to older tradition, into the ecclesiology which found expression in Pius XII's *Mystici Corporis* and in *Lumen Gentium* at the Second Vatican Council? Will the widely developed doctrine of confessions of devotion keep up practically and theologically the role it has played in the treatise on the sacrament of penance for a long time up to the present? Popes from Leo XIII onward have produced a detailed teaching on devotion to the Sacred Heart. In the nineteenth and in the present century there have been almost innumerable Roman declarations on Mary and Marian devotion. Will the official theological declarations on such devotion retain the status that they once claimed as a matter of course in the life and in the theology of the Church?

We cannot really foresee the future history of dogma and theology. If however we attempt with a little futurological imagination to form a picture of humanity in the coming centuries, to envisage its quantitative, economic, sociological, mental, and political changes, there can be no doubt that the Church's history of faith and dogma will bring with it changes which we can scarcely imagine today.

IX

It might perhaps be said that the material of the future history of faith and dogma of Christianity and the Church will differ considerably and characteristically from that of the history lying between the end of the great patristic age and the Enlightenment (the dates are very provisional and imprecise, and it might perhaps be better to speak of the Constantinian turning point and the beginning of the Imperial Church instead of the end of the great patristic age and to speak, not of the Enlightenment as such, but of the acceptance of the Enlightenment in the modern Church, an acceptance which has only now been completed and which required a hundred and fifty or two hundred years of the age in which we are still living).

The whole period, which might be thus marked out on the one hand against the first three centuries of Christianity and on the other hand against the modern age from the time of the Enlightenment, was characterized by the fact that this history of faith and dogma went on by and large in a homogeneous milieu which, despite everything new that entered into it, bore in all dimensions (even the secular) of human life the Christian imprint and was actually threatened only from outside.

The first three centuries of Christianity and perhaps the century and a half after these (as the continuation and completion of the influences of the first period) represent therefore a history of faith and dogma in a militant confrontation with and a simultaneous assimilation of a non-Christian intellectual and cultural milieu. On the other hand (despite the continued influence of ancient Platonism, despite the acceptance of Aristotelianism and the internal crises of Christianity resulting from the schism between the Eastern and Western churches and from the Reformation of the sixteenth century), this long intermediate period was a time of explication and differentiation of the substance of faith from its centre into increasingly systematized distinctions, which, because of their one starting point from within and the absence of any really serious confrontation with external opposition, could be worked out in a more or less uniform terminology accepted by all as a matter of course. This was the time of the summas and, simultaneously and for the same reason, the time when it was possible (since the whole scheme was taken for granted) to plunge with immense theological passion into individual questions and almost to be lost in them. It was at this time that the modern greater catechisms emerged and what we have come to describe as Denzinger theology. It was the time when lengthy papal encyclicals dealing with comparatively detailed questions of Christian faith could be taken as a matter of course; when the magisterium reacted meticulously and swiftly to real or supposed infringements of particular teachings from this detailed system; when it was assumed that the system as a whole was clear and scarcely open to further development (threatened at most in the present century from outside by liberal exegesis and theology and modernism) and that consequently any serious development could only be in regard to individual questions (for instance, in Mariology), so that the main work of theology was concerned retrospectively with its own history, the 'great' theologians being historians and not systematic theologians.

Today (naturally, after a long period of gestation from the Enlightenment onward, a period to which the argument conducted defensively with liberal theology and modernism belongs) we have undoubtedly entered into a new phase of the history of faith and thus also of the history of dogma and theology. It is a question today no longer of an increasingly detailed explication of the basic substance of faith within a homogeneous milieu, with its own common horizons of understanding; on the contrary, it is a question of acquiring a new understanding (while preserving, of course, the traditional substance of faith) of the faith as one and whole in a non-Christian milieu, in a new period of a global world civilisation into which new world cultures which were never Christian have entered; it is a question of a history of faith and dogma in a new diaspora where there must again be both radical confrontation and radical assimilation in face of this new situation, which bears the imprint of the most diverse forms of atheism and is marked also by a despair of the possibility of the survival of religion at all. In that sense there is a formal similarity between the period of the history of dogma now dawning and its first period, which we distinguished, even though the material and the tasks of the first and the third periods are radically different.

The history of faith and dogma will presumably go on in the future, not in the style of the second period as an evolutive explication and systematizing differentiation of the basic substance of faith, but as a transposition of this abiding faith into new and pluralistic horizons of understanding, horizons of today and tomorrow. In view of the incommensurable and not adequately synthesizable pluralism of present and future horizons of understanding of the dawning historical situation, the transposition of faith into these horizons of understanding will have to be brought about by a pluralism of theologies, a pluralism which will also be impossible to synthesize adequately, despite all the readiness for necessary dialogue on the part of these theologies with one another for the protection and continually new discovery of the one faith.

In this new period now begun the task of the magisterium therefore will scarcely consist any longer in the definition of 'new' individual dogmas, in meticulously looking out for real or alleged deviations from traditional individual teachings, but in maintaining the faith as one and whole in its basic substance; and even this, not by 'censoring', but by positively encouraging cooperation in the task imposed on us today of interpreting the old faith afresh in a new and by no means originally Christian milieu. This new task may well demand far too much from the means (material and personal) at the disposal of the Roman authorities on matters of faith; even in the last decade the Roman magisterium has continued by and large to work in the old style and with the old machinery and consequently, while maintaining its autonomy and special function in the Church, must search creatively for a new style in both its doctrinal and its disciplinary measures if it is not only to be right but also effectively to be accepted as right in the sense of faith of the people in the Church.

In brief: the history of faith and dogma will continue, since salvation history will continue in a new world history; but it will have a different character, not so much the character of a history of individual, newly articulated statements of faith and theological reflection on these, but the history of the new expression of the old basic substance of the faith confronting and assimilating the future horizons of understanding. It is obvious that this history will no longer be merely the history of dogma as formulated in the West and of its theology (to be exported to other countries), but the history of faith and dogma of a world Church, however little we can imagine its material and formal implications. What has been said does not exclude but includes the possibility that the new conception of the transposition of the substance of the Christian faith as one and whole will also have consequences for the interpretation of many or of all individual doctrines.

2

PSEUDO-PROBLEMS IN ECUMENICAL DISCUSSION

Our intention here is to say something about questions of dogmatics which remain open, although the institutional Church regards them as definitively answered. We are speaking of the institutional Church in a somewhat vague sense, in so far as it gives effect in practice to its teaching policy (in appointing professors, in censoring books—at any rate, until recently—and in other ways) in its general teaching and in its authentic doctrinal statements other than definitions. Hence it is not a question here of definitions of an absolute character of the supreme magisterium by *ex cathedra* decisions of the pope or definitions of a council. These decisions on dogmatic questions will be considered here (if at all) only if, while being absolutely binding, they can also leave open questions that were not directly answered by the definition, either because they were simply not noticed or because it was assumed that they had already been answered, although a determination of the exact meaning of the definition in question may show that this is by no means the case. In that sense even in final definitions it is possible up to a point to discover open questions which are only assumed to have been answered by the definition. But in speaking of open questions regarded by the institutional Church as already answered, we have in mind mainly authentic declarations, not definitions of the Church's magisterium. It can also be a question of those teachings which were qualified in traditional scholastic textbook theology at least up to the time of Vatican II as 'theologically certain' on the basis of a general consensus of theologians and therefore treated in practice as no longer open. These are teachings which can also properly be included here, since the Roman magisterium usually has recourse to them when it feels that a declaration is required.

Among these questions, which are only apparently settled by the magisterium while in reality remaining dogmatically still open, we are dealing here *only* with *dogmatic* questions and not with those of canon law or pastoral theology. It may, for example, be dogmatically an absolutely open question whether wheaten bread alone can be the matter of the eucharist. This is a question that can be declared open without necessarily drawing any conclusions about possible changes in the concrete practice of the Church. Consequently dogmatically open questions need not *always* be a problem for the practical action of the Church.

Our theme of course is set against an ecumenical background. In other words, the questions to be considered here will be those which are important for ecumenical discussion among the traditional Christian churches. We are therefore disregarding from the outset all questions of moral theology which are relevant today, which are dealt with by the Church's magisterium at the present time in authentic declarations put forward as definitive, although they cannot by any means claim to be such. These moral theological problems we are leaving aside here, although it cannot be denied that Roman declarations of this kind actually make ecumenical dialogue more difficult. We are also leaving aside declarations on exegesis and biblical theology from Pius X onward in which the Church's magisterium overreacted to modernism and imposed on Catholic exegetes norms that brought them into conflict with Protestant exegesis and thus certainly also made ecumenical discussion more difficult. These questions can be disregarded here since the antimodernistic doctrinal statements of the magisterium by and large have become obsolete and have been tacitly dropped by the Roman magisterium.

If we restrict ourselves therefore to dogmatic questions in the strictest sense of the term, the theme still remains far from clear. In itself it would be appropriate and useful in regard to this theme to initiate general and fundamental reflections of a theological epistemology to show (also generally and fundamentally) how and why it is continually possible in the Church's sense of faith, even though not in an absolute commitment of faith, to reach the conclusion that a certain teaching is the answer to a particular question, deciding this equation unambiguously and definitively, although this is not in fact the case. With the aid of such general and fundamental reflections of a theological epistemology the attempt might be made to show what are the reasons arising from the historical and political development of ideas why we suddenly discover that the traditional teachings do not by any means answer the questions facing us today, even though we had assumed that they would. But, in view of the brevity of these reflections and the obscurity of the general problem, we must refrain here from such an undertaking. We shall restrict ourselves therefore to a few brief observations on certain individual dogmatic questions to which the magisterium and traditional textbook theology assumed too quickly and too spontaneously that they had found an answer.

It may sound odd, but I think that we can also disregard the three great groups of questions of controversial theology which are summed up under the heatings of *sola fide, sola scriptura, sola gratia.* As far as the doctrine of justification is concerned, it can no longer be said today that the teaching of the Augustan Confession and that of the Council of Trent are certainly absolutely opposed to each other. The same holds for the idea of justification by faith alone in the sense actually understood by Lutheran theology. As for *sola scriptura,* we need do no more than refer to the fierce controversy during the Second Vatican Council, when the question of the exact relationship between Scripture and Tradition was deliberately left open, with the result that the teaching on this relationship which had become traditional since the Council of Trent was now likewise turned into an open question. I think then that we can leave aside here the traditionally fundamental controversial questions of the Western churches. At the same time of course it may be asked how all institutional churches would have to respond officially to the question of what must be done if they suddenly observed that the dissent which was once the source (and the sole source) of division between the churches has now disappeared. We shall therefore deal only with a few secondary questions which we regard, contrary to the traditional view, as open. At the same time no importance can be attached to a systematic treatment of these questions. Nor, with the questions as limited in this way, can an explicit *comparison* be made between absolutely binding Catholic positions and Protestant views. In regard to the Catholic positions, we must restrict ourselves to pointing out open questions, different possibilities of interpretation, etc., so that from this standpoint it becomes clear that an absolute contradiction of the Protestant positions is not as clear and obvious as it might seem at first sight.

We may begin with some observations on the doctrine of the sacraments in general. The Council of Trent teaches that there are seven sacraments, instituted by Christ. If as Catholics we reflect honestly today on the facts of the history of the sacraments, we shall have to say that as actual basic realizations of the nature of the Church the sacraments have their origin from Christ in the sense that the Church is 'instituted' by him, has its origin from him, without having to seek or postulate generally explicit words of institution spoken by Christ with reference to individual sacraments, even though such explicit words of institution cannot be denied in regard to the eucharist. This conception of the sacraments in general as just suggested, which sees the sacraments as actualizations in the word of the basic sacrament, the Church, which is the presence of the invincible salvific act of God in Jesus Christ, ought to be acceptable to Protestants, since in this way the true meaning of *opus operatum* can be made intelligible and the sacraments can be understood also from the Catholic standpoint as the most intensive event of the exhibitive word of the Gospel; it is possible also to point out to modern Protestant theology that, for its present-day exegesis, baptism, recognized by the Reformation as a sacrament, cannot be shown more clearly or more certainly than the other sacraments to have its origin from Jesus. In a Catholic sense, too, the fact that the sacraments are a matter of divine law must be understood as a legitimate and irreversible decision of the apostolic Church. But from this there emerges an opportunity of interpreting the Tridentine teaching on the sacraments which on the one hand seems acceptable for Protestant sacramental doctrine today, while on the other hand admittedly raising new questions on the Catholic side, but also opening up new possibilities of pastoral action which had not hitherto been considered. In a modern Catholic sacramental theology doing justice to the historical data and with a Catholic theology of the word (unfortunately only very gradually developed today) it is no longer possible and no longer necessary to portray the Catholic Church as the Church of the sacraments and the Protestant Churches as Churches of the word.

In this connection it should be noticed that the doctrine of the sacramental character as conferred in some sacraments leaves open more questions than is apparent from our textbook theology. The very fact that the Church in certain sacraments grants within itself an irrevocable status (which to all intents and purposes it will never withdraw and which it imparts as such) conveys all that we must regard as binding in the doctrine of the sacramental character without leaving scope for further speculations.

We come to the question of the understanding of ministry in the Church, in so far as here too there are very many more open questions than is commonly thought. Ministry in the Church as understood in the light of Catholic faith obviously implies that there must be a ministry of leadership in the Church as an historical and sociological reality and that its special characteristics, functions, and powers are to be derived from the nature of the Church and must be made intelligible from this standpoint. If we exclude here for the moment the papacy and its powers, in order to give them special consideration at a later stage, then the foregoing statement really covers everything that can and must be said with absolute dogmatic binding force about ministry in the Church. This holds of course in its whole extent for *those* holders of such a ministry who have the leadership of a major and (apart from its link with the Church as a whole) self-sufficient Church and are traditionally known as bishops. In practice this one ministry, as it is now sacramentally transmitted, is divided in the Roman Church into the three grades of episcopate, presbyterate, and diaconate. But it does not seem to me that this tripartite organization of ministry is absolutely certainly a matter of divine law. The triple gradation of ministry certainly does not go back to an explicit institution by the historical Jesus. I think it is possible but not absolutely certain that the triple ministry developed so irreversibly in the primitive Church of apostolic times as to be in this way a matter of divine law and unalterable. Even if these three grades are acknowledged as of divine law, the Church can nevertheless divide up its one ministry further and grant a share in it in different ways. In practice this is precisely what it does. Neither is it proved nor, in view of the medieval doctrine of the sacramentality of the minor orders, is it even probable that other forms and grades of participation in the one ministry of the Church cannot also be conferred sacramentally.

In the light of all this it is not *a priori* certain that Protestant

Churches which might want to be united with Rome would necessarily have to adopt precisely the division of ministry as it exists in the Roman Church. Neither does it seem to me to be absolutely certain, from the purely dogmatic standpoint, that episcopal authority as it has been defined from Trent to the Second Vatican Council, and as of course it will always be valid, must necessarily be held by an individual as a 'monarchical' bishop. Not of course that there is anything to be said practically and concretely against the monarchical episcopate. But when the nature of episcopal authority or the power of leadership over a major Church is described in the Church's doctrinal pronouncements, when this authority (which is and will remain valid) is described as a matter of course as held by one man, since that is the way in which it is actually exercised everywhere, this does not seem to me to imply in the sense of a dogmatic statement that episcopal authority as one and whole cannot be held also by a small collective. The Catholic doctrine of the episcopate as a whole as the supreme governing body in the Church shows that collegial constitutional structures cannot simply be *a priori* essentially alien to the nature of the Catholic Church. But for our part, at any rate, we must distinguish more clearly between the question of the nature of the Church's ministry and the question of the individual or collective holder of such a ministry. The nature of ministry must be seen in the light of the Church's nature and is by that very fact different from the nature of a function of leadership in a secular society. If this is or could be recognized by all sides in ecumenical discussion, it might be possible to agree freely on many other aspects of the concrete structuring of ministry and of its holdership in the one Church formed out of many particular churches which have had different historical patterns of growth.

If ministry in the Church stems from the Church's theological nature and *thus* from Christ, if in this sense it comes from above and not by being freely set up from the base of the Church, nevertheless the question of *how* the holders of such a ministry can and should be chosen and appointed is actually still completely open and is not properly a dogmatic question. Or it is such at most in the sense that a new holder of the episcopal ministry (if his authority is to be legitimate) needs the consent of the pope and the episcopate as a whole. But this does not mean that the actual appointment and choice of a bishop according to divine law must lie with the pope. This may be and is appropriately and usefully part of the positive law of the Church, but it is not by divine law a papal prerogative. This is evident also from the whole history of the episcopate. It can be shown that the determination of the holder of a ministry by an election from below and in fact by an historically conditioned electoral body cannot be contrary to the Church's nature, by the very fact that the appointment of the holder of the supreme ministry, the pope, comes about by an election from below, today by the very obviously historically conditioned College of Cardinals.

Of course, in whatever way he is chosen from below, a holder of the episcopal ministry only comes into the full possession of all episcopal powers when he is not only accepted into the unity and peace of the episcopate as a whole, but when he is also sacramentally ordained by other bishops and thus in this respect, too, enters into the apostolic succession. But this does not mean on the other hand that an election from below is impossible or contrary to the nature of the Church. In principle, unity and peace with the Apostolic See in Rome are indispensable. But this does not necessarily mean that the granting of this unity and this peace must necessarily as a matter of dogma be the central and essential event in the appointment of a particular holder of the episcopal ministry. The pope would renounce a prerogative that is not, dogmatically speaking, everlasting but acquired only in the course of history, if he were to refrain in a union with separated churches from appointing a bishop in the way hitherto envisaged in the Latin Code of Canon Law of the Church.

In this connection something must certainly be said about the obscure question of the recognition of the ministries of the Churches of the Reformation separated from the Roman Church. I stated my views on this question in my book on preliminary questions in regard to an ecumenical understanding of ministry (*Vorfragen zu einem ökumenischen Amtsverständnis,* Quaestiones Disputatae 65 [Freiburg, 1974]). As far as I can see, what I said there scarcely found any response and it is tacitly disavowed by declarations of the Roman magisterium and the German bishops. But, since these declarations certainly cannot claim to be irreformable, I still think that what I tentatively suggested in that book remains worth discussing. According to Vatican II there can be no doubt that these ministries as exercised in the separated churches can have a positive importance for salvation. I also think that as legitimate and at least in many cases (which of course must be distinguished from others that are not legitimate) they are also sacramental in their transmission (ordination) and in their exercise (eucharistic celebration); this is true, I think, not only of the Eastern Churches separated from Rome, but also of the Reformation Churches. If this sort of opinion is to be understood, it must first of all be remembered that these churches may not be judged now from the Catholic side, as they were judged (rightly, in principle) at the very time of the Reformation, at the point of separation, as distinct from their present separated state. Then it must also be recalled that there is a kind of essential law that is prior to statute law and simply flows from the nature of a particular individual or a society. This is something that is possible also in principle in the Church, since the latter has a nature that precedes its juridical constitution and comes to it with the definitive and irreversibly victorious event of salvation in Jesus Christ and with the faith in him unconditionally granted in that event. It is from this basic nature of the Church that realities of a sacramental character can flow—at least this is conceivable in principle, even though they do not come to be in virtue of the normal, accepted procedure, if the latter is inculpably omitted.

Unless something of this kind is assumed to have taken place, it is impossible to do justice to the facts in the history of the Church. When a priest or bishop is living in undisputed possession of his powers in the Church, is he to be denied these powers if it is assumed that, according to the normal law of the sacraments, the succession has been interrupted at some point? Was Martin V (recognized as pope by the whole Church) a legitimate pope only if it can first be established that his predecessors either were invalidly elected or actually voluntarily renounced the papacy? If a Catholic priest were to celebrate the eucharist with rice bread if and because it seemed at that point that there would be no wheaten bread in the foreseeable future, would that celebration not really be sacramental? How could medieval theologians regard confession to lay persons in an emergency as sacramental? If non-Catholic Christians marry, thereby effecting a sacrament, and if this sacrament comes into existence in virtue of the basic sacramental nature of the Church, then it is not because the pope by a positive legal act makes this form of contracting matrimony a sacramental sign for such Christians, even though the Tridentine form is not observed, that such a marriage is a sacrament today. Otherwise we would have to come to the absurd conclusion that the pope could require even these Christians to observe the Tridentine form and thus deny to non-Catholics the sacramentality of their marriage. The sacramentality of these marriages belongs to them directly in virtue of the basic sacramental nature of the Church, since these baptized Christians have a right to this sacrament, even though, in their good faith, it cannot be conveyed to them by the normal sacramental signs. It should also be remembered that the rite of conferring an ecclesial ministry is entirely at the discretion of the Church and need not by any means consist necessarily in an imposition of hands. In the light of these reflections, which of course as such ought to be much more detailed and precise, it seems to me not impossible to recognize to a much greater extent than hitherto in the traditional view the sacramental character of ordination and the exercise of the ministry based on this in the Churches of the Reformation. In regard to this question, which is of considerable importance for the possibility of a union of the Churches, I must again refer to the above-mentioned little book of mine. If as Catholic theologians we have a duty to bear in mind everything that can possibly help toward union, we should not be too readily satisfied with the traditional but superficial answers to the question of recognition of ministries in the Churches of the Reformation.

We come now to the main impediment to Church unity: the question of the papacy and the Roman primacy. Paul VI himself acknowledged that the papacy is today the greatest impediment to the union of the churches. In regard to this question also a great deal appears to be more open than is generally thought. Theologians and popes ought also today to consider more precisely what is really part of the inalienable substance of faith in the doctrine and practice of the Roman primacy and what is not. And in regard to what is not essential, although people cling to it in practice, the Catholic theologians and especially the popes ought to make their position much clearer. This is all the more important now that there is evidently a growing inclination on the part of Protestants to recognize a Petrine ministry in the Church as necessary to or at least in accordance with its nature. But there is scarcely any visible sign in Rome of a clarification of the self-limitation of the Roman primacy that is dogmatically possible and in the present situation advisable; there is no sign that the first step is being taken toward agreement on this particular question. There is no doubt at all that much of what the Roman See still claims even today by way of powers and rights acquired in the course of history is not part of the inalienable nature of the primacy. Nor of course is there any doubt about this in Rome. But Rome ought also to say clearly what is not essential in this respect and what it is prepared to give up in regard to the churches seeking unity with Rome. Whether these sacrifices are to be made only for the sake of the churches prepared for union or whether they should hold also for the Latin Church of the West is again a very different question which cannot be discussed here.

The basic question is really to be answered not by drawing up an inventory of what Rome can renounce in principle, but by circumscribing what Rome can *not* renounce in the light of fundamental dogma. If the question is answered in this way, it is of course necessary to explain also what the pope's universal primacy of jurisdiction over all the churches as ordinary power of the primacy means and what it does not. There is no need to prove expressly that very many questions remain open in this respect or that a great deal of what Rome regards as an obvious exercise of this primacy of jurisdiction is by no means obvious dogmatically. (The possibility of various ways for Rome to participate in the appointment of bishops has already been discussed. The fact has also been mentioned that to a large extent presbyteral, collective constitutional elements are not dogmatically excluded even in the Catholic Church or in its particular churches.) In regard to the unlimited authority of the Roman primacy according to the letter of the law, certain qualifications need to be considered and more explicitly stated. Unlimited as this authority may seem to be according to the letter of the law, the pope is limited, not only by the fact that he cannot change the nature of the Church insofar as this is a matter of divine law; that is, he not only cannot abolish the episcopate as it is understood by Vatican II, but neither can he in practice undermine its autonomy in such a way to reduce the bishops really to the status of mere regional representatives of the pope in a development which has not ceased to be a threat even today. A further limitation of this apparently unlimited primacy arises from another side and should be explicitly stated much more clearly than actually occurs. In other words, the exercise of the plenitude of jurisdiction of the primacy is tied to Christian moral norms, in fact to norms that are not always purely materially the same, but can be *different* in different historical situations. In practice it seems to be assumed in the Church that it is obvious and not open to any doubt that the pope always keeps to these moral restrictions of his power. And of course it is not to be denied that this is what generally happens. There may however be some doubt about whether this is *always* the case.

It is quite possible that certain moral restrictions on the pope's power inevitably emerging out of the mental climate and sociological situations today are present as such, but in practice are not seen and therefore not respected. It is, for example, quite conceivable in principle that in publishing *Humanae Vitae* Paul VI in good faith actually infringed norms for arriving at a papal judgment which were available as such. It is quite conceivable that Roman authorities may interfere in the life of the particular churches in a way that objectively infringes the principle of subsidiary function in the Church. It does not seem obvious or unquestionable to me that the law of celibacy has to be enforced uniformly from Rome in the whole Church. It is not *a priori* clear that every recourse to the universal primacy of the pope is always and in every case in practice also morally justified. (If, for instance, a ruling on celibacy from Rome alone for the universal Church is morally legitimate, then the pope has this right in principle also in regard to the Eastern Churches. Could it then seriously be asserted that the pope has the moral right also to forbid priestly marriage for all the Eastern Uniate Churches?) There can of course be disagreement on the exact details of the restrictions imposed on the pope's universal power of jurisdiction by moral principles and in particular by moral principles varying with different situations; but there ought to be an open and lucid dialogue in the Church, even if in a case of doubt and where the pope does not clearly order something positively immoral the presumption is that the pope is right. But it would be very important for the progress of ecumenism if Rome itself were to define concretely and clearly and in detail just what it could renounce in the light of its own self-understanding.

From the ecumenical standpoint the most difficult of the questions associated with the papacy is of course the definition of the pope's infallible teaching primacy. We cannot get rid of this difficulty by seeing it in the way Hans Küng sees it and more or less interpreting out of existence the infallibility of the pope when he makes an *ex cathedra* decision. But it is possible to bring out more clearly what this Catholic dogma means and what it does not mean. As far as the past is concerned, the only difficulties in regard to this infallible teaching authority of the pope that arise in practice are connected with the two Marian dogmas defined by Pius IX and Pius XII. As we hope to show later, these difficulties can certainly be cleared up. The real difficulty of Protestant Christians relates to possibilities of the future, to conceivable future *ex cathedra* decisions by the pope. In this connection, even if a Protestant is prepared in principle to recognize a Petrine ministry in the Church, he does not think that he is in a position to make out a kind of blank cheque for the future. It does not seem to him clear and unequivocal that divine providence, which keeps the Church in the truth of Christ, is necessarily bound to be effective when the pope defines something and not on other occasions or in a different way. To the Protestant, the Catholic idea of the concentration of the efficacious grace of truth, granted to the Church, precisely on a particular and juridically determinable act of the pope, seems to be a human materialization and legalization of the grace of truth, which is incredible. It seems so incredible also because history shows that on the one hand in authentic doctrinal decisions the ordinary magisterium of the popes was often involved in error, at least up to the present time, and, on the other hand, Rome put forward and insisted on such essentially reformable decisions as if there could be no doubt about their definitive truth and as if any further discussion was unbecoming for a Catholic theologian. Against such reservations on the Protestant side purely theoretical arguments on our part will have little prospect of success in practice. We could however attempt to show better than we have done hitherto that the concrete procedure before and for a papal *ex cathedra* decision now and in the future will certainly take such a form that a Protestant need not fear in practice and concretely that his blank cheque will be filled out with a papal teaching which he is bound in faith and conscience to oppose. In this respect two considerations may be useful.

First of all, it is clear and conciliar teaching that a pope, who does not receive any new revelation even for an *ex cathedra* decision, must prepare his decision by making use of all means at his disposal in that particular situation. But the moral norms implicit in this principle could be more clearly articulated and codified today, even though the observance of these norms in a concrete case would not be open to legal verification by an authority higher than that of the pope. If such norms for arriving at the truth in regard to a papal decision were not only present and observed in practice (which can be assumed on the whole to have been the case in the past, even though they could be and ought to be more differentiated now and in the future), but were also explicitly formulated and codified, there would be far less need for a Protestant to fear a future papal *ex cathedra* decision which might be contrary to his faith and conscience. If in the First and the Second Vatican Council it is said that the pope or his decision is infallible as such (*ex sese*) and not in virtue of the consent of the Church, this means merely that the pope's *ex cathedra* decision does not acquire its definitive validity only by virtue of the juridical verification of its correctness by a higher legal authority in the Church distinct from the pope. But this *ex sese* of the two Vatican Councils does not mean that the pope possesses an infallibility that is independent of God's irreversibly victorious promise to the Church as a whole.

In an *ex cathedra* decision the pope *as* head of the Church and of the episcopate as a whole acts as an authority that is restricted by the Church as a whole and its infallible faith. Consequently, in preparing *ex cathedra* decisions, the pope must necessarily have recourse to the sense of faith of the whole Church. If this were not so and if it were not necessary, a papal *ex cathedra* decision would be the proclamation of a new revelation. But the pope neither possesses nor receives any new revelation. He is the authoritative spokesman of the Church's sense of faith and for this he has the assistance of the Spirit, an assistance which must not be understood as psychological inspiration but in the last resort means the success coming from God of his recourse to the infallible sense of faith of the Church as a whole. This reference to the whole Church's sense of faith of course takes different forms at the different stages of the Church's history in the light of the opportunities available at the time. Today certainly in this respect a recourse to the episcopate as a whole is absolutely necessary, both morally and from the nature of the case. And again this recourse may take a variety of forms. But it is now not merely a laudable practice, observed by Pius IX and Pius

XII (though perhaps in ways that were not entirely satisfactory), but an absolute requirement.

Such an explicit recourse is technically quite feasible today. But in that case it is also a moral obligation. How could a pope today honestly say that he had done all that was humanly possible and morally required to be humanly certain that his teaching was a part of the assured sense of faith of the whole Church, if he had wanted to dispense with this consultation of the episcopate as a whole? It is obvious that such a consultation ought to take place and ought also to be publicly clear today in certain forms now possible of explicitness, transparency, easier dialogue, consultation of theologians, investigation of the believers' sense of faith, etc., even though it is evidently not yet clearly considered and practised in Rome, as can be seen also from very recent authentic if not defining dogmatic statements. If such procedures were clearly articulated, explicitly shown to be operative, and applied in practice, even a Protestant Christian would be largely relieved of the fear of an arbitrary manipulation of the papal teaching authority contrary to the true spirit of Jesus and the Church.

A *second* consideration may be added to the first. The Catholic faith in the existence of a papal teaching power, that is always involved in the permanent nature of the Church, does not imply that the actual exercise of this power is the same at all times (which is not true of the past), does not imply that it is independent of any historical and variable preconditions. Because of the history of dogma of the first two thousand years of the Church, we have become accustomed involuntarily to think of this history as an increasingly progressive explication and articulation of the basic substance of faith into more and more new and explicit individual statements and consequently to think naturally also of the papal teaching primacy as being actively involved in producing these new and differentiating statements. We involuntarily regard the exercise of the pope's teaching primacy, when he speaks *ex cathedra,* as an explanation of statements which, even though ultimately implied in the tradition of faith, seem materially new and were formerly scarcely explicitly perceptible: for instance, the dogma of the Immaculate Conception or the Assumption of Mary into heaven or even the doctrine of Mary as mediatrix of grace propagated some twenty years ago with a view to a dogmatic definition. But it is completely unproven and seems to me not at all probable that the exercise of the papal teaching authority will continue in this way in the future. The future history of doctrine of Christianity and the Church seems to me to be tending, not toward a further material differentiation of the substance of Christian faith, but toward a new expression of the ultimate basic substance of Christianity required and made possible by the new mental climate and sociopolitical situation. The concrete exercise of the papal teaching primacy would also have to be understood *accordingly* if it is to endure in the future.

Unfortunately, it is impossible here to offer a precise substantiation of this prognosis of the future history of dogma and thus also of the concrete way in which the papal teaching primacy will be exercised. Otherwise it would be necessary to offer a precise analysis of the mental climate of the world and of world civilisation, of the present-day irreversible pluralism in a world that is nevertheless one, and thus to clarify the secular historical background to the life of faith in the modern world-Church. But this, too, is not possible here. I am sure however that from this standpoint a prognosis would be possible for the future exercise of the papal teaching primacy, a prognosis making clear to the Protestant Christian that the papal magisterium in the future will inevitably and readily be concentrated on the defence and a new up-to-date statement of the basic substance of Christianity which is just as dear and as natural to that Christian as it is to us Catholics. To sum up, it could be said that if the future themes of the papal teaching authority and the direction of its impact were clearly and frankly stated by Rome and if at the same time the *procedure* now possible and necessary for Rome to arrive at the truth and make a decision were made clearer and more patently observed, the Vatican doctrine of the papal teaching primacy should no longer be as hitherto a spectre disturbing the faith and conscience of the Protestant Christian. At the same time the question remains entirely open whether in the foreseeable future any papal *ex cathedra* decisions at all need be expected or whether there are reasons for assuming that this is unlikely.

Finally, a word about the open questions involved in the two Marian dogmas defined by Pius IX and Pius XII. In themselves and as the only really concrete examples of *ex cathedra* decisions by the pope alone, they are also among the stumbling blocks for Protestant and Orthodox Christians in regard to the Roman Church created since Trent.

As far as the first of the Marian dogmas is concerned, I venture to suggest that a possible orthodox further development of the dogma of original sin may make it easier to prove than by an appeal to revelation in the strict sense and thus to remove also the offensive and incredible features that Protestant Christians see in it. If we want to elucidate the dogma of original sin today with reference to *all* human beings *and* at the same time equally clearly and unmistakably to grasp by faith the fact that every Adamite human being, even in an infralapsarian state, always and from the very beginning comes within the scope of God's supernaturally beneficent salvific will (a salvific will that does not merely imply an intention on God's part, but is a supernatural existential of the offer of grace presented always and everywhere), then original sinfulness is not simply a state chronologically prior to the offer of grace to freedom: it is 'dialectically' co-existent with the offer of salvation and grace as a determination of man, who is always and everywhere in his situation of freedom descended simultaneously from both Adam and Christ and freely ratifies one situation of freedom or the other. If it is recalled that Mary also is redeemed by Christ—that is, she is in need of redemption and this need is among the permanent existentials of her existence—then the normal infralapsarian human being and Mary are not really distinguished because of a difference in a period of time at the beginning of existence, but because Mary receives the offer of grace to her freedom in virtue of her predestination to be the mother of Jesus and consequently as an offer efficaciously prevailing and as such also perceptible in salvation history. A Protestant theology of pure grace, efficacious as such, should not really find this distinction offensive. The dogma of the Immaculate Conception does not necessarily imply that the beginning of grace for her is different in a temporal sense from what it is for us, who likewise do not receive grace for salvation as a permanent existential of our freedom for the first time only in baptism.

It might be almost easier to achieve an agreement with Protestant theology on the second Marian dogma. For the content of the doctrine of the Assumption does not imply that Mary's 'bodily' assumption into heaven is a privilege granted (apart from Jesus) to her alone. It was obvious, for instance, to the Fathers of the Church that the Old Testament patriarchs in limbo at the time of Christ's resurrection entered bodily into their eternal bliss. If today, as against a Platonizing interpretation of the 'separation of body and soul' at death, we may certainly hold that every human being acquires his risen body at death, 'at that very moment' (in so far as terms relating to time make sense in this respect), a view often maintained in Protestant theology and quite legitimate with the aid of a little justifiable demythologizing, then this dogma does not refer to something granted to Mary alone, but to what belongs generally to all who are saved, while appropriate to her in a special way in virtue of her function in salvation history and consequently more clearly understood in the Church's sense of faith than it is in other human beings. It can therefore be said that even in regard to these two Marian dogmas there need be no insuperable point of controversy, if the open questions undoubtedly involved also in these dogmas are clearly recognized.

On the whole, the Catholic theologian may rightly assume that there are no theological opinions today that can be shown with certainty to be absolutely binding on one side or the other in a sense that would necessitate and authorize a division of the churches. We are speaking of the present time. It might of course be said that, if there are no such diversities of opinion today justifying a division of the churches, they could not have existed in the past, which however is unlikely. Against this objection it must be said that an agreement on articles of faith, always possible in principle, needs also to be explicitly grasped as possible and this requires time and history, the length of which cannot be *a priori* decided and defined. Moreover it must be remembered that the schism of the sixteenth century involved not only the fact that no explicit agreement had been reached, but also an illegitimate disagreement in which both sides were at fault in regard to a linguistic usage on the part of the Catholic Church: a rejection of a common language which was not necessarily an objectively existing *heretical* opposition, but which in any case had a schismatic character, even though this opposition does not perhaps persist everywhere today.

If we say that present-day theology no longer sees any insuperable points of dogmatic controversy or any antagonism implying a clear and straightforward mutual contradictory opposition between the teachings of the actual churches, if, that is, we think that in ecumenical questions the task is no longer really one for theologians but for the authorities in the Church, that the latter may not regretfully shrug their shoulders and blame everything on the disagreement of the theologians, this of course does not mean that the theologians no longer have any ecumenical task. The possible, already existing, or emerging agreement between the teachings of the separated churches must of course be much better elucidated and worked out in detail. It is the task of the theologians to make clear to the Church's magisterium in Rome, which is still a long way from adequately assimilating present-day entirely orthodox theology, that in theological terms agreement already exists today or is immediately possible: these theologians must seek to gain an understanding in Rome for different theological languages which could legitimately bring the separated churches into the unity of the Church; they must gain an understanding in Rome for the fact that there is a legitimate pluralism in the theologies of the one Church of the one faith, a pluralism that can certainly have an effect on the understanding of faith and the practice of the life of the particular churches. If a dogmatic agreement of the separated churches is considered possible today, the question of course remains open as to who on the Protestant side is the authorized partner, who can decide that an agreement on faith is binding. For within the Protestant Churches there are of course groups and theologies with which this agreement cannot be established, since these groups and theologians are plainly opposed to the basic substance of Christian faith and consequently cannot be positively included in this agreement. This means of course that new questions are raised that cannot be discussed here.

Traditional neoscholastic theology, in which we were trained and which still prevails in Rome despite Vatican II more or less as a matter of course and is put forward without hesitation also in present-day Roman doctrinal statements, overlooked many questions which the binding dogma of the Church leaves open. This neglect of open questions then leads all too easily to a tacitly accepted interpretation of the binding dogma which is simply amalgamated with that dogma as if this interpretation were an intrinsic element of the dogma itself. But then there arise misunderstandings of the actual dogma which make it difficult or impossible for Protestant Christians to rediscover in Catholic teaching their own Christian faith. Here lies an important task of modern Catholic theology as a part of its ecumenical work. It is a question not only of misunderstandings existing among *Protestant* Christians in regard to Catholic dogma, but of those which *we ourselves*—Catholic Christians and theologians—have and wrongly identify with Catholic dogma. Our work therefore consists, not merely in the enlightenment of non-Catholic Christians and theologians, but before that in enlightening ourselves and in purifying our own faith from misunderstandings which we ourselves overconfidently and apathetically continue to drag along with us.

3

MAGISTERIUM AND THEOLOGY

The theme 'magisterium and theology' is certainly not without current interest for the educated Catholic, if we think of the new conflicts which have arisen recently between the Roman Congregation for the Doctrine of Faith and theologians all over the world and which have gained the interest also of a wider public. The educated Catholic is concerned with conflicts of this kind, since the questions raised are not restricted to the narrower field of specialist theology, but also affect the life of the ordinary Catholic; he is also concerned because in these cases at the present time on the one hand his sympathies are mostly on the side of the 'progressive' theologians and yet on the other hand as a devout Catholic he is prepared to respect the Church's magisterium. Our theme then may be expected to interest the educated Catholic, even if he is not a professional theologian.

It is clear in the first place that only a few observations on this theme are possible here, since a comprehensive and exhaustive treatment would require a very large book. Even then the theme might be discussed in a variety of ways. It would be possible to attempt to state more or less precisely and to justify the teaching of the Church's magisterium about itself, which alone would be a considerable and difficult task. But this is not the procedure to be adopted here. Certainly, this teaching of the magisterium about itself must be briefly recalled at the beginning. But then, as far as this is possible in a brief space, there ought to be some discussion of problems, viewpoints, and connections between theology and magisterium, which are not adequately considered in the teaching of this magisterium but are nevertheless important for the present-day relationship between magisterium and theology and have to be understood up to a point also by someone who is not a professional theologian but who shares in the life and thought of the Church.

First of all then we may recall as briefly as possible the more important theological statements made by the Church's magisterium about itself as the content of its self-understanding, assuming that these statements are presented by the magisterium on the whole as absolutely binding, as *dogma* of the Catholic Church. The Church is instituted by Jesus Christ, has its origin from him, however this institution or origin is to be precisely understood, which is also something that cannot be discussed here. As a result of this provenance the Church is to form the permanent presence of Jesus Christ in the world, the public presence of the faith that in Jesus Christ the irrevocable and victorious word of God's promise went out into the world and will never perish. The Church, understood in this way, has a sociological structure also by the very fact that it is a community of *faith*. It is not merely a community of believers forming a unity in Christ; it has a mandate and a mission to attest and proclaim this faith to the world. It can fulfill both these requirements (unity of the same faith and mission of proclamation) as a sociologically structured entity only if there is in it a concretely palpable and legally competent authority, which provides in a special (but not exclusive) sense for the task of the unity of faith in the Church and the active proclamation of this faith to the world.

It is true that such an official legal authority is obviously not something confronting the Church as superior to the latter, but is itself fundamentally sustained by the victorious power of the Spirit of Christ, who alone in the last resort guarantees the permanency of the one faith in Jesus Christ, crucified and risen, and the strength to make the Christian message effective. But this very fact means that the historical sociological character of the Church as Jesus' community of faith does not exclude but includes the presence in this community of a personal, legally competent authority, who undertakes the task above-mentioned in a special way in the power of the Spirit of Christ. According to Catholic ecclesiology, the concrete bearers of this function, who form this authority, are present in the whole episcopate of the Catholic Church with and under the Bishop of Rome, the pope; the latter is not purely and simply *primus inter pares* in the episcopal college, but (without canceling the fundamental and ultimate magisterial authority of the episcopate as a whole) as an individual official person combines in himself this teaching authority of the entire episcopate, although at the same time the pope acts precisely *as* legally competent head of this episcopate as a whole. This supreme teaching authority, itself composed of pope and total episcopate in unity, exercises its function either in the activity of what is called the ordinary magisterium (that is, by the normal doctrinal proclamation which takes place generally everywhere in the most varied shapes and forms in the Church) or in an extraordinary way (as, for instance, in councils); but we shall not be concerned with the question of which ways of utilizing this magisterium belong precisely to its ordinary or to its extraordinary activity (whether, for example, a papal encyclical represents one form or the other of the magisterium).

According to the Catholic understanding of the Church, this magisterium has also a formal authority: that is, while it obviously must justify its individual doctrinal statements from the heart of Christian faith, from Scripture, in the light of the assured faith of the whole Church, this authority of the magisterium, in order to make its impact on the faith and conscience of the individual Christian, must be recognized by the latter in a decision of faith which is not itself based on the authority of the magisterium, but has a more fundamental character. In other words, the authority of this magisterium for the Catholic Christian is not justified merely by the weight of the relevant arguments presented by the magisterium for its individual doctrinal statements or by the appreciation of the individual Catholic of the importance of these arguments, but by the very fact that this teaching authority as it is grasped in principle from the outset in faith speaks in virtue of the legitimate utilization of its mandate. It is impossible here to develop the Catholic teaching on the *criteria* according to which the formal legitimacy of this magisterium can and in principle also must be established for the particular case.

In its ordinary and extraordinary teaching, however, the magisterium can make use of its authority in very varying degrees and in fact simply cannot concretely avoid this gradation. It can speak with ultimate binding force (that is, it can demand for its teaching a real and definitive assent of faith) and in this sense impose its teaching as irreformable and finally binding: it can proclaim a dogma. But it can also teach in such a way that a theological doctrine is put forward as 'authentic' (as it is usually described) and yet not as ultimately binding, and thus the question remains open (even though this is generally not expressly stated) as to whether this teaching may not turn out later to be in need of completion or even to be erroneous. It is important for the educated Catholic today to understand that the magisterium can not only exercise its function by proclaiming dogmas properly so-called, that is, it need not be faced from the outset by the dilemma of proclaiming a dogma or simply of being silent. In order to be able to present the Christian faith as one and whole concretely, vividly and in a way that corresponds to particular historical situations, the magisterium must be able to put forward also provisional, more or less problematic and yet not simply nonbinding statements, since without these the Christian faith as one and whole cannot be vividly conveyed and really assimilated by the faithful in a particular historical situation. The sense of faith of the Church as a whole is like the self-understanding of a particular individual, which is always a synthesis involved in an historical process, a synthesis on the one hand of maxims grasped with absolute assent and on the other of provisional understandings formed by a person to the best of his knowledge and judgment: a self-understanding that is quite impossible without such a synthesis.

Even though theology formulates quite manageable principles, according to which it is possible to distinguish between a dogma and a merely authentic teaching, in the concrete case doubts and differences of opinion can persist also in regard to this distinction, particularly since the concrete practice of the Roman magisterium today with reference to these merely authentic declarations is almost always to avoid any explicit statement to the effect that it is a question merely of an authentic but not definitive comment of the Church's magisterium. It cannot be denied that such an authentic doctrinal pronouncement not only *can* in principle be erroneous, but in the course of history often *has been* actually erroneous; this is expressly admitted in a pastoral letter of the German episcopate on the magisterium, even though the Roman authorities on the doctrine of faith scarcely ever explicitly withdraw such concrete errors at a later date and prefer tacitly to bury them. Even according to the teaching of the Second Vatican Council the Catholic theologian is not simply free and uncommitted in regard to such an authentic teaching of the magisterium, he owes it respect. But *how exactly* this respect for the teaching can co-exist with the possibility of error in that teaching (that is, with the possibility and necessity of allowing for error and thus with the progress of theological discussion) is something on which no sufficiently clear information can be found in the teaching of the Church's magisterium. In their pastoral letter previously mentioned, the German bishops made some suggestions in this respect which were important for their Königstein declaration on *Humanae Vitae*. But the Roman magisterium itself can hardly be said to have spoken at all hitherto about the precise question of how the acknowledgment of a certain binding force of a purely authentic doctrinal declaration on the one hand can co-exist with the necessity and possibility of allowing for an error in that declaration on the other hand in the theoretical consciousness and in the conscience of the theologian and the believer, without cancelling each other out. To facilitate the understanding of such a possibility, we may certainly point to the situation in practical life of an individual consciousness where there are norms and principles of action which are understood and regarded as provisionally valid with the reservation that a later and better insight may lead to their revision.

As we said, the holder of this teaching authority in the Church is the episcopate as a whole with and under the pope. But, in connection with their teaching, the theologians, too, of course have a definite and necessary function in the Church, particularly if in the light of the Church's history it is assumed as an inescapable fact that the function of the theologian and that of the holder of the teaching office properly so-called are generally not combined in one person, but in practice today and for a long time have been assigned to different persons. From the nature of the case there will be more to be said later about this function of the theologians. There has been some talk here and there of a 'magisterium' of theologians and even attempts to refer to biblical evidence for this. But, without prejudice to a real and indispensable function of the theologians, it is better to avoid the term 'magisterium' in this connection, because it leads to misunderstandings arising from the fact that in one and the same society with reference to the same task there cannot really be two *offices* distinct from one another. In statements by the magisterium of the nineteenth and twentieth centuries the relationship between magisterium and theologians is described on the whole in a way that assigns to theologians only a function of further and more subtle interpretation of the teaching of the magisterium and of defending this teaching by showing that it is contained in the original sources of revelation: theologians are thus assigned merely a subordinate auxiliary function in the service of the magisterium. We shall see shortly that this view, taken by itself, does not do justice to the actual data or requirements of the Church's proclamation. But what has been said up to now may suffice to indicate the traditional teaching of the Church's magisterium about itself. We are coming only now to our proper subject matter which, as we pointed out at the beginning, does not consist in the repetition and substantiation of the Church's teaching on the magisterium as it actually exists, but is concerned with a further and unclarified question which may be of interest, not only to the professional theologian, but also to the educated Catholic of the present time.

It is not easy to pinpoint in advance in a few words what is to be the object of our reflections, to state the 'thesis' to be defended here, to indicate from what different aspects the matter under consideration can be approached. Without putting forward a systematically formulated thesis, we may now suggest a number of observations which seem to be important for a more exact clarification of the relationship between magisterium and theology, but without setting out these observations systematically. First of all, in the whole history of dogma and theology it can be observed that the actual dogmatic substance of faith as put forward by the magisterium in the Church's proclamation is itself always theology. In this statement 'theology' means the fact or circumstance that the dogma to be stated and proclaimed is formulated with the aid of concepts, horizons of understanding, terminologies, selective considerations, shifts of emphasis, etc., which in a particular mental climate are or can be quite legitimately and concretely unavoidable and necessary, but on their own account do not themselves possess the dignity of dogma as such. The dogma is inevitably always formulated with the aid of theology, which itself is not dogma: that is, it is not as such revealed and irreformable. Even dogma properly so called is always a synthesis of what is properly and originally revealed and of human reflection, which is not actually revealed but is, precisely, theology. The *successful achievement* of such a synthesis, when it is a question of a dogma properly so called, can be guaranteed by the defining authority of the magisterium, but a statement of this kind always remains a synthesis: a statement whose dogmatic validity and irreformability does not exclude but includes the fact that, despite its inerrancy, it is open to the future for a new form of expression, to be worked out with the tools of a different theology, to be stated in different terms, against different backgrounds of understanding, under the influence of different theological truths, etc. If this were not the case we could not speak even of a legitimate pluralism of theologies in Scripture, new and hitherto unknown terms now sanctioned by the magisterium could not appear in dogmatic statements: in a word, there would be no history of *dogma*, but at most a history of theology.

Unfortunately it cannot be illustrated here by concrete examples from the history of dogma, but the fact is that theology is always at work in the formation of dogma itself, that theology cannot simply be *merely* the subsequent reflection on dogma, not affecting the dogma itself. Theology therefore is an intrinsic element of that very process which is behind the Church's proclamation and carried out by the magisterium. This is true even when concretely and in practice the representatives of the magisterium and the representatives of speculative theology are not identical. When representatives of the magisterium teach and define, they have themselves also been theologians or have made use, explicitly or implicitly, of the help of theologians. This can be seen even more clearly when we consider that the actual history of the activity of the magisterium has scarcely been under the latter's own control. In practice in its defining or authentic doctrinal statements the magisterium sanctions a development of the Church's sense of faith which had been stimulated and sustained by unofficial theology *before* this sanctioning. In this respect the magisterium is always and in principle dependent on theology, even though this dependence is not of a *legal* character, even though it follows from this very fact that the representative of the magisterium in the exercise of his task cannot by any means avoid being himself something of a theologian, since (as it is stressed, for instance, in the Second Vatican Council) he must make sure that his decision is authorized by the original sources and data of revelation, by Scripture and binding tradition, by Christian teaching as a whole; in other words, the function of his office may not be confused with a magico-mechanical process on the basis of its purely formal authority.

Theology does not merely *precede* the proclamation of the magisterium in the sense described (since any proclamation from the very outset inevitably contains an element of reflection, which as such is not simply identical with the primordial event of revelation) but also necessarily *follows after* this proclamation, a subsequent reflection which cannot be regarded as unimportant for the proclamation of the magisterium itself. Any dogmatic proclamation of the Church by the ordinary or extraordinary magisterium, if it is really to be understood, must be able to 'get across', must always also be interpreted, explained, adapted to the general and even secular horizons of understanding of those who hear it, although this task could not be said or expected to be adequately accomplished solely by the magisterium itself in its official proclamation. This is not the case, nor could so much be expected from the magisterium when it is actually teaching authoritatively. The very fact that this teaching is imposed as binding means that it inevitably falls short to some extent of the presentation of the proclamation of faith as the latter actually 'gets across' to the particular hearer in his own intellectual, cultural, and historical situation.

Strictly binding formulation of doctrine by the magisterium, valid for the Church as a whole, is inevitably something traditional in an 'old fashioned' way; it brings the Church's memory with binding force into the present, without on that account being able always to make this memory completely an actual possession of the present time. This of course does not mean that a pope or bishop cannot preach in a way that will make the message completely topical. But by that very fact such a representative of the magisterium is acting as a theologian, he works with terms, horizons of understanding and ways of access to the message which belong to the present time and with which at least generally he has no absolute guarantee that his synthesis between the binding content of his message and his present-day means of expression will certainly and entirely succeed; at the same time he is also necessarily always 'only' a theologian who speaks on his own account and at his own risk and must wait to see whether and how the concrete shape of his preaching and proclamation is recognized in the Church's sense of faith as a successful synthesis of the old faith and the present-day understanding of it.

A further task of theology, subsequent to the Church's teaching but indispensable and continually to be observed in its actual achievement, consists in examining again and again the synthesis just mentioned between what is really consciously accepted in faith and its historically conditioned means of expression, to see whether it can still be adequately assimilated in faith or whether it needs to be expressed in ways more easily accessible today; it is particularly necessary to discover whether the older formulations, while remaining permanently valid, do not actually contain amalgams which, notwithstanding the normative character of the formulations, can and even must be eliminated. In this connection some of the many concrete examples from the history of dogma would facilitate a better understanding, but it is impossible to cite them here. At least one example however can be mentioned.

Up to the time of Pius XII all formulations of the permanent Catholic teaching on original sin had taken monogenism for granted. Today we can and must see that this assumption is uncertain or false, that it is an amalgam which is not binding and can be eliminated from the permanent teaching on original sin, precisely in order to render credible the proclamation of this dogma. From this indispensable task of theology, subsequent to the function of the magisterium, it becomes clear that statements of the magisterium (not only authentic statements but also definitions of dogma) do not simply represent an endpoint, a conclusion which needs only to be repeated and defended, but are continually involved in an unfinished and never to be completed process which itself is not actually inaugurated and cannot be completely controlled by the magisterium and the results of which in the future cannot clearly be foreseen. This continuing process—as the history of dogma shows—can of course again lead to new statements which are put forward as binding by the magisterium itself and guaranteed by the latter's formal authority. It can often but need not always be like this. But, either way, the history of faith with reference to a particular reality of faith is not closed but continues.

Even from these few observations, which can be made in regard to the Church's history of dogma and doctrine and which might be complemented by many others more exact, it can be seen how complicated is the relationship between magisterium and theology. For faith and its history the magisterium is not the primary and most fundamental datum, since its existence and formal authority must be established and grasped by revelation and faith as prior to the magisterium itself; the magisterium always works with a theology which always precedes it as the means of its own proclamation, although this theology may not be adequately and thoroughly considered in its origin, in its usefulness, and in its pluralism by the magisterium, but is used by the latter in a trust in the power of the self-revealing Spirit of God who is not really subject to the reflection of the magisterium. If and when the magisterium has fulfilled its function for the time being on any particular occasion, the work of theology continues and does not consist merely in proving the legitimate derivation of statements of the magisterium from the sources of revelation and in defending these statements in face of critical reason, but also always leads again beyond the statements and by that very fact provides the magisterium again with an opportunity to say something new and not merely to repeat the old formulations. The magisterium and its statements are therefore a normative authority for theology, but conversely theology is an indispensable condition of existence and effective survival for the magisterium, without which the latter itself could not exist or act at all. Between magisterium and theology then there is a relationship of *mutual* dependence with a character of course proper to each occasion: a mutual dependence in which neither of the two elements can be completely derived from the other, a mutual dependence whose indissoluble unity is guaranteed in the last resort, not by the magisterium itself, but only by the unity of the Church, by revelation itself and the power of the Spirit of God. Within this unity the magisterium has its own and necessary function, but it is not the whole and not really the most fundamental datum from which all the rest could be deduced. Despite the commission of the apostles and their episcopal successors, its function from God and Jesus Christ is only a *partial* function in the Church, which is conceivable only in the totality of the Church (which is more than the magisterium) and can be shown to be legitimate and become actually effective only within this totality.

Between the individual constitutive elements of the Church (original revelation, continually renewed reflection on it in practice and theory, magisterium as event of perceptible unity concretely coming to be again and again in faith, sacrament, etc.) there exists a continual reciprocal causality, which is the history of the truth of the

Church and as such history sustained, controlled, and freely governed by the Spirit of God and not in the last resort by the magisterium itself. This history, never completely under the control of human beings, not even of officeholders in the Church, also always contains the relationship between magisterium and theology within its ceaseless course and thus always implies also an irremoveable historicity of the magisterium itself, of theology in the Church, of the mutual relationship between these two, a historicity consequently which maintains their permanency while continually transforming the concrete shape of their relationship, without any possibility of foreseeing clearly what this concrete shape will be in the future. The legal structure of the magisterium therefore, despite a formal definability in itself and in its relationship to theology, in its concreteness is always involved also in a process of historical change. What must be *concretely* the relationship of the magisterium to theology and of theology to the magisterium is not something clearly evident once and for all, but is always to be discovered afresh through new experiences in new forms.

I am acutely aware of the fact that I have spoken very abstractly about the relationship between magisterium and theology. Unfortunate as it may be, it was not possible to elucidate the meaning of this with the aid of concrete examples and individual cases. It may all become a little more clear and understandable if in what follows an attempt is made to put forward some more or less concrete and practical *conclusions* from these considerations of principle, which may be of some importance also for the non-theologian.

(1) Not only on the part of theologians, but also on the part of representatives of the magisterium, there must be a genuine will for dialogue. It has often been said and not entirely incorrectly that the magisterium does not discuss, but decides. It is of course true that it is not a question here of a dialogue in which the partners have the same function. But it would be wrong to suggest that the magisterium itself is dispensed from practising theology in this dialogue, that it can rely as if by magic on its formal authority and the justification of this *alone,* that it need not allow for error in its purely authentic doctrinal statements, that it cannot also fall short in decisions involving a definition; it would be wrong to assume that even definitions cannot turn out better or worse, may not be more or less easy to assimilate, that they cannot integrate into themselves to a

greater or lesser extent the totality of what was to be defined; it would also be wrong to claim that even definitions may not include assumptions, use terminology, or imply amalgams that are inadequate or even false and therefore can be eliminated, even though these need not always be noticed explicitly by the representatives of the magisterium at the time of the definition. If the representatives of the magisterium are clearly aware of all this, it will become clear that they can exercise their function properly only in a genuine dialogue with theology, even though the partners to the dialogue do not have the same function in this respect.

(2) From this it follows certainly that declarations of the magisterium today and in future will have to show more evidence than was generally shown formerly of the necessary preceding dialogue with theology and a greater readiness for dialogue on the part of representatives of the magisterium. It may and must indeed be *definitely established* that these declarations of the magisterium are not simply expressions of opinion on the part of a few Roman theologians who happen to be engaged in dialogue with one another, expressions of opinion which are worth no more than the arguments put forward, the importance of which is to be judged wholly and entirely by those to whom they are submitted. But none of this excludes the necessity for the magisterium today also to put forward expressly and clearly arguments of its own, which of course it must have, and the desirability of an explicit indication by the magisterium in its declaration of the extent to which its teaching is binding, in other words, whether the declaration is presented as authentic or as dogma properly so-called. Any such explicit qualification has been omitted by the Roman authorities up to the present time. It is assumed that the qualification will be immediately obvious to theologians in the light of the traditional rules; an explicit qualification is omitted evidently because it is thought that an official dogmatic statement will not be taken sufficiently seriously or respected if it is expressly assigned by the teaching authorities themselves the quality of merely an authentic (that is, in principle reformable) teaching, if the impression is not created that the teaching put forward is basically irreformable.

Apart however from the fact that a procedure of this kind creates among theologians and other believers the impression of a certain lack of sincerity and can lead to conflicts of conscience which are objectively entirely superfluous (we may recall, for instance, *Huma-*

nae Vitae), the method does not help the dialogue between magisterium and theology. Even when it is a question of teaching that is absolutely binding, of a dogma, this dialogue is not closed but can and must always be carried forward; but it is particularly appropriate when it is a question of merely authentic statements of the magisterium. But the exact form of dialogue is often different and the opportunities are greater when it is settled from the outset and clearly and expressly stated that it is a question merely of authentic teaching, which certainly must be taken seriously by the theologian and which acquires in virtue of the formal authority of the magisterium a different importance from that of any odd theological opinion; nevertheless it is in principle reformable and can be scrutinized and questioned by theologians in an entirely different way from what is possible with a dogma properly so-called, which cannot really be doubted, even though it can and occasionally must always be open to an interpretation leading with the aid of different conceptual methods to a better, more comprehensively integrating formulation. The Roman authorities on faith should not think that they are forfeiting their effectiveness and power if they make immediately clear by such a qualification the possible and justified continuation of dialogue with the theologians. Even faith and still more purely authentic teachings of the Church, which at least hitherto have been just that, are involved in a history that is not and cannot be closed. This history however should not be carried on by confrontations between magisterium and heretical positions of theologians, but by dialogue in which both partners unequivocally respect the unrenounceable function of whoever happens to be the other partner at the time. This respect demands from the magisterium in theory and practice an appreciation of the fact that theology is not merely the executive assistant of the magisterium, does not merely prepare the way for it or define it, but has a critical function that goes further and is irreplaceable. This is all the more important since the Church's sense of faith in practice and theology is much richer, more differentiated and active than could be objectified and set out by declarations of the magisterium *alone*.

(3) In this dialogue magisterium and theology must always allow for the fact that they take up positions in regard to one another which are absolutely correct, even binding in faith, and are expressly presented as such, but which nevertheless (although this is

not always immediately noticed by both sides) are amalgamated with ideas, terms, horizons of understanding, etc., which are not binding in faith and perhaps can be and, at a particular stage in the history of ideas, must be eliminated. If and when on the one hand such amalgams have perhaps turned up in statements actually binding in faith, but on the other hand were not noticed by one or other or both partners to the dialogue, there emerge the real situations of tension between magisterium and theology would could by no means have been avoided from the very outset, even though they are solvable in principle. The important thing in this respect of course is not the term 'amalgam'. In a more subtle and exact philosophical and theological theory of truth and its historicity it would certainly be possible to dispense with the term 'amalgam' and replace it by something better. But, since a theory of this kind is not possible here, this term can bring out our meaning sufficiently.

If, for example, it is stated as teaching binding in faith that the Church is founded by Jesus, that the sacraments are likewise instituted by him, that a conversion of the substance of bread and wine takes place in the eucharist, that three 'persons' must be really distinguished in the unity of the one God, etc., the fact is that in former times it was more or less taken for granted that terms like 'institution', 'substance', 'person', used in these formulations were quite unambiguous and clear and consequently that there could be no doubt about the exact meaning of such statements. But today in the light of history, biblical theology, and the history of ideas we can see that such terms are not as unequivocal as they were once thought and assumed to be and that on the contrary particular forms of imagery, traditional assumptions, and horizons of understanding spontaneously occur, reverberate, or are implied in them, which have by no means the binding force of irreformable statements of faith but can or must be eliminated. Without questioning, for example, the dogma of transsubstantiation as defined at the Council of Trent, we cannot think of the substance of bread today in exactly the same way as the Fathers of Trent thought of it in the concrete. In view of Jesus' imminent expectation of the kingdom of God, admitted today even in Catholic biblical theology, it is impossible to understand what is meant concretely by his institution of the Church in precisely the same way as the magisterium and theology implied in former times when they proclaimed their assurance that Jesus founded the Church, which (as we also obviously maintain) has its origin from Jesus and the enduring faith in his unsurpassable importance for salvation. In the light of the ever continuing history of ideas (not, obviously, under the control of the magisterium), it may well be doubted whether the term 'person' today in the doctrine of the Trinity produces more clarity and lucidity than misunderstanding and obscurity, without at the same time raising any doubts about the permanent binding force of the dogma of the Trinity.

The amalgamations just indicated between permanent dogma and historically conditioned terminology, conceptual models and assumptions, really provide perhaps the most important object of the dialogue between magisterium and theology. Up to the present time this has occurred, as can easily be understood, particularly in the field of morality, since in its traditional formulations (for example, with reference to what is known as 'natural law', to sexual morality and socio-ethical principles) inevitably very many historically conditioned elements are contained which can have no claim to permanent validity. In this connection the question of religious freedom discussed at the Second Vatican Council would be a good example, since the processes of elimination of amalgams from the hitherto traditional teaching here took place at the council itself. None of this means that the magisterium cannot also have the right and duty to draw attention to newly formulated positions of theologians which not only eliminate time-conditioned amalgams, but perhaps even violate what must be the permanent substance of the dogma concerned. If, for example, a theologian were to deny outright the real and necessary origin of the Church and the sacraments from Jesus or to formulate a theory of God which simply eradicated what belongs to the essence of the dogma of the Trinity, the magisterium would then obviously have the right and duty unambiguously to oppose such positions. But, since in a dialogue of this kind between magisterium and theology it may often remain uncertain for a long time whether a new formulation by a theologian merely legitimately eliminates traditional amalgams or violates or denies the substance of the dogma, it is not surprising that these dialogues need time, involve conflicts, lead to justified and also unjustified and avoidable disciplinary measures of the Church going as far as the removal of a theologian from office, and cannot quickly be ended on one side or another by an authoritative decision, which theologians also often permit themselves.

Hearing of these conflicts with their unnecessarily lengthy processes of clarification, the person who is not an expert in theology, the ordinary believer, can scarcely avoid a feeling of insecurity or impatience; he is inclined to declare that everything has become confused and blurred in the Church's life of faith and in its proclamation, that he no longer knows where he stands. Objectively speaking, this is not entirely true since, for the Christian who really wants to believe and who respects the magisterium of the Church, the real basic substance of his faith even today remains clear and obvious, and since, when periods of uncertainty and of controversies between magisterium and theology have to be endured, patience and confidence can be required also from the normal Christian. This is all the more obvious since a close examination reveals the fact that there were similar periods in early Church history and we may well think that they were brought to an end too quickly as a result of a pronouncement of the magisterium on one question or another, so that at least contradictions which were verbal but looked like objective heresies were consolidated, although they really could have been avoided if only more patience and readiness for dialogue had been shown on all sides at those times.

In any case the question of a new and more exact interpretation of the Church's teaching and also of its dogmas with the aid of a possible elimination of amalgams handed down at the same time is one of the most important objects of the dialogue between magisterium and theology and inevitably brings with it conflicts that are not always easy to settle between magisterium and theologians, conflicts that are simply part of the historicity of revelation. These conflicts cannot be avoided if only because a theologian before publishing his views cannot inquire first from the magisterium whether these are acceptable and because processes of learning are unavoidable and necessary also for representatives of the magisterium itself: for their own and (properly understood) normative sense of faith is not simply a rigid norm free from all historicity, but has itself a history. Of course the demand for dialogue does not mean (as theologians today often seem to think it means) that 'dialogue' has to go on until agreement is reached between like-minded people, rendering any actual decision of the magisterium superfluous. In a dialogue of this kind real decisions of the magisterium can and sometimes must be made in virtue of its formal authority, they must be respected by theologians to the extent required by their particular binding force.

But neither does the fact of such a decision and the duty of theologians to respect it mean that after these declarations of the magisterium all dialogue is at an end and the theologians have nothing more to do but to hand on and defend the decision. Even after such a decision the dialogue can and must go on, albeit with new assumptions. For such a decision does not leave everything quite clear, since respect for it still leaves open the question of what it does and does not contain, whether it also implicitly transmits amalgams which are not purely and simply binding, how the decision can be conveyed to the Christian of today in a way that is perhaps better than the way adopted by the magisterium itself, whether there may not be an error in purely authentic doctrinal statements. The dialogue can and must go on.

(4) In such a dialogue between magisterium and theology something else is desirable, on which we touched at an earlier stage. When the magisterium claims to be exercising its formal authority, it would be desirable and it would help toward a more exact shaping of the continuing dialogue if the magisterium itself were to state explicitly and in a new, hitherto undeveloped and unconsidered way the degree of binding force (which is not always the same) to be attached to its declaration, thus making clear what is known as the theological qualification of the latter.

This of course has happened in the course of the last hundred and thirty years when there was a question of properly *ex cathedra* decisions involving a definition. But ultimately binding decisions of this kind are rare and have actually occurred only twice in the course of the centuries since the Council of Trent. In former times however, at least up to the beginning of the nineteenth century, a theological qualification was often added to declarations of the magisterium; but after that, it was almost always omitted. In earlier times there was an enormous number of such abstract and formal theological qualifications, the terminology and meaning of which can now be grasped only with difficulty. Today certainly there is not much to be done with these traditional qualifications. It would therefore be a task for theologians, which has not yet been tackled at all, to produce a meaningful and manageable system of these formal qualifications: a task which could be accomplished by the magisterium only with difficulty. But if a theologically well-founded, simple and yet meaningfully articulated scheme of such graded qualifications was freshly worked out from the very beginning and was available, the magisterium could be expected to add an explicit qualification indicating the degree of binding force to be attached to its individual declarations. The theologian and also the interested non-theologian would then know better for theology and practice what was really involved, exactly what measure of respect (certainly not the same in every case) they had to bring to such a declaration; neither would then so easily get the impression that the magisterium was demanding a higher and more binding degree of assent than can be required in the light of its own general principles. In this question the magisterium should not tacitly assume that its declaration would not be respected at all and would simply disappear in the subsequent dialogue, if it were itself to note explicitly in a new and really practicable way the limits of the binding force of that declaration. To get to this stage however, the theologians would have to do some preliminary work that they have not yet really tackled.

(5) A final point should be noted with reference to the relationship between theology and magisterium: we cannot restrict the formal legal competence of the latter as such more closely than it is restricted by the magisterium itself. But the magisterium defines its competence as extending to all that has to do with faith and Christian morality (*de rebus fidei et morum*), even though this does not clearly answer in every respect the question as to exactly what in the field of morality falls within the competence of the magisterium (as recent controversies have shown about the competence of the magisterium in regard to what is known as natural law, when the latter as such cannot simply be declared to be revealed) and even though it means that the question of the competence which the magisterium claims for itself seems to be still obscure and unsettled. But, however that may be, the fact remains that the task of the magisterium changes in practice to no small extent with the changing mental climate in which it has to operate in the course of history.

In our time we are faced by a pluralism that can no longer be adequately integrated —of philosophies, anthropologies, cultures not now restricted only to Europe—existing even within the Church itself, so that in the light of all these things theologies, too, are slowly but increasingly clearly emerging in the plural in the Church, theologies which, although centered on one and the same Christian faith, cannot be adequately integrated into one and the same theology as it existed more or less until the middle of the present century, when in Japan, Africa, and Australia in the priests' seminaries the same theological textbooks as in Europe were used without any hesitation. Assuming that the existing Roman magisterium in all its necessary and also active efforts to gain an understanding and contact with all these plural theologies will continue at least in the immediate future to bear a European stamp and cannot represent all of them uniformly, then it can certainly be understood that the task of this magisterium in the time that is coming will not be so much the supervision of the detailed work of theology as the defence and vivid and up-to-date expression of the basic substance of the Christian faith. For the most varied reasons, which cannot be explained in detail here but largely result from the mental climate of the present time, we cannot in practice expect in the foreseeable future really new definitions like the two Marian dogmas of the nineteenth and twentieth centuries. This is evident from the fact that the Second Vatican Council refrained from such dogmatic definitions in the strict sense of the term. For quite practical reasons in the immediate future the magisterium will have no other option but to leave for a longer time and more patiently to the theologians themselves and their work and discussion many individual theological questions in which it intervened very quickly and very decidedly in the nineteenth century and in the first half of the twentieth. Any other way would simply be impossible and would represent a dangerous waste of the practical effectiveness of the authority of the magisterium. This does not mean that the importance and the task of the magisterium are diminished, but only that they are moved into another field, which is much more fundamental and important.

At a time of worldwide secularism and atheism, threatening the basic substance of Christianity and at the same time giving a fresh shape to its themes, the magisterium ought constantly and with all the resources of the Spirit to find a way of conveying both uncurtailed and vividly that basic substance to today's and tomorrow's humanity, and particularly outside Europe. This is something which the magisterium has really scarcely attempted in the past centuries; it has been occupied with marginal areas in the hierarchy of truths of the Christian faith and beyond that has perhaps encouraged a number of special forms of Christian piety and Christian life, but very largely left the living testimony of the Christian faith in its basic substance to preachers, teachers of Christian spirituality, and theologians. It seems that in this respect the task of the magisterium will have to change. It will have to be not so much merely doctrinal in regard to traditional teaching, but prophetic in such a way that the old faith and the questions of the day are brought into both vital and critical contact with each other. What this means concretely and how it could be concretely carried out is something that cannot be considered here. But it might perhaps be said that the magisterium could well become a little more theological, could undertake up to a point and in its own way tasks of the theologians that it may hitherto have left too much to the theologians and the preachers of the faith who were dependent on them. If we keep in mind the interconnection and mutual dependence of magisterium and theology of which we spoke, this new orientation of the task of the magisterium need not in the future come up against the protest that what is demanded of it is a living theology instead of the fulfillment of its specific task, which is not quite the same thing as theology. In the power of the Spirit of Christ, by common consent, magisterium and theology must work at the one task: to bear living witness to God and his crucified and risen Christ, to witness to the faith in which the final destiny of the world in the glory of God himself is victoriously grasped for all time.

Between magisterium and theology then there exists a very special relationship that makes it impossible to regard the magisterium as a factor with an impetus entirely of its own, as completely self-sufficient. If we may apply a trite comparison, it is a relationship akin to that between the bones and muscles of the body. The two differ in nature and function. And yet the bones can exercise their proper function only with the aid of the muscles and vice versa. The coordination of the two as such is guaranteed neither by the bones nor by the muscles alone, but only by the totality which is prior to the two factors, and lies in the power neither of the one nor of the other independently. So, too, not only is theology dependent on the magisterium, but the magisterium is also dependent on theology and inconceivable without the latter; and the connection and unity of the two is again not under the control of the magisterium but only under that of the Spirit, who directs the whole course of history.

4

ON BAD ARGUMENTS
IN MORAL THEOLOGY

This article is intended to deal with an epistemological question in the field of moral theology, admittedly with the reservation that only a few vague remarks are possible in so brief an article on such a difficult theme, a theme that inevitably thrusts us very quickly from the particular concern with which we started into the most general questions of philosophical and theological epistemology.

It is a question in the first place of a quite straightforward observation which, at least in the author's opinion, continually occurs to anyone who is occupied with questions of moral theology. Moral theology contains arguments. In order to substantiate moral precepts, proofs, often very rigorous and subtle, are adduced; and yet we gain the impression that these proofs tacitly and without reflection really assume from the outset the very conclusion at which they aim, that the conclusions are, so to speak, smuggled into the premises of the argument (in good faith, of course) and that the proofs are convincing only to someone who was convinced of what was to be proved even before any proof was forthcoming.

We are not going to produce examples here to support the correctness of this observation. The reason for this omission *here* is easy to understand: we should otherwise have to enter into lengthy discussions as to whether the example fitted, whether, that is, the proof of a moral precept is evident only to someone who is convinced that the maxim is true prior to any proof. If then we wanted to produce proof of the appropriateness of the example to the observation just made, we would have to enter into considerations which go beyond the scope of our present reflections. The reader is therefore requested to look for such examples from his own experience of moral theological discussions. If he finds them, well and good. If he thinks that he has never met with such experiences in his moral theology, this article has not in fact been written for him.

If however the observation to which we appealed is correct, it cannot be dismissed as the sort of trivial remark that occurs as a matter of course in any field of human study, simply because *petitiones principii* are found *everywhere*. In the light of an innocuous, normal logic of ordinary life and learning, it could indeed be said that this sort of thing does of course occur in moral theology, but only because it is part of the whole field of human error and must be eliminated as far as possible by continual strenuous efforts.

It is not however as simple as that—least of all in moral theology. Even though cases of this kind occur not only in moral theology, they are particularly evident there and for reasons that belong to the very nature of moral theology itself, in so far as the latter is a theoretical science which studies the *practical* behaviour of human beings. Here then we shall consider briefly the right and limits, not precisely of the observation from which we started out, but of what lies behind it and is not simply false. We are speaking of right and limits.

First of all there is the *right* of what lies behind the observation or indeed of what is in fact observed. When moral theology seeks with the aid of reflex argumentation to establish precepts for action, it is a question always (or almost always, or in ordinary life) of precepts which were put into practice in a person's behaviour even before they were given expression in theory. Theoretical reflections on norms of practical behaviour emerge from and are necessitated by what has already always occurred in practice. But, since it is supposed to be responsible and moral and when it is such, this practice has in itself in principle its own immanent experience of its rectitude. Hence (this is a truism, but one which is often overlooked in academic moral theological polemics on both sides of a dispute about the conclusiveness of a particular argument) it is possible that a necessarily subsequent theoretical reflection on a previous practice possibly containing its intrinsic evidence in itself does not by any means take in this evidence, interprets and conceptually objectifies it wrongly or inadequately, and yet the badly interpreted and badly substantiated precept is right. Of course, this is always apparent to formal logic which insists that a conclusion can be true even if it does not follow from the premises, whether because the premises are false or not proved, or simply because this conclusion does not logically follow from correct premises.

This reference to formal logic however does not touch the real heart of the matter. For it in no way indicates whether and how the truth of the 'conclusion' can be known otherwise than by a correct argument. But in principle this is possible in the field of morality. In that field there can be a global, still implicit, but perhaps entirely correct and effective insight which is prior to theory, to conceptual articulation and objectification, which is itself the inner light of practice as such. This is something not to be forgotten in the appraisal of a moral theological argument. The appraisal may suggest that in a particular case this argument (taken purely in its explicit conceptuality and logical coherence) is wrong or not conclusive; but in such an appraisal it must not be forgotten that the argument criticized is really (also and in the first place) to be read as an appeal and reference to a global experience in which more can be contained than what becomes conceptually and logically explicit in the course of the argument. Any attempt to deny this would in principle mean starting out from an understanding of the relationship between practice and theory that is problematic or even false. (Here of course it is impossible to go into the difficult epistemological problems of the relationship between theory and practice, problems which constitute a large part of modern philosophy and fundamental theology.)

A bad argument in moral theology then is not simply 'disposed of' by showing that it is not logically conclusive. The person who rejects it must at least explain the fact of its existence and whether it is sufficient to say that it is false or not conclusive and only reveals the stupidity of those who argue in this way; the one who rejects the argument can be asked if he cannot see behind the terminology and conceptual reasoning the wisdom of a more fundamental experience struggling to break through its clumsy expression. A counter-question of this kind is justified and important particularly when the argument declared to be false or not conclusive is upheld, not merely by a single individual, but by many people, and was even perhaps put forward without opposition for centuries in the Church and is still widely maintained.

If these further questions are not raised, going behind the disputed arguments of moral theology, there is a danger of a moral theological nihilism or scepticism *or* of a commonplace moral theological positivism, appealing solely to the simple fact of the existence of these badly proved convictions in the Church and leaving it at that. In other words, people see everywhere in moral theology an empty formalism with nothing but bad arguments and hair-splitting, insinuating what cannot really be proved; then they become sceptical in regard to all 'legality' (taking refuge in a *pure* 'situation ethic') *or* simply entrench themselves behind the formal authority of the magisterium, forgetting that this very magisterium in its purely authentic declarations can be subject to time- and situation-conditioned errors.

Seen more closely, what this sort of argument, inadequate in itself, implicitly indicates can be different in kind and quality. It can be a global knowledge of revelation, badly objectified in detail; it can be a question of an 'instinctive' human insight of a 'natural' character, which itself can be understood as taking on a variety of forms and perhaps as coming to be in a variety of ways in the course of the history of humanity.

The justifiable 'respect' given to a bad argument is bound to vary according to the special character of the truth that may lie behind it. If, for example, a correct global understanding of Christian *revelation* can be presumed behind an argument questionable in itself, then the latter must obviously be treated differently from another argument open to criticism where it is obvious from the outset that behind it there is a purely human preconception, which itself, much more easily than in the first case, can be problematic and historically or sociologically or culturally conditioned.

Admittedly, in order to be able to distinguish from the outset between the two approaches, it is necessary to have formally a principle to decide what can (and what cannot) really be regarded from the beginning as divine revelation. But this problem of a formal criterion has never or scarcely ever been considered in normal textbook theology, even though for understandable reasons it could be of great importance particularly for moral theology, if only because the competence of the Church's magisterium in the field of revelation properly so called is certainly not identical with its competence in the field of what is known as (pure) natural law. But these of course are problems that cannot be pursued further here.

If then the Church's magisterium defends a particular moral pre-

cept and (which is quite possible) does so with bad arguments, the
critic of these arguments, the individual moral theologian, must certainly allow for this possibility. He may perhaps therefore have the
task also of defending the correct precept with better arguments and
of making it more intelligible than the magisterium is able to do, for
in these things the latter cannot expect to bring a higher enlightenment to its reasoning but must make use of the arguments generally
found in the Church's moral theology.

So much then on the 'right' that can exist behind a bad argument
in moral theology, presented perhaps in a certain way without meet-
ing any opposition and often sustained by a long history of moral
theological teaching in the Church, since the conviction of the correctness of what was to be proved prevailed long before the appearance of the proof itself—now however we must look at the *limits* of
this right. And these are perhaps more important for the practice of
the Church's moral theology and of the Church's magisterium. The
tacitly and implicitly operating prior conviction of the correctness of
what is to be proved can also arise from causes which are quite
problematic or which have led, as a result of their own historical
relativity, to false global prescientific convictions. There are also
false (historically time-conditioned, global, instinctively operating)
convictions which then seek objective expression in explicit conceptual 'proofs', so that to anyone who shares these convictions the
proofs are very obvious and they are put forward and defended with
the absoluteness with which people cling to such a prescientific
global conviction, even though the latter is false or at least questionable. In life, too, prior to any scientific reflection, there are judgments that are not inspired by the wisdom of experience but are
'prejudgments', which are historically, culturally, and sociologically
conditioned, are changeable, can be erroneous always or in a different situation. The actual development and history of moral theology
in the Church has to do largely, not only with the destruction of
incorrect or uncertain theological arguments purely as such, but
with the demolition of such prescientific instinctive convictions
which are false or unproved, but hitherto made the explicit arguments seem 'obvious'.

At the same time unfortunately the untenability of such moral
theological arguments is actually realized and recognized very often
(even though not always) in the Church only when the global presci-

entific conviction, based on *other* reasons (of history, of sociological changes, of changes in the human psyche, etc.), *behind* the arguments has been demolished. Examples might perhaps be cited also of explicit counter-arguments against the reasons used to support false moral precepts, counter-arguments which led to the breakdown of these false global convictions; it will often also be necessary to allow for a long historical process in the course of which in many questions there is a *mutual* interaction between rational counter-arguments and a breakdown of preconceptions for other reasons. But it may certainly be honestly admitted that the Church's moral theology and its arguments very often cleared the field of certain positions and recognized the untenability of earlier arguments for these positions only *after other* historical factors had already destroyed the preconceptions on which, whether they noticed it or not, people had based their arguments. This may be understandable, but it is not very edifying for the historian of the Church's moral theology. It may be said that the Church is conservative in the light of its task of safeguarding the deposit of faith, that this conservatism gives it a legitimate albeit limited function in the history of ideas which is not to be underestimated and may not be depreciated from the very outset. But it is in fact also part of the tragic and impenetrable historicity of the Church that in practice and theory it defended moral precepts with bad arguments, based on problematic, historically conditioned preconceptions, 'prejudgments', which it did not itself abandon but which other historical causes eliminated; only then did the Church finally find the new conviction obvious and (unfortunately) proceeded to act as if the new global conviction was obvious and the Church had never had any doubts about it.

How many examples can a moral theologican produce without more ado of occasions when the Church's magisterium also *expressly* acknowledged such revisions of its own standpoint and at the same time admitted that it owed this better understanding to causes other than its own efforts to break down prejudices? I do not think that the average moral theologian could produce many such examples immediately. But it would be fine if things were different.

This dark tragedy of the Church's history of ideas is all the more depressing, since it always or often involved questions which have a profound influence on the concrete life of human beings, for such false precepts (which objectively were never valid or had long become obsolete through cultural and economic changes not at first recognized by the institutional Church) imposed burdens on human beings (at the same time endangering their salvation) which were not at all legitimate in the light of the freedom of the Gospel.

If what we have said is more or less right, it means that moral theology in its own field has the task of analyzing much more closely, critically, and courageously the provenance and historico-sociological relativity of those preliminary decisions which are at work behind the arguments of traditional textbook theology and also of the Church's magisterium. More concretely it means that a distinction is to be made especially in the field of moral theology much more clearly and courageously between a tradition that really carries on an indubitable divine revelation and one that is merely 'human' and possesses no guarantee of its correctness and supratemporal validity, even if it has been held universally and unquestioningly in the previous history of Christianity and the Church. In regard to the critical distinction between these two 'traditions' it must also be remembered that a 'human' tradition may even have been absolutely right for a particular time, because it deduced the right precepts *for that time* from the human and sociological conditions and the fact of the situation which then prevailed but were not themselves unchangeable. Under certain conditions such an instinctive basic conviction was indeed morally binding for that time, but *only* for that time. If we consider such changes and possibilities of change, if in the light of an established (but not yet sufficiently thoroughly considered) theory of the real nature of strictly supernatural revelation we perceive that only very few individual moral precepts (which?) are a part of actual revelation as such, then we can have an idea of the changes possible in 'Christian' morality, despite the history of these prior convictions enduring almost two thousand years but largely containing only 'human' tradition.

If then it is entirely a task for moral theology in a good conservative spirit perhaps often to preserve the genuinely human element of historical moral tradition, even if the content of that tradition is historically conditioned and is explicitly recognized as changeable in itself (since not everything that is changeable must necessarily be changed), it is also the task of academic moral theology, not only to expose as such what is unproved in the course of the argument, but also to work to break down the preconceptions behind it, if these are themselves historically conditioned and no longer correspond to the concrete 'reality' they are meant to support and which they reproduce without further consideration. This is a difficult task for which the Church's magisterium with its conservative attitude (understandable but perhaps also unjustified) generally shows little gratitude.

If moral theology thus has a history in its actual process of knowledge (which is by no means conditioned solely by theoretical reflection and argument since it is also conditioned by factors that do not belong to the field of theoretical reflection at all and for that reason alone simply *cannot* be eliminated and since theory always rests on a pretheoretical realization of human and Christian existence) then moral theology is an ongoing process which in the last resort cannot be foreseen, which cannot exclude all friction, conflict, and danger, indissolubly linked as these are with the history of ideas. The courage to take risks, to face opposition and criticism, is therefore among the virtues of the moral theologian (as we respect and admire them, for instance, in a person like Bernard Häring) since, for the reasons indicated, the moral theologian cannot be merely the interpreter and defender of the traditional teaching of the magisterium, but also its critic who helps the magisterium to understand better and more effectively to defend before humanity the teaching of Christian revelation and of man's self-understanding in the history of his morality.

It would be possible to develop the suggested starting point further. It would be possible to reflect on the fact that the concepts used in *any* moral theological argument always form a unity of concept and image and the argument is based on a *conversio ad phantasma* (to adopt the terminology of Aquinas) and is impossible otherwise; that any argument, if it is to be understood at all, always appeals *also* to the concrete reality already grasped in experience and action, that is always also culturally and sociologically (in fact historically) conditioned. (For when the moral theologian speaks of money, authority, family, truth in intercommunication, sexuality, and so on in the course of his argument, how can he prevent the involvement or reverberation in these terms of something that is historically conditioned and not perennially valid?) Of course in an argument so unavoidably historically conditioned something of these historically conditioned representational and visual models becomes explicitly visible, can be criticized and perhaps eliminated and replaced by a different (again necessary) representational model, which admittedly itself remains historically conditioned, so that it is impossible to aim at a 'chemical purity' of the concept as such as distinct from the visual model. But the critical discrimination between concept and image is always possible only up to a point and is never completed. There is always some part of a representational model that is not seen and considered in its historical relativity, but is nevertheless secretly at work in such a moral theological argument. Hence there are two points which the moral theologian must keep in mind in his arguments.

First, the argumentative process (which must take the form of a dialogue) never reaches an absolutely definitive conclusion; the concrete representational models (especially those in a transitional stage), without which any concept would be empty, must continually be investigated under new historical conditions for their validity, their changeability and the possibility of their elimination; the experience must continually be made and permitted of the constant temptation in a moral theological argument (which is a historical process) to get away from what is really being considered, because the latter has changed in the meantime or is actually being changed.

Second, a moral theological argument is always or frequently (although mostly implicitly but unavoidably) also an appeal in a historical decision to uphold that concrete although historically conditioned reality which, as concrete, lies behind even the abstract argument as its 'visualization', without which there is no concept and no argument. Whether a latent appeal of this kind, implicit in the argument, reaches it's goal, persists, and brings it about that a future history (at least history in the immediate future) also really *wills* it to remain not only as 'proved' in the argument but also as implicitly *required* as a postulate of practical reason, the future will decide, not the person who is arguing. He may be successful or he may not. He can indeed be convinced that his argument will continue to be effective also in the future, *if* and insofar as that argument gets to the really metaphysical, transcendentally necessary nature of the case (that is, of man). But, since he cannot ascertain this with utter clarity by an absolutely adequate distinction between (metaphysical) concept and (historically conditioned) visualization, he still cannot be absolutely clear as to whether the argument which he firmly maintains as valid is one that is really metaphysically conclusive, one that will continue to be effective for all future time and that participates in the permanent validity of the metaphysical nature attained by it, or one that can be regarded as valid only if and insofar as the factor of an appeal (explicit or implicit) is also accepted.

The moral theologian need not be upset about this situation. For in principle he certainly has the right involved in every free, always unavoidable historical decision to want the concreteness of the visualization, to which he perhaps appeals without reflection or really adequate discrimination, to persist and not to be changed, even though he does not know whether this historical will of his own (that is perhaps also still concealed in such an abstract argumentation) will actually be effective. But in any case it becomes clear that the theory to be supported by argument is itself also a part of practice, whether this is known or not.

In our reflections up to now we started out from the tacit assumption that there are purely and simply *two* kinds of argumentation in moral theology: right and wrong (or unproved). But now we certainly ought to make some more precise distinctions. Right (correct, true) can *either* be one that gets at the transcendentally necessary nature of man and is consequently bound to proceed in the hope that it will continually be effective. (We are leaving aside here the question of whether and how there are positive precepts given by divine supernatural revelation which in themselves and in their demonstration do not really come under the first type of argumentation and yet possess the hope and the claim to continually enduring validity.) *Or* the argumentation can be right, because and if it derives its correctness (explicitly or mostly implicitly) also from the representational model with which the concepts of the argumentation are put forward.

If an argument of this kind is or is supposed to be right, two further possibilities can be conceived. (1) *Either* this representational model is generally accepted and undisputed, even by those against whom the argument is directed; in other words, the argumentation proceeds in the light of an anthropological, cultural, and sociological situation which generally prevails and is recognized within the concrete milieu of the argumentation, even though as such it is historically conditioned and not of metaphysical necessity. In such cases for the most part no absolutely clear borderline can be

drawn at all between the metaphysical element of the concepts used
and the historically conditioned visual model. This kind of argumentation may certainly be described as true, particularly since even
historically conditioned situations, as long as they remain unchal-
lenged, can really give rise to a moral imperative, even though the
latter need not be always and perennially valid. (2) *Or* the visual
model used (explicitly or mostly unthematically) in the argumentation is actually imperiled in the situation of the person arguing, but in
itself it is meaningful; in a case like this the argument carries an
implicit 'appeal' (as we described it) for the maintenance of the
situation envisaged by him in his historical decision, whether this
character of an appeal as part of the argument is deliberately intended or (which frequently or mostly will be the case) not. If there
is a chance in the foreseeable future that the appeal implicit in such
an argumentation will be successful, the argument can safely be
described as 'true', even though this 'truth' is also established by a
(meaningful if not also theoretically conclusive) decision of practical
reason itself, which is also implied in its own right in apparently
purely theoretical argumentation. It may be admitted that the qualification of this kind of argumentation as 'true' presupposes a conception of the relationship between theory and practice in which practice is not purely and simply the application of the precepts of
theoretical moral reason, but has also an underivable autonomous
status, sets up truth and does not merely accept it. But these are
problems of course which cannot be pursued further here.

A moral theological argument is false, untrue, not only if it cannot
deduce what it asserts from the transcendentally necessary nature of
reality, but also when even the representational model is lacking
with which it has to work in order to be able to be recognized as true.
The absence of such a really sustaining representational model can
again be understood in *two* ways, even though these two ways coincide up to a point.

Either (*first way*) an appeal is made in this argument to an historically conditioned state of man (which provides the representational
model) which is simply no longer universally valid (for the group
involved in this dialogue) and is taken for granted as universally
valid by the person who makes this appeal only because of his
historical and sociological backwardness and his failure to keep up
with the times, although (and this is presupposed) it cannot by any

means be said that man's historically conditioned state is required by his metaphysical nature or that it is disregarded only through man's (objective) fault. With the lack of historical and cultural simultaneity on the part of human beings, despite their chronological simultaneity, it cannot be denied that wrong arguments of this kind frequently occur also in the Church and are at the bottom of a good many moral theological controversies.

Or, the *second way* in which this wrong argumentation occurs lies in the fact that it not only cannot legitimately deduce its assertion from man's metaphysical nature, but implies an appeal to an historical decision that in practice has no serious chance of success, because the historical situation to which the appeal is made is admittedly not yet passed, but is so imperiled, so patently disintegrating, that it can be foreseen that in the long run this appeal will in fact remain ineffective. The argumentation in this second way can be described as untrue for the same reasons as those on account of which an argument with an implicit appeal to an implicit historical decision offering ample prospects was previously described as true. The two forms of wrong argumentation in moral theology naturally tend to overlap, without being able to be distinguished with absolute certainty from one another, since the judgment on the chances of success of the appeal mentioned is a matter of practical reason and can have no theoretical certainty.

All that we wanted to do here was to put forward a few considerations and ideas about bad arguments in moral theology. If these reflections once more give rise to the most obscure and difficult questions of human knowledge of the most general character (questions which were noted here without attempting to provide a clear and certain answer to them) this lies in the nature of the case. The moral theologian knows that actions which are to be described concretely as immoral always, contrary to their intention, implicitly affirm the incomparability of good in relation to evil, the inescapable dependence of man on the absolute good, the sacred dignity of conscience. But all this really means also or makes immediately evident the fact that, even in a wrong moral theological argument, at least implicitly, but really, that light is affirmed which is inherent in freedom and love and which in the last resort comes from the absolute love and freedom which we call God.

PART TWO

Theology of God and Christology

5

THE HUMAN QUESTION OF MEANING IN FACE OF THE ABSOLUTE MYSTERY OF GOD

E very age has a number of expressions, key terms which serve to sum up its task and its longings in the light of the special character of its own situation. Christians will always count faith, hope, and love among these key terms, even though they have varied the emphasis from one to another of them in the course of the history of Christianity. Logos was certainly one of the many key terms; it played an important part in the history of ideas in late antiquity. Order was regarded as a key term in the philosophy and theology of the High Middle Ages, particularly in the work of Aquinas. Enlightenment, emancipation from self-alienation, utopia, and hope are also terms of crucial importance intended to invoke human existence as a whole and ringing in our ears today. Whether key terms are genuinely of Christian origin or come to Christianity and the Church more or less from outside, critically, perhaps accusing, and in any case challenging, Christians and their theologians are certainly called upon to confront the proclamation of the Christian message with them, to measure the message by them and them by the message and thus bring about a historical kairos which satisfies both Christianity and its unsurpassable message and also the task and longing of the particular historical moment.

Among such key terms, with their evocative power and their terrible ambiguity, the term 'meaning' may also be included. Christian theology at the service of the Church's proclamation is therefore called upon to look at what this term is supposed to convey, to examine it critically, to be examined by it critically, even to struggle with the term as Jacob struggled with the angel, so that out of the struggle a blessing may come both for the person looking for meaning and for theology itself and thus also for proclamation. In the following brief reflections there can be no question (this would require more space than is available) of summoning up all the resources of theology in order to confront them with the question of meaning. Instead, we shall restrict ourselves to a single datum of Catholic theology in order to relate it to the question of meaning. This one datum is God's incomprehensibility—here, always, and for all eternity. We are asking then: What is its relevance to the question of meaning within a Christian theology and proclamation, when as Christians we acknowledge the incomprehensibility of God? In such a question of course, however much it expressly refers to 'meaning' and looks for an understanding of that term in the light of God's incomprehensibility, the term 'incomprehensibility' in its turn is also called in question.

GOD'S INCOMPREHENSIBILITY IN DOCTRINE AND THEOLOGICAL TRADITION

First of all, some observations must be put forward on the doctrine of God's incomprehensibility, but without confronting this teaching for the time being with the question of meaning. The Church's teaching refers quite frequently to the incomprehensibility and ineffability of God. The word *incomprehensibilis* occurs at an early stage of the history of the Church, in Leo the Great (DS 294), likewise in Martin I (DS 501); in the Eleventh Council of Toledo in 675 it is said that God is ineffable in his essence (DS 525). In the famous profession of faith of the Fourth Lateran Council in 1215 God is described as incomprehensible and ineffable (DS 800, 804). Likewise in the declaration of the First Vatican Council, God is called incomprehensible and it is said of him that he is ineffably exalted above all that is or can be conceived apart from him (DS 3001).

In the Church's professions of faith, then, it is taken for granted that incomprehensibility and ineffability are among the attributes of God which are meant to bring out what is really to be understood by God as such. This incomprehensibility of God, which appears even in the Old Testament, not however as the incomprehensibility of his nature, but as that of his creative action on his world and its history, is celebrated in the same sense in Paul's letters when he not only extols God's saving deed as a whole in Christ as mystery, but also expressly describes it as impenetrable and inscrutable (Rom. 11:33). From this starting point, 'negative theology' then developed the idea of the incomprehensibility of God's nature, in the East particularly with the Cappadocians and in the West with Augustine.

This negative theology of the incomprehensibility of God's nature, justified as it is, must however not be allowed to obscure the fact that incomprehensibility is also characteristic of God's free decrees and that it was from this source that the appreciation of his incomprehensibility as such was originally acquired. Leaving aside here the Franciscan metaphysic of freedom and love, which as such certainly has a fundamental importance for our question, it can be said in the light of Pius Siller's research that in medieval philosophy and theology the doctrine of God's incomprehensibility likewise acquires an outstanding place and rank in the work of Aquinas.[1] For the latter it comes within the scope, not so much of a metaphysical characterization of God, as of revealed theology, in anthropological eschatology, Christology, and theological hermeneutics; it is this incomprehensibility of God alone which for Aquinas makes possible the revelation of God as such, without man becoming God.

Here we shall refrain from developing more closely the subtle theology of God's incomprehensibility in Aquinas and thus also in Siller and refer the reader to these two authors themselves for a discussion of this precise question of incomprehensibility as a mode of understanding in general and of the incomprehensibility of God in particular. We may be satisfied here with a rather simpler idea of the incomprehensibility of God, particularly since the Church's official theology and theology generally do not take too much trouble to explain this concept. Here in the first place it need only be observed that according to this traditional teaching the incomprehensibility of God persists also in the immediate face-to-face vision of God: that is, it is not merely something peculiar to the knowledge of God in the

[1] Cf. the essay of the present author 'An Investigation of the Incomprehensibility of God in St Thomas Aquinas' in *Theological Investigations,* vol. 16 (London/New York, 1979), pp. 244–54. In this essay I was grateful to be able to make use of the researches of my student Pius Siller in his dissertation 'Die Incomprehensibilitas Dei bei Thomas von Aquin' (Innsbruck, 1963).

pilgrim's earthly life, but also determines his relationship to God in its eternal consummation.

HOW CAN THE ETERNALLY INCOMPREHENSIBLE GOD BE THE MEANING OF OUR LIFE?

We can be satisfied with these few hints, since we have to reflect, not really on this incomprehensibility of God in itself, but on the human question of meaning (admittedly insofar as the latter is confronted with the dogmatic teaching on faith on the incomprehensibility of God). Obviously the situation cannot but be one in which a confrontation of this kind occurs continuously in religious experience, in a metaphysic and in theology, in which the *adoro te devote latens Deitas* ('the devout adoration of the hidden deity') is a basic determination of religious experience and speculation. This is certainly not to be denied. Nevertheless it may be said that in the Church's official teaching and in traditional textbook theology the incomprehensibility of God is *one* of God's attributes *in addition* to many others, is taught as a particular theme, but does not actually occupy a really systematically and completely dominating position, sustaining everything else, for the totality of the teaching on God and our relationship to him. When a good deal has been said and many things have been discussed about God and our relationship to him in nature and grace, it is then *also* added that he is incomprehensible; we talk of God, his existence and his knowability, his relationship to us in nature and grace, without from the very outset making God's incomprehensibility the starting point always and everywhere determining the understanding of his nature and of its peculiar and unique character. Moreover, when we acclaim the immediate vision of God as the one, proper and alone fulfilling goal of man, when we pray *ut te revelata cernens facie visu sim beatus tuae gloriae* ('that I may see your face unveiled, be blessed in the vision of your glory'), we have forgotten in practice that this blessedness of eternal glory means coming immediately into the presence of the *incomprehensibility* of God. After extolling the pure infinite light of the eternal deity, which finally descends into the mind and heart of the creature and drives all earthly darkness away for ever, we gently observe as a kind of afterthought that even here God remains incomprehensible;

but this incomprehensibility is regarded more or less as a marginal phenomenon, as a tribute to be paid to our own finite creatureliness in a beatitude as enjoyment of what is seen and comprehended in God. God's incomprehensibility is not what is seen, but what is not seen, from which we avert our gaze.

If then God's incomprehensibility, which is nowhere denied in Christianity, is seen from this odd twofold aspect, even though merely implicitly and unthematically and basically in a way contrary to its proper meaning, it is not surprising that the theme of God's incomprehensibility is not brought out really clearly and firmly in the traditional treatment of the question of meaning.

This forgetting of God's incomprehensibility at the point where we recognize God as ultimate, sole, all-illuminating answer to man's radical question of meaning seems to me to be blatant. For us the person who does not know God is wandering in darkness; but that person walks in the light who knows God and brings him into his calculations for living as the item that throws light on all the rest of his accounts. God is extolled by us as the one comprehensive meaning of our existence, ultimately solving all our dilemmas, in which alone all partial experiences of meaning find their true place and their integration. God enlightens, combines, organizes, resolves discords, is the refuge-tower abiding in a blessed, pure unity in himself: the stronghold in which we can take refuge away from all that is unreconciled in life and knowledge. For us he is light, eternal peace, reconciliation, unity purely and simply, the point (which is in fact attainable for us) from which all the terrible discords of nature and history blend in a pure, meaningful harmony. He is *meaning* pure and simple and, when we make this statement, which is of course correct in itself, we think spontaneously of meaning in our sense, as that which is seen, that which is understood, controlled, that which is justified in *our* sight and is given into our hands, put at our disposal, so that finally the pain of the emptiness of meaning of the unanswered question ceases.

All this invocation of God as the one and comprehensive answer to the one and entire infinite question that is man is really not to be rejected. Difficult as it may be to say explicitly what is really to be understood by meaning, there are partial experiences of meaning and all these partial experiences show the way to the one point lying within the infinite at which the particular experiences of meaning come together, are anticipated and reconciled with one another in a fundamental unity, so that we rightly call this most fundamental, all-unifying, utopian, and for that very reason most real meaning purely and simply God. But when we thus sense and demand the highest with all our strength of mind and heart, in theory and practice, do we not again then fall from the supreme height of our existence into the empty abyss of meaninglessness, if we say that this highest is incomprehensible? How can the incomprehensible and nameless be the meaning that *we* have? We cannot however understand this incomprehensibility as a special characteristic of God, which he has *together with* the other attributes different from that, which then yield the fullness of meaning for which we yearn. These other attributes of God, which we declare to be the meaning of our existence, are themselves incomprehensible; this incomprehensibility is not one attribute of God alongside others, but the attribute of his attributes. The question then remains of how this incomprehensibility can be our meaning.

As a precaution a specifically theological observation must be made at this point. On the ground of Christian faith we cannot say that God is the guarantor and content of the meaning of our existence only in so far as he creatively produces a finite something that (*formaliter,* as the scholastics would say, as distinct from *efficienter*) amounts on the one hand to our fulfillment of meaning and on the other hand, being finite and consequently not incomprehensible, escapes the apparently insurmountable hopelessness in which we are involved. A solution of this kind is impossible because for Christian faith it is not a finite reality, even though created by God, but God in himself that is, even though by sheer grace, man's immediacy, goal, and fulfillment of meaning.

In order to clarify the difficulty, it must moreover be added that this incomprehensibility obviously radically determines, not only those peculiar characteristics of God which belong to him solely as he is in himself, but also his attributes as 'relative' to us, that is, the decrees of his freedom, his justice, his mercy, his fidelity, etc. If we do not at once and from the very start understand as incomprehensible also these attributes of God (existentially decisive up to a point for ourselves) which are relative to us, such a statement is mistaken from the outset and does not refer to the true God at all. But are we really doing justice to this insight by working out an apologetical theodicy of the terrible course of world events and the horror of the history of humanity, asserting quickly and unctuously that the good meaning of the course of world events and of mankind's history will dawn upon us in heaven with blinding clarity? Are we not forgetting that, at the very stage when we see God face to face, he is the incomprehensible also in his freedom in which he guides world history and that this very incomprehensibility under which we suffer shines out more especially there in all its terrible splendour? If we take seriously the decisions of the free God, is not what the psalmist says (94:6 in the Vulgate version) particularly true for heaven: 'O come, let us worship and bow down, let us kneel before the Lord, our maker'? Does not Paul say, particularly in regard to God's free salvific action, that his judgments are inpenetrable and his ways inscrutable (Rom. 11:33)? Is this true only as long as we are on pilgrimage on these ways or is it not true particularly when we have reached the end of these ways?

With the question of meaning it is not so simple to appeal to God and at the same time to think that everything is clear, all darkness bright, all problems solved, all the pure fullness of meaning brought out, when God is called the Word. If we really understand this word, we might just as well say that it is out of the question now and for all eternity to think of seeking and finding a meaning in any reality that is perceptible and comprehensible to us.

What shall we say? One thing is certain. If we raise the question of meaning and attempt to answer it in the light of the modern ideal of knowledge, according to which knowledge gains its true nature and reaches its goal only when it sees through and thus dominates what is known, when it breaks down into what for us is unquestionable and obvious, when it seeks to work only with clear ideas and seeks to reflect to the very last detail the conditions of its own possibility, when as autonomous it seeks itself to decide the limits of what concerns it and what does not, when it seeks to be silent about those things on which it is impossible to speak clearly, when it is interested only in the functional connections of the details of its world of experience—in a word, when the modern ideal of knowledge prevails as a matter of course and without any need of justification—then any talk of God's incomprehensibility can be understood only as a sentence of death on the question of meaning and how we want to cope with life in face of this prohibition of a universal question of meaning is irrelevant.

TWO BASIC QUESTIONS ON THE CLEAR-OBSCURE 'SOLUTION' OF THE DILEMMA

On the one hand, then, we uphold as inescapable and legitimate the *universal* question of meaning and on the other hand we not only speak of the incomprehensibility of God *somewhere* within the theological system, but also acknowledge the power of this expression over everything else and confront it with this question of meaning. On these assumptions, it seems to us that two questions especially must be raised. First, how must the nature of human knowledge be understood in principle and *a priori,* so that it can raise the question of God's incomprehensibility at all, so that it becomes clear that it cannot regard it as out of the question from the very outset to be occupied with the incomprehensibility of God? Second, how precisely must the act of man be understood in which he allows for God's incomprehensibility without being broken by this incomprehensibility or putting it aside as irrelevant for himself? These two questions of course are closely connected, but are not simply identical, since it is only the second question that makes clear how knowledge as such must transcend itself, must be raised up into the totality of human existence, when it is faced with the incomprehensibility of God.

It is clear without more ado that answering these two questions has something to do with the appropriate statement of the question of meaning and its understanding. For us, absolute meaning exists only in God and for that reason the question of meaning can be rightly understood and answered only if God's incomprehensibility is simultaneously considered and therefore also the two questions just now formulated. Here of course in regard to these two questions it is possible to put forward only a couple of suggestions from which, from the nature of the case, too much is continually expected.

(1) How must knowledge be understood even in its initial stages if it is to be able to have anything at all to do with God's incomprehen-

sibility? If reason from the very start were the power to know the individual realities of consciousness and their reciprocal functional connections, the incomprehensibility of God could not even be considered either as a question or as a statement or it would have to be set aside from the very outset as a nonconcept, like that of a square circle, and be rejected as an expression for what could only apparently be conceived.

Man's knowing mind cannot be understood merely as coming across what we call God in the course of its activities and then assigning to this contingent object the predicate 'incomprehensible' as one attribute among others that belongs to this accidentally discovered individual object of knowledge. If man's reason is thus understood in a modern way, *a posteriori*, positivistically, functionally (even if the rules of the functioning of reason so conceived are developed epistemologically), this reason can never be the power of knowing God's incomprehensibility, if only because God himself cannot be understood as a particular individual object among other data of consciousness and because a reason that has to do *purely and simply in the first place* with what can be defined by functional connections cannot subsequently come to deal with something that absolutely contradicts what is thus understood as the *a priori* character of possible data of consciousness. Reason must be understood more fundamentally as precisely the capacity of the incomprehensible, as the capacity of being seized by what is always insurmountable, not essentially as the power of comprehending, of gaining the mastery and subjugating. Reason must be understood (to use Aquinas's terminology) as the capacity of *excessus,* as going out into the inaccessible. If reason is not understood from the very outset as the capacity of incomprehensibility, of unfathomable mystery, as perception of the ineffable, then all subsequent talk of the incomprehensibility of God comes too late, falls on deaf ears, and can be understood only as an intimation of what happens to remain of objectivity, of what has not yet been processed by all-consuming reason but will sooner or perhaps later be so processed.

Actually however reason is of this nature, even if it is inclined to stop at what is clearly understood and comprehended and to linger there, even if it always forgets where the clear brightness of its individual perceptions comes from. For when it grasps and understands any object, it has already transcended the latter into an infinity that is present as unexplored, precisely as such and not otherwise; it always seizes the individual object by being tacitly aware of the fact that the object always is and remains more than what is grasped of it. It locates the individual object within reference systems which themselves are not precisely fixed and determined and in which such an individual reality has a place without being absolutely and for ever settled there. It always has a bad conscience (which, if admitted and accepted, becomes a good conscience) that it has itself never adequately understood and authorized its own assumptions, although to do this would enable it to rely absolutely on its individual perceptions. It perceives, and every perception that gives expression to an individual reality is accompanied by a terrible awareness of its provisional character. It is only because we do not know that we can attempt to know something, only because we direct our questions to what is unanswered and thus in the last resort to the ineffable, that we can hear answers which, the better they are, the more they raise new questions.

Wanting to understand and, consequently, the question aimed at comprehension as such (and in all this the rational subject demanding an explanation from the very outset) are themselves put in question with every answer, so that incomprehension becomes incomprehensibility and the boundless question the sole point at which the question itself becomes the answer, the domicile where incomprehensibility (called God) resides and alone shelters us. If we want to regard it as darkness always to be already beyond the individual object of knowledge as the condition of the possibility of our knowledge, since there can be no point anywhere at which it comes to a stop, then we can confidently say that this darkness is the condition of the light that illumines an individual object, then we can say that it is only in falling into an unfathomable abyss that we grasp the individual reality to which we think we can cling. In brief: the simple fact (inevitably freshly asserted in every perception) that any individual perception is possible only within an infinite process which as far as we are concerned is never ended (and which in theological terms can be ended only by its own goal, approached asymptotically, if this is itself present, but then as naked and unveiled incomprehensibility), always asserting afresh that what is grasped lives by the incomprehensible and that understanding is governed by incomprehensibility.

If we want, we can dismiss all this as idle dialectic and cheap paradox, with the invitation to stick to what is clear and comprehensible. But we can do this only with the aid of rationalistic theory and (whether we want it or not) the bitterness of life's frustrations brings us up continually against this marginal experience, so that at most we may wonder whether what is beyond this field of clear knowledge and autonomously practicable plans amounts to a fall into an abysmal meaninglessness or to being caught up by a sheltering incomprehensibility relieving us purely and simply of ourselves and our question.

(2) We thus come to the second question, which of course is directly connected with the first. We have been asking about the knowing reason and we defined it in advance of its function of definitively comprehending as the power of coming face to face with incomprehensibility itself. If this is the fundamental definition of cognitive reason itself and not simply what happens to it unexpectedly as it reaches the end of its activity, this does not mean that we are irrationalists; for this fundamental state of being exposed to incomprehensibility is understood precisely as the condition of the possibility of conceptually elaborating, delimiting, and discriminating knowledge. But when we describe reason in this way, we have already gone beyond it; precisely in order to define its nature fundamentally, we have transcended it to reach something greater and more comprehensive, because—in the last resort no one who believes in God can doubt this—it is always possible to comprehend the nature of something in the last resort only by transcending that nature. Once again then we must face our second question. How exactly must the act of man be understood in which he can allow for the incomprehensibility of God without being broken by this incomprehensibility or putting it aside as irrelevant for himself?

Before attempting to answer this question more precisely, we may put forward one or two preliminary observations to protect the answer to this question from the very outset against objections and misunderstandings.

With Aquinas we are absolutely convinced that knowledge on the one hand and will (as freedom and love) on the other can be distinguished as powers emerging as distinct out of an ultimate substantial unity of man and kept together in this unity in a kind of perichoresis ('mutual interpenetration'), to make use analogously of a term of trinitarian theology. At the same time we are sure that Aquinas gets to the depths of this question of the difference of these two powers from one another, not at the point where he marks out one from the other and draws the obvious conclusions (for example, that the essential nature of the beatific vision of God consists in the act of intellect as such) but where he discusses objectively the unity and the mutual interdependence (even though within a system analogous to that which exists in the divine trinity) of the transcendentals *verum* ('truth') and *bonum* ('goodness'). When we consider and take seriously the metaphysics of these transcendentals in their unity and mutual interdependence and in their differentiation, we can give a good Thomistic answer to our question. This act in which man can allow for and accept God's incomprehensibility (and thus the comprehensive meaning of his own existence), without being broken by it and without taking refuge in the banality of his clear knowledge and of a demand for meaning based solely on this complete knowledge as open to manipulation, is the act of self-surrendering love trusting entirely in this very incomprehensibility, in which knowledge surpasses itself, rising to its supernature, and is aware of itself only by becoming love.

This statement, which still requires elucidation, may sound paradoxical, but it does no more than express the paradox of the ultimate unity of man's diverse powers in which in the last resort each power becomes aware of itself only when it is raised up into the other and in which the whole is named after the final element in the system of these elements (it is in this way that we say 'God is Spirit', giving him the name of his third mode of subsistence).

We may adopt the opposite approach in order to make the answer to the second question intelligible, by asking what kind of an act it must be in which man as reason can bear the incomprehensibility of God and does not regard this incomprehensibility as the infinitely high wall, enclosing the small field of his blessedness on all sides, so that he can enjoy his happiness in this small area only by nervously casting his eyes down in order not to have anything to do with this wall looming up to high heaven. What must the act be called (if it exists at all) in which the occurrence of the incomprehensible mystery in its inexorable unambiguity and finality itself amounts to eternal blessedness and not its all-annihilating frontier? We can only answer that, if this act exists at all, if it exists because we simply cannot do without it, if we look for a name for it derived from our basic experiences, we can speak only of 'love'. Admittedly, that very thing which we call love must not be defined in the light of anything else, but only in the light of *that* experience which we have in the occurrence of the incomprehensible mystery. In the last resort love is precisely the acceptance of the incomprehensibility which we call God, in his nature and his freedom, as sheltering, as affirmed as for ever valid, as accepting us.

But this nature of God's love, which is revealed particularly and ultimately only in the acceptance of his incomprehensibility as beatifying and not as annihilating, is also accessible to us in the light of lesser experiences that we have otherwise in personal love. At the point where one person encounters another in really personal love is there not an acceptance of what is not comprehended, an acceptance of what we have not ourselves perceived and consequently not mastered in the other person, the person who is loved? Is not personal love a trusting surrender without reassurance to the other person, precisely in so far as the latter is and remains free and incalculable? This is not to say that the absolutely unique love of God, in its real, univocal sense, can be subsumed under an interpersonal love that we can easily experience; the two factors have only an analogous similarity, that is, a similarity in which a greater dissimilarity continually appears (to vary the terminology of the Fourth Lateran Council on the relationship between God and creatures). But interpersonal love nevertheless gives us a hint of our relationship to God; it justifies us in saying that the act in which the subject, leaving aside itself and its own claims, surrenders itself to the incomprehensible and for ever persistently incomprehensible mystery can at best be called love, since knowledge purely as such in our ordinary field of experience (even though not in its fundamental nature) bears in itself the character of appropriation and domination of what is known, while this is not the case in genuine interpersonal love, even in the empirical area of life. At the same time it remains true that only in the act of resigned and self-forsaking surrender of the subject to the incomprehensibility of God as such (which then ceases to be a limitation and becomes the very content of our relationship to God) does the most fundamental nature of love really dawn upon us, of which interpersonal love is merely a creaturely reflection.

Certainly the relationship of the basic act of human beings in regard to the incomprehensibility of God, insofar as this act is knowledge and insofar as it is free love surpassing knowledge, has not yet really been adequately defined. But, as already indicated, this basic definition of the relationship is not to be put forward on the plane of a theory of faculties, as in Aquinas, but with the aid of a theory of the transcendentals 'true' and 'good' and their relationship with one another. For only in this way can it be made clear that love (praxis)—perhaps today we would also say freedom—can be and must be also the condition of knowledge of the true (theory), so that this very relationship of a perichoresis of the two transcendentals reaches its most radical essential realization in the presence of the incomprehensibility of God.

ULTIMATE FULFILLMENT OF MEANING
ONLY IN THE FREE AND LOVING ACCEPTANCE
OF THE INCOMPREHENSIBILITY OF GOD

In the course of our reflections on the act of accepting God's incomprehensibility, we seem to have lost sight of the human question of meaning. In reality however this is not so. We may make this clear with one or two closing remarks. Although there is a particular experience of meaning directly in the field of human experience and prior to the question of God, we assume that the question of meaning as a whole can be answered positively only with what we call God, in the sense not only that the fulfillment of the human question of meaning is guaranteed and creatively effected by God, but consists in a gracious self-communication of God in his most intimate reality. But this self-communication of God, that alone radically answers the question of meaning, seen from man's standpoint, is and remains the immediate coming into the presence of God's incomprehensibility, which, if we are to talk seriously and without reservation about real and not merely passive fulfillment, must itself be understood and realized, not as the limit but as the content of the final blessed fulfillment of meaning.

If however this is the situation, it is one to which the concrete mode of the promise in Christian proclamation of an ultimate fulfillment of meaning must also really correspond. In this proclamation there cannot be an offer of a God who is secretly subject to human selfishness, not even to the sublime selfishness of human rationality. The God of fulfillment of meaning must be proclaimed as the one who cannot be fitted into the calculations of our life, who simply cannot be regarded as the last item in our bookkeeping, bringing out the meaning of the whole series of our accounts. Our proclamation must boldly declare that the ultimate question of meaning is correctly stated only as the question of free love, which can get away from itself and experience the incomprehensible as what is wondrously and blessedly obvious. The question of meaning must itself be relentlessly clarified as a question by being confronted with the incomprehensibility of God and thus turned into a question of whether it is capable of being understood as the question of an incomprehensibility that brings final happiness or, since a third meaning is impossible, seeks to understand God's incomprehensibility merely as another expression for the empty absurdity of existence.

In this question 'objective' knowledge and ultimate free decision cannot be separated. And it is this very fact that proclamation must clearly show to be inescapably involved in any theory from the very outset; it must make clear that knowledge, too, is itself good or bad according to whether it seeks to understand the incomprehensibility of existence, which is derived from the incomprehensibility of God, as bringing final bliss or in the last resort as hateful. Present-day proclamation, particularly when it recognizes God as the ultimate answer to the question of meaning, is tempted to make God a tiny means for the small man, to permit God only what seems to shortsightedly selfish man to be useful to himself, without radically grasping and proclaiming that man can reach final bliss only with a God who is incomprehensibly greater than himself and for that very reason the true blessedness of man.

Where today does Christian proclamation speak clearly and firmly of the God of judgment, of the eternally incomprehensible ways and decrees of his freedom? Certainly Christianity is the proclamation of the victory of God's grace and not actually merely the ambivalent offer to man's freedom of two possibilities, of salvation or of eternal perdition. But this very message of God's gracious freedom is more powerful than man's freedom and is always ahead of the latter, without destroying it, only if it is heard as the event of the incomprehensibility of God's freedom and not as an obvious insight with which to outwit God's judgments, if it is heard as an appeal to man's freedom to trust entirely in God's incomprehensibility without reservation and without reassurance, since it is only in this way that freedom becomes free and blessed. Recourse to God as answer to the question of meaning of man in his wholeness is right and indispensable. But it becomes the creation of a human idol if it does not bring man, forsaking himself, self-surrendering, and blessed only in that way, into the presence of the incomprehensibility of God.

6

ONENESS AND THREEFOLDNESS
OF GOD IN DISCUSSION
WITH ISLAM

The question of God's oneness is certainly one theme (if not the most crucial) that must be discussed in an encounter between Islamic and Christian theologians. The religions of Israel, Christianity, and Islam are the three great world religions which profess a primary monotheism, explicitly regarded by Christianity and Islam as derived from Old Testament monotheism. But, in a history of faith and theology that has become increasingly clear and explicit, Christianity acknowledges the threefoldness of the one God and consequently faces the question from Old Testament monotheism and the faith of Islam and its theology as to whether the profession of faith in the triune God does not amount basically to an absolutely pernicious tritheism and whether the Christian acknowledgment of the oneness of God is no more than a disguise for such tritheism or (if it is not to be stated so radically) simply a doctrine that cannot really be implemented religiously and logically by someone for whom the acknowledgment of the oneness of God is not merely a proposition maintained verbally and theoretically but the very heart of his existence in theory and practice. On the other hand of course this question as such could be put by Christianity to the other two world religions: that is, it could be asked (assuming an actual history of revelation in which the one and basic content of the substance of faith is slowly more clearly articulated in forms that cannot afterward be forgotten) whether these two world religions have not failed to achieve that elucidation and radicalization of monotheism which finds expression precisely in the doctrine of the Trinity. But for the task with which I propose to deal the first way of approaching the question will suffice.

All that we are asking here then is why the Christian doctrine of the Trinity does not cancel or threaten any real acknowledgment of the oneness of God. If the question is stated in this way, it is obvious that not each and every thing can be made equally explicit in the answer, that the doctrine of the Trinity simply cannot in itself be treated expressly thematically in all its fullness and vitality. If, as far as it is given expression here, it seems to the Christian theologian to be put forward somewhat pallidly and with a kind of sceptical restraint, this can be admitted from the outset and is justified by the limited scope of the following reflections. In the task attempted here it is quite impossible to avoid putting forward theologoumena and interpretations of the Christian doctrine of the Trinity that may up to a point be matters of controversy among Christian theologians. We are starting out from the conviction that we shall not do justice to the task before us if we simply repeat the Church's defined doctrine on the Trinity without at the same time interpreting it as theologians on our own account and at our own risk. At the moment when we attempt to present the official teaching of the Church on the Trinity in a way calculated to win the sympathy of an Islamic theologian, we must avert possible misunderstandings of this doctrine which on the one hand do not seem to be entirely removed simply by repeating the Church's official teaching but which on the other hand can certainly be overcome only in a theological reflection which the Christian theologian must admittedly accomplish largely on his own account and at his own risk.

In this undertaking of mine the following points must also be stressed. Unfortunately I am not an expert on Islamic theology. This means that any attempt at an explicit confrontation between Christian and Islamic theology is excluded from the very outset, since Islamic monotheism would then have to be presented and interpreted in its basic teaching, its variations and its history. This however is absolutely impossible for me. I can therefore put forward only a few considerations on the relationship between Christian monotheism and the Christian doctrine of the Trinity and at the same time hope that these preliminary considerations may be useful for an explicit discussion between Islamic and Christian monotheism, so that the discussion does not break down at the very beginning as a result of misunderstandings of the Christian doctrine of the Trinity. It is also my intention not to permit the drift of these merely preliminary considerations to be lost in a purely abstract conceptual dialectic, but, as far as this is possible in a brief space, not to lose sight of what all the sublime and by no means simply avoidable conceptualities in the doctrine of the one and triune God imply existentially and religiously. After these preliminary observations we shall turn immediately to the essential question, without announcing in advance a formal structure of these reflections, since the actual course of the reflections must be justified by its own development.

Christianity is a primarily and not merely secondarily monotheistic religion. It acknowledges the oneness of God, of the God whom the Christian worships, by whom he knows he is created and called to salvation, whom he worships in absolute obedience, in faith, hope, and love. According to the evidence of the Christian Scriptures and the creed of Christendom this belief in the one sole God is not merely any sort of doctrine which *happens* to occur in the diversity of Christian articles of faith, but purely and simply the really basic dogma of Christianity. In regard to the understanding of this basic dogma it must be noted that the acknowledgment of the oneness of God is not primarily a metaphysical statement, even though this acknowledgment necessarily implies something of the kind. It is a question of a statement that is part of the history of salvation and revelation and must be acknowledged within that history. Christianity does not say primarily that there is only one sole absolute, but that he alone is God who is manifested as acting on us in the history of salvation and revelation; to this one alone can we really have that relationship of absolute devotion which constitutes the fundamental nature of religion. The statement on the oneness of God refers therefore not to an abstract absolute, alongside which any other is unthinkable from the very outset, from the very nature of the case, but to the God experienced concretely in his action on us, to the God of Abraham, of Isaac, to the God of the prophets, the God of Jesus.

This however is a statement that is anything but metaphysically obvious; it is not one that could be denied only by someone who had not understood at all the statement about the necessary oneness of an absolute or who thought he could accept in a gnostic or manicheistic sense the metaphysical absurdity of a good and a bad abso-

lute existing side by side. The Christian proposition of God's oneness refers to a concrete absolute. And in this sense it is anything
but obvious. For it then implies *either* that whatever is the object of
a religious—really radically religious—experience, wherever it appears in the history of religion and is genuine, is the same thing, is
that which as one holds together and authenticates by its oneness all
history of religious and numinous experience, which in the last resort then turns the diversity and apparent contradictoriness of the
history of religion into a *universal* history of salvation; *or* that this
religious intentionality purely and simply misses its goal, worships
an idol and not God. And again, understood in this way, the statement is anything but obvious. People have always been tempted to
attribute their numinous experiences, because of their diversity and
inconsistency, to different absolutes, to interpret the pluralism of
their religious experiences as an ultimate datum, to be polytheists
explicitly or implicitly; or, if for metaphysical reasons they did not
venture to take up this attitude, they were inclined to banish the
ultimate unity behind this pluralism of religious experiences and
their object into a region where it ceased to have any religious implications. But the monotheistic religions—which are not the same
thing as monotheistic metaphysics—claim that this ultimate, most
fundamental unity, which sustains everything, is infinite and omnip-
otent, does not merely dwell in a remote solitude in principle outside
the reach of man, but, without dissipating its oneness, can as itself
penetrate into the pluralism even of this world and be present there,
can itself become concrete.

The monotheism of Christianity and of the two other world religions therefore must be understood both as concrete monotheism
and also as universal, since the concrete God, who appears actively
in an authentic religion, is as such the one and absolute and, since
this very God because of his absoluteness and oneness is the God of
the whole world and because of his universal salvific will, is active
everywhere in his world. Understood in this way the monotheism of
the genuine monotheistic religions must therefore either see the
trend of other numinous experiences and religions as directed to
their own concrete God, or reject them as missing their goal, or
radically relativize such numinous experiences and set them apart
from theism properly so called by interpreting them (as can be observed in all three monotheistic world religions) as experiences of

created angelic powers of a good or evil nature. If the God of religious monotheism, despite his infinity, incomprehensibility, and (as Creator) preeminence over the world, is nevertheless the concrete God who appears precisely where we are, without himself disintegrating into a pluralism of numinous powers, then all these three monotheistic religions, each in its own way and more or less radically, have inevitably (in Christian terms) an incarnatory character, since the concreteness of the God who acts in history is meant to allow him to be present precisely in his sole real divinity itself. Whether then this incarnatory character, which is involved in monotheism understood in this way, is related to a 'covenant', to a sacred book that is really God's book itself, to a definite person who is the presence of God—all these are further questions which of course cannot be pursued here.

After these brief indications of the meaning of Christian monotheism, we now ask whether it is compatible with the Christian doctrine of the Trinity of God or not. Is the doctrine of monotheism and that of the divine Trinity to be made compatible only by verbal artifice? Can these two statements be shown to give simultaneous expression to a single, indisputable religious fact? Our basic thesis, put forward here, is meant to show that the doctrine of the Trinity can and must be understood not as a supplement or an attenuation of Christian monotheism, but as its radicalization, assuming only that this monotheism is itself taken really seriously as concrete monotheism based on the experience of salvation history which does not banish God in his oneness out of Christianity's experience of salvation history and into a metaphysically abstract solitude.

With this basic thesis, which must be understood in a positive and not necessarily exclusive sense, our concern, as indicated from the beginning, is not with the assertion that (from the aspect of this thesis about the Trinity as radicalness of monotheism and not as its supplement or attenuation) the whole fullness of the Christian doctrine of the Trinity can be accepted as a datum or whether it must be said that this is not the case. We can leave this question aside here. Before we turn directly to this basic thesis of ours, elucidating and substantiating it, it seems appropriate to attempt to clear up some perhaps crude misunderstandings of this Christian doctrine of the Trinity. These misunderstandings are widespread, not only outside orthodox Christianity (even in liberal theologies from Unitarianism onward, which are meant to be Christian), but also seem to make themselves felt subcutaneously, latent in theologies of Christianity which as such and in principle are orthodox, although it is impossible to produce detailed evidence of this here.

Of course, it is impossible to repeat here the long, difficult and varied history of the doctrine of the Trinity, which objectively (insofar as it is dogma properly speaking) found its dogmatically binding and hitherto final formulation in the age of the great Fathers, was stated again summarily at the Council of Florence, and received further profound interpretations in high scholasticism and afterward; but all this is theology and not dogma of Christianity. All that we propose to do here, presupposing this official, binding teaching of the Church and its history, is to put forward a few remarks directed against possible or real misunderstandings inside and outside Christian orthodoxy.

I would like first of all to say frankly and sincerely that the term 'person' in the doctrine of the Trinity seems to me to be misleading or open to misunderstanding. This is not to deny that the term involves a binding linguistic usage for the Catholic theologian, that the proposition, 'The one God in his one sole nature subsists in three persons', rightly understood, is correct and is a defined truth of faith. But even if this is taken for granted, the fact remains that the term 'person' can be and has constantly been misunderstood. It must continually be recalled that the history in dogmatic statements of a particular term (which as actually understood does not retain purely and simply the meaning that the Church wants to give to it) is not a history that has been or can be guided solely by the Church's magisterium. Consequently the possibility is not as such and *a priori* excluded that the continued course of such a history of terminology, taking place outside the sphere of faith and nevertheless influencing the actual understanding of these terms in a dogmatic statement, may threaten or almost destroy the usefulness and intelligibility of terms used officially by the Church and that this sort of thing can be maintained only by difficult and arduous measures of support, put forward specially and subsequently, for the meaning of such a term as understood by the Church. This, it seems to me, is today and has for a long time been the situation with the term 'person'.

If someone today, whether Christian or not, hears the statement that there are three persons in God, he will think instinctively of three subjects differing from one another in their subjectivity, knowledge, and freedom, and wonder what kind of logic it is that permits three persons understood in this way to be simultaneously one and the same God. Even if this modern man uses the definition of official textbook theology, that personality is the subsistence of a rational nature, and if he is told that the rational nature need not be increased numerically in line with the plurality of subsistences, he is still in danger of thinking of the rationality of these subsistences as sharing their plurality, of thinking of them as three reciprocally related centres of mental action, related to one another as such. Or, conversely, if the person hearing about the Trinity does not appreciate these logical difficulties and more or less forgets the proposition about the oneness of the divine nature, if he begins to speak of the three divine persons, he imagines these persons distinct from one another as three realities with reciprocal relationships which are understood in their diversity as at least also founded on or constituted by elements which are by no means really distinct from one another according to the Christian dogma of the Trinity, but belong to the essential sphere of God, which exists in strict identity only as one, this fact however being more or less forgotten in this conception (especially under the tacit but effective influence of a modern notion of person).

This popular, unelaborated idea of the three persons, latent even at the highest levels of theology, but heterodox if thought out radically to the end, is meant (inevitably) to fill out speculatively the reciprocal relationality of the three persons (which, according to the Council of Florence, constitutes them as 'persons') and at the same time consciously or unconsciously borrows from the content of God's essentiality, although it is in fact recognized that this nature of God and all that it contains is absolutely one and unique and that the dogma of this uniqueness of the divine nature must be completely upheld. In this conception the 'persons' know one another, have a mutual love of each other, speak with each other, and so on. If however we get to work on such elucidations of the diversity of the three 'persons', we bring into this reciprocity of their relations as constituting itself the diversity of the persons (at any rate in the light of the modern idea of person which is thrust upon us) essential realities of God which truly exist only as one and which simply cannot constitute distinctions. If, for example, it is said that between the divine persons there exists a mutual knowledge and love, this is not to be rejected as heterodox; but it may be asked what precisely statements of this kind are supposed to mean if knowledge and love in any case belong in the first place to the sphere of the one nature of God, if it is not clear what we are to understand by a threefold personal relativity in knowledge and love, if and insofar as this relationality is clearly (if only conceptually) distinguished from the essentiality of knowing and loving, if, for example, it is also considered (for example, in the proposition that the Holy Spirit is the mutual love of Father and Son) that Father and Son by the very fact of possessing the divine nature are necessarily essential love and must be regarded strictly as only a single principle in the spiration of the Spirit. The embarrassment arising from the use of the term 'person' in the theology of the Trinity (at least when the modern notion of person continually and today inevitably comes to mind) was evident in the classical theory of the Trinity as taught by Augustine and in the Middle Ages. According to this theory, it must be said that the Father knows himself *because* he is in possession of the original nature of God, he utters the Logos *because* he is by his nature in his unoriginated knowing self-possession, and nevertheless we want to explain that the Father knows himself *in* and *through* uttering the eternal Logos as distinct from himself. These problems cannot be pursued further or set out in detail here.

It cannot of course be denied that in principle the problems might be endured in the last resort by appealing to the unfathomable mystery of the trinitarian God, without investigating them in a strictly logical way. But an appeal of this kind cannot be allowed to relieve us the problems when they perhaps arise, not inevitably because of the mystery, but as a result of an indiscriminate and speculatively too little considered use of the term 'person'. In the last resort, the above remarks may at least amount to a warning about the problems of an indiscriminate use of the term 'person' in the doctrine of the Trinity.

This warning may be explained from another aspect. In the Church's official teaching on the Trinity 'person' and 'hypostasis' ('subsistence') are used synonymously, if the fact is disregarded that the hypostasis of a person means the subsistence of an intellectual nature (and in God there is only one such nature). Nevertheless, these terms are not simply synonymous either in their historical origins or in their use on the one hand predominantly in Latin theology and on the other hand predominantly by the Greek Fathers, as also in the subsequent history of the formulation of the doctrine of the Trinity; they are distinguished from one another at least by clearly perceptible nuances. In any case the idea of hypostasis has not developed in the same way as the idea of person, which is now more closely associated with a modern understanding of subjectivity, so that personality and subjectivity come to the fore to such an extent that the use of the term 'person' in the doctrine of the Trinity becomes increasingly problematic, both in the popular understanding of the doctrine outside orthodox Christianity and also in its speculative utilization inside a theology of the Trinity which seeks to be orthodox and not to obscure the oneness of the divine nature. In view of all this, without questioning the legitimacy of the Church's traditional official linguistic usage, speaking of three persons in God, we might wonder if it would be more appropriate to speak of three hypostases in God (or, to express it in a more modern form, of three modes of subsistence of the one God in his one sole nature) and in this way more easily to prevent popular misunderstandings of the doctrine of the Trinity and also in what really amounts to indiscriminate speculative interpretations of this doctrine in current theology. It seems to me (if it is not too presumptuous on the part of an individual theologian to say this) that the term 'hypostasis' or 'mode of subsistence' on the one hand is quite suitable to express and retain the real substance of the dogma of the Trinity and on the other hand involves fewer dangers of what is in the last resort a tritheistic misunderstanding of the trinitarian dogma. All this however amounts and can amount to no more than very brief and awkwardly expressed suggestions.

At any rate we cannot be content to make use of any kind of blurred, indistinct concept of 'person', continually in a process of historical development, when speaking about three persons in God, and then to assume that we have understood and correctly expressed the dogma of the Trinity. This warning was really the sole point of these somewhat lengthy reflections. But it is a warning that seems important to me. Even an Islamic theologian may and must allow for the possibility that his denial of the Christian doctrine of the Trinity may be no more than a denial of a proposition that by no means expresses the content of that doctrine, since even a Christian theologian does not find it easy in his own thinking to avoid misunderstandings of the term 'person' which he is continually using.

Coming now at last more immediately and more perceptibly to the basic thesis formulated earlier, that the doctrine of the Trinity is not a supplement or an attenuation, but a radicalization of Christian monotheism, we begin again from a different standpoint. We are starting out from the proposition that the economic Trinity *is* the immanent Trinity and vice versa. I do not know exactly when and by whom this theological axiom was formulated for the first time. But it seems to be established in theology today or is at least a theologoumenon that cannot be *a priori* rejected as heterodox, but can safely be used in theological reflection. No Christian can seriously deny that there is an understanding of the doctrine of the Trinity in terms of the economy of salvation, that there is an experience of the history of salvation and revelation of a threefold kind. The history of revelation and salvation brings us up against the ineffable mystery of the unencompassable, unoriginated God who is called Father, who does not live and remain in a metaphysical remoteness, but who seeks in all his incomprehensibility and sovereignty and freedom to impart himself to the creature as its eternal life in truth and love. This one and incomprehensible God is unsurpassably close to man historically in Jesus Christ, who is not simply one prophet in a still continuing series of prophets but the final and unsurpassable self-promise of this one God in history. And this one and the same God imparts himself to man in the innermost centre of human existence as Holy Spirit for salvation and for the consummation which is God himself. For Christian faith then there are two utterly radical and definitive and unsurpassable factualities, modes of existence, of the one God in the world, factualities which are the final salvation freely granted by God to the world, in history and transcendence.

As permanent, these two factualities are always to be distinguished, even though (and this is not to be specially explained here) they are mutually dependent. It is of course not clearly obvious from the outset that there are only *two* such factualities of God himself *in* himself *for* his creation. If we could presuppose the doctrine of the immanent Trinity on the two internal divine processions as *only* two, it would be easy to answer the question of the exclusiveness of the two divine modes of factuality for the world. But, since we must first of all here understand the economic Trinity as immanent, the question is not so easy to answer at this point. But (and this may suffice here) we could say that the diversity, unity, and mutual dependence of man's historicity and transcendality provide an adequate aid to understanding for the distinction, unity, and exclusiveness of the two factualities of God, assuming however that we regard man from the outset as the image of God and do not forget that this image 'man' must from the outset be such that he can be the recipient of God's self-communication: that is, what is to be communicated must necessarily correspond to the nature of the recipient of the communication, and vice versa. If, with all the unity and mutual interdependence, there is really a permanent duality of the divine modes of factuality in God's self-communication to the world, this mens at least that there is what we describe as the economic Trinity. The unoriginated God, who imparts himself in two different modes of factuality and because of the unity and diversity of these two modes and because of the unencompassable sovereignty which he retains even in his self-communication, may not be understood simply in a lifeless identity with these two factualities. In this salvific economic Trinity the unoriginated and permanently sovereign God is called Father; in his self-communication to history, Logos; in his self-communication to man's transcendentality, Holy Spirit. (We prefer to use here the term 'Logos', which is also authorized by the New Testament, since at this point we want to avoid the question of whether the 'Son' of the Father, who is Jesus according to the New Testament, designates even in the earliest New Testament statements, as distinct from later statements of the New Testament or of the magisterium, an exclusive salvific economic mode of factuality of God and thus an immanent mode of subsistence of God, or more fundamentally the unique unity of the man Jesus with God-Father as such.) For the Christian, then, there is undoubtedly a salvific economic Trinity.

In regard to this statement however it is essential to see and acknowledge that the duality of God's factualities for us does not get in the way of the factuality of God in himself or that the latter is not mediated by something that is not God. Logos and Holy Spirit are not to be regarded as mediating modalities which are different from the one God. For since Christianity rejects any neoplatonic, Plotinian, gnostic or similar idea of a descending self-emptying God, they would then have to be regarded as created realities, which, like all other created realities, would by their nature point to the God who always remains remote, but would not mediate God as such in his innermost reality. In God's *self*-communication to the creature, radically understood, the mediation itself must be God and cannot amount to a creaturely mediation. These reflections however would seem largely irrelevant even to a religious person who is a theist, if he wants to remain obediently and humbly alone looking to the incomprehensible God from an infinite distance, not venturing at all to realize that this infinite and incomprehensible God might also be the God who is utterly close and immediate and not only the infinitely remote Creator-God. But if and when the thirst for God in himself imparted to man by God himself is admitted, if and when the ultimate unsurpassable statement of revelation that God himself as such wills to give himself to men is heard and accepted, in the sense in which this statement emerges clearly in the New Testament in the experience of Jesus and his Spirit, then it is impossible to avoid the admission that there is a twofold self-communication of God in diversity and unity, the modalities of which in their unity and distinction are again God himself strictly as such. But this means first of all in the dimension of the salvific economic Trinity that the statement that the Logos and the Holy Spirit are God himself is not an attenuation or obscuration of monotheism rightly understood, but its radicalization.

In describing monotheism at the beginning as religious and theological, we said that it was not an abstract metaphysical theory about a remote absolute, but a statement about the sole absolute, about the God with whom we have to deal concretely in salvation history. If this God of concrete salvation history realizes there his absolute and unconditional self-communication in history and transcendence, then on the one hand the diversity of these modes of factuality cannot be denied, but on the other hand this mode of factuality cannot be thrust between the one God and the creature graced by God as something merely created, which would then establish God's remoteness and not his closeness. If and insofar as (and this of course cannot be questioned) creaturely mediations between God and men can be conceived and do in fact exist and when these occur in the field of man's religious relationship to God and thus have a numinous quality, there is really always a danger of an explicit or disguised polytheism. Man seizes on such a mediation, grasps it absolutely firmly, affirms it at least implicitly in this firm grasp as God himself, and yet in truth it is no more than a finite creature that cannot by any means convey God in himself.

For the Christian then the religious monotheist is inescapably confronted by certain alternatives. He may demythologize in a theoretical monotheism all (even permanent and unavoidable) mediations of his relationship to God (whether these are understood as word, Scripture, sacrament, or institution, etc.) as purely created, in the last resort thrusting the absolute God into an infinite remoteness; thus he becomes a merely theoretical monotheist, for whom God is as distant as the supreme divinity among ancient and primitive religious figures, because in the concrete he has to cling to these particular and finite mediations of explicitly or surreptitiously polytheistic character; *in practice* then religion becomes again devotion belonging to the present world and is simply a numinous transfiguration of that world. *Or* the person takes radical monotheism seriously, but at the same time for his own part refuses to see the mode of factuality of the monotheistic God as itself divine, and then he must see God's mode of factuality as radically creaturely and finite and lying on this side of the abyss between God and creature; thus he ends up again with a merely theoretical and abstract monotheism, which places God at an infinite distance, and in the actual practice of religion necessarily clings to these created mediations as all that he can regard concretely as properly religious, whether they are called commandment, Scripture, covenant of God, or anything else. In either case he will hesitate uncertainly between an abstract monotheism, which simply cannot take entirely seriously what is proper to religious monotheism, and a concealed polytheism, which in practice makes absolute those created realities which are supposed to convey God to him, although they are finite. (It seems to me that we might follow this hesitation between an abstract monotheism and an unadmitted polytheism up to the modern Western history of ideas, in Hölderlin, Rilke, Kerenyi, Heidegger and others.) There is a continual attempt to distinguish between the divine and the gods. *Or,* finally, the religious monotheist, sustained by God's grace itself, has absolute confidence that the absolute God as such has come absolutely close to him. But then he must consider the mediating modes of factuality as themselves divine in the strict sense of the term. He must say both these things, even though he cannot offer for this dual statement any higher synthesis, surpassing it, making intelligible from a more fundamental standpoint the statement that the one sole God as himself is close to man in two modes of factuality and that these two modes of factuality are themselves God.

This absolutely comprehensive dual statement is therefore the radicalization of that monotheism which comes within a religious dimension. For the monotheistic God is the God who is close to us in concrete salvation history. It is only when created modes of mediation (although these *also* exist) in the ultimate sense are denied to him that he is really the sole God, close to us, who is present as himself in salvation history. The proposition of the identity of God's modes of factuality with God himself is only the converse of the proposition that any purely created mediation between God and man removes this God into an absolute remoteness, turns a concrete into an abstract monotheism and permits man to be implicitly polytheistic in the concreteness of his religious life. God must mediate to himself through himself; otherwise he remains remote in the last resort and in this remoteness is present only by the divisive multiplicity of created realities which point to God's remoteness. This is the meaning of the proposition on the divinity of the two fundamental modes of God's factuality in the world and it thus also means that concrete monotheism is taken completely seriously.

When we reassert at this point in our reflections the axiom invoked at an earlier stage of the identity of the salvific economic and the immanent Trinity, we are brought directly to the classical Christian theology of the Trinity. Since these two modes of factuality of the one God in and despite their diversity are themselves God and not something created and different from him, they must belong always and eternally to God himself as such. In order to bring out clearly that they belong to God himself as such, they are called in classical trinitarian theology internal divine processions. The unoriginated God (called 'Father') has from eternity the opportunity of an historical self-expression and likewise the opportunity of establishing himself as himself at the innermost centre of the intellectual creature as the latter's dynamism and goal. These two eternal possibilities (which are pure actuality) are God, are to be distinguished from each other, and are to be distinguished by this distinction also from the unoriginated God. Insofar as they belong to God himself as such, since they simply could not otherwise be God himself, they

can be called modes of subsistence, in order to make clear that the
two modes of factuality of God himself as such in regard to the world
really belong to himself as such and do not mean a modality which
would be brought into existence by a free decree of God and would
consequently belong inevitably to the sphere of what is created and
finite and not of God himself. It cannot of course be shown here that
the classical doctrine of the Trinity could be made intelligible from
this starting point. But a traditional Christian theologian could not
deny this possibility, if he considers the connection between the two
'missions' and the two 'processions' in God.

In my humble opinion, it cannot be denied that it is possible from
our starting point to arrive at a theology of the Trinity which does
not *a priori* have to work with the traditional concept of person, but
can make use of the concepts of hypostases (as distinct from persons), of modes of subsistence of one and the same God. But we
referred earlier to the problems created by the use of the term 'person' in the theology of the Trinity, so that the starting point suggested here cannot *a priori* be regarded with suspicion merely because it does not from the very outset quite clearly lead to a triad
precisely of persons. This does not mean at all that it is impossible to
arrive at the concept of person from our starting point, assuming of
course that this notion of person is itself really clarified and remains
continually clear of those misunderstandings which, as we said, at
least today tend to cling to it. These however are all questions that
could be discussed only in a highly developed theology of the Trinity
and not in these brief reflections.

In conclusion, in this apologetic for a correctly understood doctrine of the Trinity compatible with an unambiguous monotheism,
we must refer to one or two points to which, for instance, Aquinas
himself also drew attention. For the most part, we Christians talk a
little too ingenuously of *three* divine persons and then say that each
one of these three is God, so that (as we should readily admit to
ourselves) we are exposed to the danger of being regarded as trithe-
ists. In the logic of ordinary speech it is possible to add together a
number of things only if they are seen as similar, but not different
things seen precisely as different. If then we speak of three persons
in God, we suggest involuntarily that one and the same term 'person' applies in strictly the same way to Father, Logos, and Spirit
and that there is a threefold occurrence of this sameness. But this is

contrary to dogmatic teaching on the Trinity, since Father, Logos, and Spirit are absolutely identical at every point where they are the same, so that this sameness exists strictly speaking only once, and since they are *only* distinguished by that in which they differ and consequently cannot really be counted together under one figure. Without wanting to abolish the traditional modes of expression in the doctrine of the Trinity, the difficulty of finding appropriate terms must be kept in mind when we are talking about the mystery of the Trinity in the presence of strict monotheists. Even if we completely respect the linguistic usages of the classical theology of the Trinity, we might say that it is by no means absolutely necessary to speak of *'three persons'* even in regard to the Trinity (a usage which is not to be found anyway in the New Testament) in order to explain what Christianity really means by this doctrine. In religious language we could safely speak of the Father who is ineffably close as himself in his Logos in history and in his Spirit in ourselves; we could admit that this Logos and this Spirit, however much they are to be distinguished from him and from one another and cannot be reduced to a lifeless sameness, are God himself and not intermediate beings, which would have to be regarded as creatures or would introduce a subordinationist process of evolution into God.

If we admitted this and so kept more closely to the linguistic usage of the New Testament, we would—I think—express the substance of the Christian dogma of the Trinity and perhaps be able more easily to allay the misgivings of other monotheists, even though it remains true that these other monotheists must continually be urged to make an effort to understand correctly the Christian doctrine of the Trinity, however imperfectly and inevitably also misleadingly it may be formulated. If then the question arises of a formulation of the dogma of the Trinity which strategically and didactically is as easy as possible to assimilate outside the sphere of Christianity and if at the same time restrained formulations are recommended, not to conceal but to avoid superfluous misunderstandings, then of course Christian theology must not be prevented from going more deeply into the mystery of the immanent Trinity on the lines of the speculation of the Greek Fathers, of Augustine, and of medieval theology from Aquinas to Richard of St. Victor, assuming however that it will also consider the same mystery of the salvific economic Trinity

really with the utmost intellectual vigour and love and make it fruit-
ful for Christian religious life.

As I said at the very beginning, I am aware that I have not really
carried out a dialogue with Islamic theology, but only indicated a
few points from the problems within Christianity with reference to
monotheism and the doctrine of the Trinity, in the modest hope that
it might perhaps be remotely useful for a real dialogue in which
Islamic and Christian theologians would talk about a joint profession
of faith in the one sole God and ask at the same time why this
profession is not curtailed or threatened by the Christian doctrine of
the threefoldness of this one sole God.

7

DIALOGUE WITH GOD?

Anyone who reads pious Christian literature or listens to sermons on prayer will be familiar with the statement that prayer is a 'dialogue with God'. Consequently there is no need here expressly to produce evidence of this stock theme of Christian spirituality and the theology of prayer.[1] But perhaps it is not entirely pointless to offer some reflections on the question of whether and in what sense prayer can be described as a dialogue with God. For the term 'dialogue' presupposes that in prayer, not only man, but also God himself speaks, addresses us and responds in his own words to what we say. The question which is to occupy us here is not the more general and comprehensive question of the possibility and the preconditions of prayer as such—that is, of the personal address which man directs to God (certainly not a simple problem today)—but only a question of whether and in what sense it can be said that in prayer God addresses man, so that we can really describe prayer as a dialogue between God and man.[2]

Modern man certainly has great difficulty in seeing and acknowledging that in prayer he experiences something like a personal approach of God. If (as is justified in this brief article) we disregard the more comprehensive questions of a personal experience of God as

[1] From the very beginning, the present author has been continually occupied with the subject of prayer in his publications. We need only refer to the book *Von der Not und dem Segen des Gebetes* ('On the Burden and the Blessing of Prayer'), which appeared for the first time in 1949, and also to the appropriate articles in the volumes of *Theological Investigations*.

[2] For a general survey of the theme of prayer, the reader may consult the article 'Prayer' by J. Sudbrack in *Sacramentum Mundi*, vol. 5 (London/New York, 1970), pp. 74–81, who also touches briefly on our chosen theme, but then refers for further details to the article 'Word of God' by L. Scheffczyk in *Sacramentum Mundi*, vol. 6 (London/New York, 1970), pp. 362–68.

existing and of the relationship between God on the one hand and man and the world on the other[3]—that is, the more comprehensive questions which seem difficult enough to man today—the difficulty of experiencing prayer as dialogue lies in the fact that what people are accustomed or inclined to interpret in an unsophisticated piety as God's speaking to us in prayer is experienced in the first place as their own mental state or activity (which is undoubtedly true, cannot be denied and today can no longer be naively overlooked), and the question may be asked how this can be understood as a special manifestation of God, as his speaking to us. Modern man has the impression up to a point of talking to himself in prayer and of wondering whether this conversation with himself may also be passing *over* God, whether his reflection on himself perhaps takes place *'in the presence of'* God. If he experiences in prayer certain sudden, unexpected, and powerful irruptions and outbursts of new insights and impulses (which, of course, certainly happen), modern man will interpret such occurrences in the first place as events within his own person, as deeper mental processes seeking expression, as the emergence of what has hitherto been suppressed, as a fortunate coordination of subconscious associations, or something of the kind. He will point to the fact that the same somewhat extraordinary mental processes are also present when there is no question of specifically religious contents, in artistic intuitions and fresh ideas that cannot really be preprogrammed, in sudden transformations of the whole person which are not expressly religiously motivated, and so on. Whether he is right or not entirely right is something that need not be investigated here; in any case modern man has the impression that it would mean accepting miracles or old-fashioned mythology, if he were to regard an unexpected and powerful mental experience, because of its suddenness, intensity, and significance, at once as the result of an isolated intervention of God in space and time into the normal course of the history of his consciousness. All this seems to him, at least as a general rule, to be as improbable in the mental

[3]See the article 'Experience' by K. Lehmann in *Sacramentum Mundi*, vol. 2 (London/New York, 1968), pp. 307–9. But as far as we are concerned, all this involves the problems connected with the term 'person' (cf. 'Person' in *Sacramentum Mundi*, vol. 4 [London/New York, 1969], especially pp. 404–9) and its application to God, which has been discussed in detail from different aspects, particularly in recent times. Cf. 'Observations on the Doctrine of God in Catholic Dogmatics' in *Theological Investigations*, vol. 9 (London/New York, 1972), pp. 127–44.

sphere as the assumption that miracles occur in the external world as new interventions of God 'from outside' into his world.[4] Even if he acknowledges the existence of God, he explains the course of his inner life by intramundane causes, which still remain intramundane even when they produce less ordinary phenomena in the sphere of consciousness.

Even today however there are many people in the Church, especially in the many groups cherishing an enthusiastic piety, who unhesitatingly regard certain mental experiences, particularly in speaking with tongues, baptism of the Spirit, in complete conversion, etc., as charismatic interventions of the Holy Spirit 'from outside',[5] who more or less ignore the simple fact that all such occurrences are primarily *their own* and (at least until there is conclusive proof of the opposite, which has not yet been produced even by parapsychological phenomena) must be explained as effects of conditions of an internal or external character present in themselves. Moreover, for the outsider, all such enthusiastic phenomena have their parallels in religions outside Christianity which clearly display the singularity, the horizon of consciousness, the language and the limitations of all these mental causes, so that it is scarcely possible to discover or seek there anything that would necessarily have to be attributed to a special and miraculous intervention of God. As a result of these and similar considerations, it is very difficult for modern man to discover in his conscious prayer anything that he might simply interpret as God's speaking as distinct from his own words. To him prayer seems to be a monologue or at best a conversation with himself, not a dialogue with God, not an event that could be described seriously and without too many qualifications as conversation or dialogue.[6]

---

[4] The suddenness of the occurrence of these phenomena—the causes of which have not been grasped and for the most part can be understood only with difficulty—is an aspect which is discussed in connection with miracles, even though not comprehensively or conclusively. Here we can do no more than allude to it. As far as prayer is concerned, in my opinion this aspect has been considered only infrequently and inadequately. There will be more to be said about this in what follows.

[5] Here we need only recall movements like 'Jesus People' and the Pentecostal movement, among others, which are evidently becoming increasingly established in Europe.

[6] On the clarification of the question of how 'conversation' as such is to be understood, cf. the article 'Gespräch' by J. B. Metz in *Lexikon für Theologie und Kirche*, vol. 4 (Freiburg, 1960), cols. 836–37. In our context it is also useful to consider J. B. Metz, 'Akt, religiöser Akt' in *LThK*, vol. 1 (Freiburg, 1975), cols. 256–59, and also K. Rahner, 'Gebet IV. Dogmatisch' in *LThK*, vol. 4, cols. 542–45.

In this difficult situation we might be tempted to interpret prayer as dialogue with God in the sense that it means coming to terms with the word of God (reading, applying, etc.) which is present in revelation and in Scripture.[7] God speaks to us in Scripture, prayer as meditation on Scripture responds to this word, and thus there is a conversation, a dialogue with God in prayer. For the Christian, who regards Scripture as the word of God, this view certainly makes sense. But this explanation too has its difficulties. On closer examination it is clear that it only shifts the problem. For revelation received in a person's mind (it is not revelation at all unless it 'gets there') and revelation objectified in Scripture are both in principle exposed to the same uncertainty: that is, how a content of consciousness in a person's subjectivity and carrying with it all the limitations of that subjectivity, which must in the first place be interpreted as the effect of this human causality, can be heard and understood as God's word.[8] But, apart from this vast problem, which cannot be pursued further here, there is yet another difficulty about this explanation.

The devout person thinks he perceives in prayer a concrete approach of God, calling him in his individuality and individual life's decision. But if the person praying had to regard the application of the word of Scripture (as such universal) to himself and his concrete situation in life as his own work, undertaken on his own account and at his own risk, merely as the application of universal norms to a concrete situation for an individual decision (where the important thing is what goes beyond the universal), then there would be no dialogue in the sense understood when prayer is described as such. There would be no more than a purely human application of a universal divine word to an individual and the concrete, always unique questions relating to his own life. The person praying remains in a conversation with himself, even though with the aid of a universal divine word. The transition from universal revelation to the concrete

[7] A first approach to the vast field of 'meditation' opened up here can be found in section III.A of the article 'Spirituality' in *Sacramentum Mundi,* vol. 6 (London/New York, 1970), pp. 157–60.

[8] The author dealt with the fundamental questions of hearing revelation in his work *Hearers of the Word* (London/New York, 1969). This book later came up against a certain amount of criticism. We hope that our remarks here will make a modest contribution to clearing up misunderstandings and to a further development of some of our initiatives.

imperative is the work of that person alone, even if the transition is understood as coming about with the aid of divine grace, as long as it is not clear how the assistance of grace in the application of the word of Scripture to himself and his life's questions can be interpreted as a divine address, how then also the concrete imperative calling the person praying can be understood as a call of God.

This assistance of grace for concrete decision is known in theology as 'illumination' and 'inspiration', but it is not certain what exactly is meant by this expression. For there is at least one important school in theology[9] which interprets this illumination and inspiration, insofar as they are the condition of salvific acts, as purely 'entitative' and outside consciousness, so that nothing is gained for an understanding of God's speaking to us in prayer. Even if it is said that such an occurrence in prayer, in which a salvific decision is achieved, is accompanied, together with the entitative supernatural grace sustaining it, by 'healing' graces which urge this event on toward a salvific decision,[10] this still does not get us much further with our question. For this healing grace is interpreted as natural in itself and in the first place as the limit of intramundane causes, so that for the question of being addressed by God in prayer it is exposed to the same difficulties from which it started out at the very beginning. This healing grace too is part of intramundane reality involved in the interconnection of causes and effects and in this sense can certainly be understood (like everything else in the world) as God's creation, by which God intends our salvation, but for that very reason no more God's speech to us than is anything else that we encounter in our history.

Not infrequently we try to make the question easy for ourselves by first assuming a knowledge of the personality of God and immediately drawing the conclusion that he can be addressed by us. If we

---

[9]On this cf. the surveys by L. Casutt and J. Auer in the articles 'Erleuchtung' and 'Erleuchtungsgnade' in *LThK,* vol. 3 (Freiburg, 1959), cols. 1014–16. In this connection also two publications by the present author may be considered and compared with one another: *Inspiration in the Bible* (Quaestiones Disputatae 1; London/New York, 1958) and *Visions and Prophecies* (QD 10; London/New York, 1963). These references are meant only to underline the fact that there is still more to be done in the treatment of these questions.

[10]These aids were called 'healing graces' (*gratiae sanantes*) in the sense that they turn a free will that is 'sick' because of concupiscence into a 'healthy' free will. Cf. *Indiculus* 9, DS 248: *'liberum arbitrum . . . de languido sanum'* ('free will . . . is brought . . . from sickness to health' [Neuner and Dupuis, *The Christian Faith* (Dublin, 1973), n. 1914]).

get so far, it seems that we are already in a state of dialogue that can immediately be actualized. But, even if we assume the knowledge that God is to be regarded in himself as wholly and entirely 'personal', this still does not justify the two further steps necessary for an actual dialogue with God. It is still by no means clear that this personal God can be addressed by us; and even more does it need to be made clear that he responds to our approach and does not remain silent. Even if we say in regard to the second step that he has come out of his silence, has spoken and imparted himself to us by his verbal revelation, there remains the question already raised, as to why the dialogue in prayer is more than a conversation with ourselves about God's universal revelation in his history of revelation, why it is more than the acceptance on our own account and at our own risk of what is said to us in this revelation.[11]

We must attempt to get further in a different way. The assumption hitherto taken for granted in our reflections on prayer as dialogue with God was that in prayer God tells us 'something'. The assumption behind our statement of the problem was that a certain individual, categorial content of consciousness, alongside many others, as directly effected in a special and outstanding way by God and in this special effectedness, constitutes something like a dialogue with God. And this assumption carried with it the difficulties of which we were speaking up to now. But how would it be if we were to say and could say that in prayer we experience ourselves as those who are spoken by God, who in the concreteness of our existence have our origin in and are at the disposal of God's supreme freedom? What if we say that what God tells us first of all in prayer we are ourselves in the determinedness of our freedom, in the indeterminability of our future, in the never completely revocable and never functionally rationalizable facticity of our past and present?[12] If in all these reflections we understand our question in this way, this means of

---

[11]These ideas are certainly not difficult to understand, but they make clear by their unusualness how very much we are inclined here to take for granted in our thinking and arguing certain assumptions which on closer examination turn out to be far less defensible than we would wish. It is almost self-evident for this reason and in this sense that criticism is an indispensable task for a modern theology.

[12]The questions formulated here are by no means as artificial and arbitrary as they might seem at first sight. These working hypotheses—at this point they are not suggested to the reader as anything else—will turn out in the further course of this train of thought to be intrinsically and objectively substantiated, at least in the sense that such a conception cannot be rejected in principle as impossible and unjustified.

course *a priori* that this relationship between God and ourselves as 'partnership' and 'dialogue' is one that is unique and unparalleled and cannot simply be understood univocally according to the pattern of a relationship between human beings in the form of a partnership and a dialogue, so that of course from this standpoint also for our question the idea of 'dialogue' has the character of uniqueness and incomparability if it is meant to characterize the peculiarity of prayer.[13] If we can answer positively the questions now raised, then we are (in our transcendality which as such is experienced as derived, as we might say) ourselves the statement and address of God as heard.

This however is not to be understood simply as a universal proposition, but is a statement about a particular individual in his quite definite, unique, and historical concreteness, who is committed to himself and *in this way* experiences himself as the one spoken by God to himself. God's most fundamental word to us in our free uniqueness is not a word that occurs as something additional or as a single object among other objects of experience, categorically, at a definite point within the wider field of our consciousness; it is we ourselves in unity, totality, and dependence on the incomprehensible mystery that we call God, the word of God that we ourselves are and that as such is spoken to us. As soon as we read these propositions (which apparently sound purely existentially ontological), while assuming that this transcendentality is always from the outset and everywhere (because of God's universal salvific will) raised and radicalized toward God's *immediacy* by what we call supernatural grace as God's self-communication, they are seen to be directly theological statements.[14] If, by mind and grace in one, man experiences himself as the one spoken by God himself and this constitutes his actual nature, in the concreteness of which the free grace of God's self-communication also participates, and if he allows in prayer for this existence and freely accepts it as God's word in which God promises himself in his *word* to man, then by this very

---

[13]This will have to be stressed in regard to a way of thinking that neglects the analogical character of such speaking and deals too directly with these structures. This is not to deny the fundamental right to do so; in fact we are attempting here to say something about this relationship as partnership and dialogue.

[14]This means that a genuine, if specific, concreteness is asserted of the reality under consideration.

fact prayer (in a primary sense, to be further widened below) is dialogic, a conversation with God. Man hears himself then as God's address, which is filled with God's promise of himself by faith, hope, and love, in God's gracious self-communication. He does not hear 'something' additional to himself as to someone presupposed in his inert facticity, but himself as the word spoken to him, in which God constitutes him a hearer and to whom he promises himself as answer.

It cannot be our task here of course to substantiate the statements just made in terms of a theological or philosophical anthropology.[15] If that could be done here, it would be necessary to see that these statements were made and substantiated not only as objective statements appropriate to man as such and which occur to him only when he thinks and speaks about them in subsequent statements. Statements of this kind ought to be understood and substantiated as transcendental, that is, here simply as propositions whose content is established and known everywhere and always in man's mental and free self-realization as the unthematic condition of the possibility of all human existence, so that this transcendental dialogic existence can be admitted, thematicized up to a point and also accepted in explicit freedom in prayer, and thus prayer can be understood as dialogue. But, as we said, the meaning of these statements can neither be more closely explained nor more precisely substantiated. For that the reader must be referred to an anthropology developed elsewhere.[16]

So far, however, we have mentioned only one aspect of prayer, the 'transcendental' aspect, which enables us to see prayer as dialogue in a quite definite sense. We must now add a second aspect which both provides a real justification of the general understanding of prayer and dialogue and also clears up any mythological or miraculous misunderstandings. If, that is, man accepts unconditionally and genuinely this absolute openness toward God, derived from God

[15]The article 'Man (Anthropology)' by J. Splett, R. Pesch and K. Rahner in *Sacramentum Mundi*, vol. 3 (London/New York, 1969), pp. 358–70, provides a useful introduction to the subject. It includes a bibliography.

[16]Two articles by the present author may be helpful in this respect: 'The Experience of God Today' in *Theological Investigations*, vol. 11 (London/New York, 1974), pp. 149–65, and 'Experience of Self and Experience of God' in *Theological Investigations*, vol. 13 (London/New York, 1975), pp. 122–32.

and his freedom (which is God's original word to man), if it is not concealed, distorted, or misused by man's prior decision in regard to quite definite categorial contents of his consciousness, then (if I may be allowed what may seem like an arbitrary leap in thought) we have what Ignatius of Loyola described in his *Spiritual Exercises* as 'in-difference' and (when this indifference is really radically freely achieved and maintained) 'consolation . . . without any preceding cause'.[17] If, within such an ultimate dialogic freedom, a particular individual object of choice is encountered, which, even after long spiritual experience and questioning, does not distort, confuse, or restrict this pure openness to God, if it is experienced precisely as the medium by which this indifferent openness to God is accepted and remains intact in unconditional surrender to him—that is (con-versely), in unconditional acceptance of God's word, that we our-selves are—then this categorial object of choice (however intramun-dane and relative it may be in itself) can and may be understood as a factor in this dialogic relationship between God and man, because and insofar as this chosen object is incorporated into the totality of the dialogic conversation, without imperiling or removing the lat-ter's boundless and absolute openness. Seen objectively, as purely intramundane and categorial, such a categorial chosen object, on which a person decides in prayer, can always remain problematical, may perhaps turn out later (measured by man's intramundane needs and structures) to be inadequate, provisional, replaceable, and even detrimental; nevertheless, it is here and now the best medium of this indifferent, transcendental openness in which man knows himself as God's spoken word and consequently salvifically God's will.

In this kind of logic of existential knowledge and freedom[18] prayer becomes dialogic even in regard to its categorial individual contents. What appears in consciousness with a kind of surprising suddenness

---

[17]Cf. *The Text of the Spiritual Exercises of St Ignatius*, translated by John Morris and others (5th ed.; London, 1952), nos. 23 and 330.

[18]The author put forward some ideas on this theme some time ago, in the light of a different starting point and with a different objective, in *The Dynamic Element in the Church* (London/New York, 1964), where the initiative in particular of Ignatius of Loyola was used to bring out the knowledge of God's concrete will in a specific situation. For further reflections on these lines cf. 'Observations on the Factor of the Charismatic in the Church' in *Theological Investigations,* vol. 12 (London/New York, 1974), pp. 81–97, and also the article in the *Festschrift* for J. Salaverri, entitled 'Einige Bemerkungen zu einer neuen Aufgabe der Fundamentaltheologie'.

and unexpectedness or as sentimental feeling is not to be regarded simply for that reason as an effect of the Spirit and thus as an approach of God and consequently as needing today to be enthusiastically highly stylized in face of a down-to-earth and sceptical psychology. Where however the particular reality in consciousness, for which we decide, can be sustained as a positive medium in the face of a permanent and unconditional openness toward God (or, as we might say, in the face of an absolute critical freedom), this same particular object can be regarded as spoken to us by God in and together with that fundamental address of God to ourselves which we are ourselves and which we perceive and accept in prayer.

We are not claiming here that the two aspects of prayer, which we tried very briefly to outline, adequately establish the dialogic character of prayer. We shall be satisfied if it is agreed that we have elucidated a little more the dialogic character of prayer. Nor of course is it possible to explain the consequences of this conception of prayer as dialogue.[19] If it now seems more difficult than is generally assumed to see prayer seriously and realistically as dialogue with God and especially to experience it in practice thus 'demythologized' as dialogue, that is not to say that the ordinary believer has to keep all the reflections developed here explicitly in mind in his daily routine. After going through these considerations and this disenchantment, he may experience prayer in a kind of fresh naïvety as dialogue with God, simply because that is what it is in truth.

[19]It may however be permitted to refer quite generally to 'Theses on the theme: faith and prayer' in *Opportunities for Faith* (London/New York, 1974), pp. 53–61, where the author attempted to formulate a few requirements for prayer today.

8

THE DEATH OF JESUS AND
THE CLOSURE OF REVELATION

There is an old and well-known axiom in Catholic theology that Christian revelation, as addressed with binding force 'publicly' and 'officially' to everyone, was closed with the death of the last apostle and thus the history of revelation properly so-called came to an end, even though the history of the understanding of revelation, the history of faith in this revelation and the history of theology continue. Hence the Second Vatican Council says in *Dei Verbum* no. 4: 'The Christian dispensation, therefore, as the new and definitive covenant, will never pass away, and we now await no further new public revelation before the glorious manifestation of our Lord Jesus Christ'. This axiom of the completeness of public divine revelation is substantiated in the council with the reference to Jesus Christ, the Word of God made flesh, who completed the work of salvation, in whose life, death, and resurrection and sending of the Spirit the Father is seen. In this declaration in the Second Vatican Council on the definitiveness of Christian revelation there is no explicit reference to the apostles or to the end of the apostolic age with the death of the last apostle. But, since in the conciliar text it is not a question so much of a precise chronological determination of the end as of indicating the reason for this end, the traditional formulation that revelation was closed with the death of the last apostle is not disowned by the council. On the other hand, however, it is not claimed that this formulation is clear or that it easily stands up to any critical questioning. No lesser person than Cardinal Bea, for example, drew from this axiom in its traditional formulation the conclusion that all the canonical Scriptures of the New Testament would have had to be written before the death of the last apostle, since otherwise there would have been no one to make known the original revelation of the inspiredness of the last of the writings of the New Testament. But if, conversely, the emergence of the last of the inspired writings of the New Testament is placed *after* the presumed death of the last apostle and at the same time inspiration and the knowledge of inspiredness is understood in the traditional sense (a sense which is not immediately obvious), then all that remains to be said is that Christian revelation was closed with the end of the apostolic age, but that this age can safely be extended to the time of the emergence of the last of the writings of the New Testament. But however the end of the epoch of Jesus and his apostles is to be precisely chronologically determined (the age of the Church's coming to be as distinct from that of the fully established Church) the basic substance of the axiom in any case remains clear. God's revelation in Jesus Christ occurred historically once and for all, occupies a definite and limited spatio-temporal position in history, and is nevertheless unsurpassable and for all subsequent time irrevocably valid, so that nothing that is really 'new' can ever again occur in the history of revelation.

This axiom (given more precise expression, which is desirable but cannot be provided here) must be regarded in the light of the doctrine of the new and *eternal* covenant in Jesus Christ as Christian and Catholic dogma, but this certainly does not make it any easier for a modern mentality to assimilate. Joseph Ratzinger draws attention in his commentary on *Dei Verbum* to this difficulty of understanding for modern man. Here we cannot explain more closely either the difficulty or its solution. But, since this difficulty is important for our present question concerning the connection between Jesus' death and the completion of revelation, we must at least briefly give some attention to it. Modern man sees himself as existing in history, as a being absolutely open to the future, as a person who does not simply possess his nature from the beginning as something to which merely accidental modifications are added in the course of history, not permitting this statically conceived nature to be itself truly historical. He sees the necessity of coming to be in freedom, not as the stigma of his finiteness, but as the distinguishing mark of his freedom that is always freshly and surprisingly realized in self-transcendence into the future. Consequently man today will always regard the history of religion (particularly if he does not dismiss this as a now obsolete and finished period within his history of emancipation) as opening out on to an unknown future. And if as a Christian he sees the history of *revelation* as always and every-where at work, at least in the past, in this history of religion, since history is always salvation history and since salvation history is not possible without faith or, consequently, without revelation, then the proposition about the end of the history of revelation in the midst of the continuing course of history as a whole seems to him at least difficult to understand. To say that the history of revelation is at an end seems to him to deprive history as a whole of its ultimate depth and dignity.

If in response to this difficulty it is pointed out that the Spirit of God of course always continues to lead the Church into all truth, that the history of the acceptance of revelation, of its adaptation to the ever new human person, the history of *faith,* continues, then at least it becomes easier than it usually is to see how to work out in theology the unity and continuity of (completed) revelation history and (continuing) history of faith, and thus up to a point to modify more clearly and legitimately the caesura laid down by the axiom. If it is said that the axiom teaches not so much the completeness as the unsurpassability of revelation in Jesus Christ (*Dei Verbum* has *oeconomia christiana . . . nunquam praeteribit,* translated 'the Christian dispensation . . . will never pass away'), then a termino-logical aid to understanding the axiom is certainly provided for mod-ern man, since the latter can grasp the possibility of a chronologi-cally fixed historical event being authoritative for all later times (but particularly for a genuine future) more easily than a historical event that is itself simply finished, does not continue, and yet claims a significance for later times. If however the axiom is understood in this sense of an historical unsurpassability, it needs to be given first of all a more exact formal explanation in terms of the philosophy and theology of history (something that has not yet been adequately considered in theology) and there must be an indication of the *con-tent* implied in this unsurpassability of revelation in the Christ event.

In regard to this latter task, admittedly, a great deal has been done in theology and also in the Second Vatican Council. Since in Vatican II revelation is no longer understood as a mere communication of propositions (as it used generally to be), but as history (of which of course propositions are also a part), the question of the unsurpassa-bility of Christian revelation has become the question of the unsur-passability of the Christ event. Then of course it can be claimed that nothing further is said after Jesus Christ, not in the sense that a good deal more remains unsaid, but in the sense that all has been said, all is in fact given in the beloved Son in whom God and the world have become one. Then it can be said that God has irrevocably promised himself as historically perceptible in Jesus Christ to the world as its effective salvation in a self-communication of the absolute God him-self as the absolute future of the world, a self-communication which from God's side effectively and irreversibly prevails in the world; then, too, it can be said that this promise is unsurpassable, because it is the self-promise of the absolute God in himself to the world. This promise then is not actually closed but opens out into an infinite future and in this sense is unsurpassable. History remains open in all its dimensions, even those of grace and revelation, and now moves in its openness within the historically accomplished promise of an absolute salvation, a promise which, from God's side, encompasses victoriously the ambivalence of the world's freedom for salvation or perdition.

As we said earlier, it is not our intention in these reflections to reconcile this axiom in detail and comprehensively with modern man's self-understanding. For this, something more would be re-quired than the few and fragmentary suggestions just put forward. What will occupy us here is only the specific question as to whether and how the *death* of Jesus as such has a significance for the unsur-passability of the revelation event in Jesus Christ, and how in this light it is possible to make a contribution to the reconciliation of the modern mentality of an open future with the dogma of the unsurpas-sability and 'completedness' of Christian revelation. The latest offi-cial formulation of this axiom by the Church (as above-mentioned) at Vatican II does in fact refer to Jesus' death and resurrection in the statements preceding this conciliar axiom. But it is not clear whether this reference to the death (and resurrection) of Jesus occurs only because a mention of Jesus' death and resurrection cannot be omit-ted in a description of the final bearer of the original revelation or whether the death *as such* (completed of course in the resurrection) has an essential and irreplaceable significance for the establishment of this unsurpassability of Christian revelation.

It is the latter explanation which is upheld in the thesis we are attempting to put forward and substantiate here. The thesis might also be formulated in this way: it is only by the cross of Jesus as such that the unsurpassability of Christian revelation can be and is established; the theology of the cross is an internal constituent of the doctrine of the unsurpassability of the Christian revelation as one and whole. That of course does not mean at all that the theology of the cross is exhausted in this function. What we are saying is that in the reality of man presented in this revelation and in the continuing course of history, the 'end' of a revelation history can come only in the death of the person who is revelation bearer and revelation event in one. The theology of the cross has this aspect and this function, even though it does not come to an end there.

Let us look more closely at what has been said. If history as history of man's freedom is to continue and to persist as salvation history, and thus in a broad sense (that is, implying also the history of faith) as revelation history (since otherwise the history of man as a *whole* in *all* his dimensions would not continue), then the 'conclusive' and 'unsurpassable' character of a revelation event in the continuing course of history can only consist in the historical manifestation of the absolute self-promise of God as such and in fact as the goal of this history itself. Any other 'word' of God that, being finite, is not himself, could essentially be only provisional, leaving the way open for further new words of God, replacing (or perhaps, in the Hegelian sense of *aufheben,* 'canceling and preserving') the earlier word. Otherwise such a word with its finite content would have to be understood as linked with a merely declaratory explanation that it is final because of God's arbitrary decision, even though in principle there could certainly be further new words of revelation. But anything of this kind would not only deny the openness of man's history as he understands it today, but would also in the last resort debase revelation to the state of a now incredible mythologem, would postulate an arbitrary God who would suddenly cease to be a partner in the history in which he had previously become involved. It might also be said, if the terminology is approved, that a *prophetic* word of revelation is always and essentially provisional; the *eschatological* word of revelation can consist only in God's self-promise as the absolute future of the world, leaving open here the question of whether also every prophetic word—if it is to be a personal word of a 'supernatural' character—must carry with it a reference to the future and openness *toward* God's eschatological word, in order to be really God's genuine word of revelation in the Christian sense at all. The (sole) eschatological word of God's self-promise as such, as the absolute goal of history, as the absolute future, implies a further peculiarity which needs to be considered.

God does not offer this eschatological word of his merely as the supreme and unsurpassable opportunity for man's freedom and his history in freedom, leaving open the question of *how* the history of freedom of mankind as a whole will react to the opportunity thus offered. It is God's offer as such—an *opportunity* that alone establishes the history of mankind's freedom as it is in fact, as a whole and always and everywhere, not as an individual event in the history of revelation by which the latter enters into an unsurpassable, an eschatological phase. The eschatological word of God's self-promise to the world must be the irreversible triumph of this offer of God of himself to the world, must in a sense be the proclamation, not merely of sufficient grace, but also of efficacious grace, for the world and its history as a whole, even though of course (as the doctrine of the co-existence of efficacious grace from God and of man's freedom implies) the freedom of the history of humanity is not nullified and the proclamation of the victory of God's offer of himself does not involve a theoretical statement by God in favour of the *individual* in regard to the latter's destiny in this history. In the eschatological word God promises himself to the world, not merely as its final and unsurpassable opportunity, but as his own effective fulfillment of this opportunity. This, I think, is also the meaning of Jesus' message that in him a victorious immediacy of God's kingdom is present, as it had not formerly been present and consequently cannot consist solely in the opportunity already existing, albeit through grace, of freedom to decide for God.

How then are we to think concretely of this one eschatological and unsurpassable word of revelation? For the sake of simplicity we assume here that 'this plan of revelation is realized by deeds (*gestis*) and words having an inner unity', as *Dei Verbum* (no. 2) of the Second Vatican Council states. We also assume that the history of humanity has from God and in itself a unity and solidarity of its events among themselves of such a kind that a single event in the course of that history has some meaning and also 'speaks' for all the rest. In the light of these assumptions, we are faced with the question of how God's eschatological word of the irreversible victoriousness of God's promise is to be conceived, if this victorious self-promise of God is to appear historically and in fact in the still continuing course of history? Allowing for these assumptions, we may say somewhat briefly that God's self-promise, if it is to be not merely words but also deeds, can be granted only in a person who has accepted this self-promise freely and definitively. Only in this way can the victoriousness of God's self-promise be seen, can be deeds and not merely words. In addition of course it is necessary for the free and definitive acceptance of this self-promise of God by a human being to become historically perceptible for us.

Before we go on from this point, if our train of thought is to be protected against misunderstandings and any suspicion of heresy, an incidental remark is necessary. It cannot be our task here to work out a Christology uniformly in all its aspects: that is, to show that the bringer of absolute salvation—the reality and the bearer of the absolute, irreversible, and victorious self-promise of God to the world in historical perceptibility—is necessarily the person described in the classical Christology of the hypostatic union. All that is important for us in regard to this question is that this historically manifested self-promise of God to the world (if it is to be eschatological, not merely an offer but the victoriously prevailing offer of God by God himself) must necessarily occur in a person who freely and definitively accepts this self-promise. And this acceptance as definitive must be made historically perceptible for us.

To me all this seems really obvious. A mere word, in which a self-promise of God was thought to be taking place, would in fact be a mere offer to the addressee of this word, an offer to man's freedom; it would then be an offer whose definitive acceptance was still uncertain. If it is said that this word of God assures us also that it is actually accepted and prevails, we may still ask when this acceptance in fact takes place, whether it has already happened or is still to come in the course of history, whether as past or future (if it is not itself the salvation of the world as a whole and thus the end of history) this acceptance occurs in such a way that the blessed outcome of history as a whole is irreversibly decided by a single event in that history. The word of God as such, that guarantees God eschatologically as the actually victorious end of history, must then necessarily occur through an historical event, an event that can occur only in the factual and definitive acceptance of this offer by God of himself to the world by a person who of course must be seen as so constituted that *his* acceptance of this self-offering in obedient and increasingly definitive freedom guarantees the salvation of the world as a whole. This might be the starting point for the classical Christology of the hypostatic union, which however would have to be completed in greater detail and more precisely by a theology in which the solidarity of this God-man with all humanity and its history would need to be brought out.

Here, however, only one question remains: how are we to conceive more exactly and concretely this free and definitive acceptance of God's offer of himself as the absolute future of all history, the acceptance by which alone God's offer becomes the eschatologically definitive word of God to humanity? To which the answer must be that this free and definitive acceptance of God's offer of himself, which makes God's word to the world eschatological and predestines world history to salvation, can come about only by the *death* of the person who freely accepts that offer: a death of course which must be seen as redeemed and more palpably as redeemed, that is, taken together with what we describe as the resurrection of Jesus. In this sense the *death* of Jesus is an internal constitutive element of God's eschatological self-promise to the world.

It is of course impossible here to work out a detailed and precise theology of death in general, which was presupposed to the basic thesis, above-stated, of our reflections. In this connection we must refer to other studies of the theology of death in general. But here it is sufficient to say that death (which is something that goes on throughout the whole of life to its very end) understood in wholly human and theological terms, is not a merely biological occurrence at the end, a medical exitus, but a self-realization of creaturely-human freedom in which man faces God and disposes of himself completely and finally for or against God: this he does in that final state of creaturely powerlessness that reaches its uttermost realization and manifestation in what we commonly experience as death. For the Christian understanding of freedom, the one act of freedom that centres on finality in a human life takes place in the course of actually dying and not independently of this, even though, as far as our experience goes, the act of freedom of the one life definitively

disposing of the person cannot necessarily be chronologically localized at the very moment of its medico-biological termination. For
Christian anthropology a definitive self-realization of freedom is inconceivable either as happening independently of death somewhere
within the ordinary course of life (in a mystical act, for instance, not
continued into death) or as occurring only after death. At the same
time the concrete way in which a person dies is in principle irrelevant. But the acceptance of the concrete way in which ultimately
death uncontrollably occurs is also part of the successful definitive
act of freedom that we describe as death. And a theologian should
not be forbidden (if, indeed, he is not required) to consider why and
how the concreteness of Jesus' death (its violence in the conflict
with the political and religious authorities, the extreme God-forsakenness of this death, etc.) is also essential and significant for the
salvific import of this death for Jesus himself and even more for us.
But even then the decisive factor is that death, for Jesus also, must
be understood fundamentally as the act of supreme freedom in absolute powerlessness, centred at the same time on finality.

If then the final and definitive acceptance of God's offer of himself
is supposed to take place in Jesus and he is thus to be the eschatologically victorious word of God to the world, this can come about
only in and through his death. Of course the successful achievement
of this acceptance in the powerlessness of death must also become
perceptible for us in faith; in other words, it must be seen together
with his resurrection.

The death of Jesus and consequently his passion as a whole is a
necessary constitutive element in the eschatological word of God's
self-promise to the world as its absolute future. If, as we said earlier,
this word of God and this alone is unsurpassable, if this word and
this word alone is the now the unsurpassable revelation of God
which reaches its close by itself opening up the infinite incomprehensibility of God as such and makes possible and authorizes by this
very fact a still continuing history (since the latter now has an infinite goal as victoriously prevailing), then it can and must be said that
the death of Jesus is this disclosing closure of revelation and without
that death the closure is quite impossible. While textbook theology
usually says that revelation was closed with the death of the last
apostle, it would be better and more exact to say that revelation
closed with the achievement of the death of Jesus, crucified and

risen, that is, with the cross, since God himself promised himself irrevocably there to history and God can add nothing more to this final word of God, even though within this final word history also continues as God's revelation—the history that we usually describe as history of the Church and history of faith, which is the history of this final word of God and thus, rightly understood, can also continue to be described as history of revelation.

If the cross as Jesus' death achieved to the point of resurrection must be described as the end of the history of revelation, this is not to deny, but implicitly to assert, that in this cross as the victory of God's offer of himself to the world, the Church, too, of course is established as the historical and (as public) institutional palpability of faith in the crucified and risen Christ, a faith without which God's self-promise to the world in Jesus would not be victorious at all. Today also then it may be said that public Christian revelation was completed with the end of the apostolic age, assuming that this 'completedness' is rightly understood and that this apostolic age is seen as centred in the cross of Christ as such, the cross that is not merely one of the events within this phase but also its gnoseological axis. In the cross of Jesus the transcendental and historical dimensions of man are definitively and irrevocably reconciled; man's absolute dependence on the self-bestowing mystery of God becomes an historical event, realized in fact in the death achieved there as such, and otherwise impossible. That man's transcendence toward God in his immediacy is really finally achieved through God himself and carries the person away beyond all detailed and provisional classifications: this is the substance of the Christian revelation that became an event in the cross of Jesus and was made evident there. And for that reason the cross is the completion of Christian revelation.

We can look at what has been said from a somewhat different standpoint and thus examine again expressly the problems with which these reflections opened. I mean the problems arising from the contrast between the modern mentality of an absolute will for a boundless future on the one hand and the doctrine on the other hand of the completedness of public revelation, which is nevertheless the ultimate content of history itself. As we said, these are problems which cannot be treated comprehensively or adequately here. But if it is the will of modern man not merely to exist like his ancestors as the same person, even though under somewhat different conditions, but also in creative freedom to establish really new futures (individually and collectively, while embracing these two dimensions), then this will of man today is nevertheless continually repudiated and foiled by death, which, by its very contradiction to what is up to a point a new will of man, acquires a new distinctive character and radicalness. This fatal contradiction between man's absolute will for boundless freedom and the death to which he is doomed becomes obvious, even though it is suppressed in all the ideologies of our time and is not compensated for the individual in his own existence by thinking of the succession of the generations of those doomed to death as continuing indefinitely. The fatal contradiction does not become acceptable when understood as continuing for ever and when each generation is seen to be merely the pedestal on which the statue of victory is erected by the next generation, a generation that likewise perishes with its victory.

Each person has a responsibility, not only for those who are to come, but also for the dead who went before; not only for his own life, but also for his own death. If it is not to lie, the modern mentality of an absolute will for the future must therefore recognize the fact that it is foiled by death. If then it is possible at all to conceive and hope for a vindication of the intersection of all history by death, it can lie only in the fact that death itself is not the nullifying end of history, but the event in which history is dissolved by God's own act into the infinite freedom of God. That death can be this event, that it has already been achieved as such and as such is promised also in regard to our own death: this the faith of the Christian learns at the cross of Jesus.

9

WHAT DOES IT MEAN TODAY
TO BELIEVE IN JESUS CHRIST?

In regard to this theme I think it is appropriate to begin with some
preliminary observations.

First, it is obviously impossible to provide anything like an
exhaustive treatment of the theme. It is a theme that aims at Christianity in its wholeness and in its essence, at the totality of human
and Christian existence with its unfathomable mystery and with all
its dimensions. The theme is concerned especially with the Christology which has been believed, lived, prayed, and sustained for two
thousand years, which the best minds of Western history have considered over and over again; it is a theme that really presupposes an
entire anthropology and theology, that as such demands the most
detailed knowledge of biblical studies and of the history of dogma; it
needs to be considered in the light of the present situation of our
own time and of the world in which we live. In view of all this, it is
obviously impossible to do more in regard to the theme than to put
forward a few observations which are inevitably arbitrarily chosen
and thus carry with them the danger that precisely what is left unsaid
might have been more helpful to the reader than what is actually
said.

Second, it is a theme that would fail from the very outset to cover
its subject matter if it did not invoke the one whole and mysterious
existence of man, if it were understood as one particular object of
man's questioning curiosity among countless other equally important objects of his questioning and searching. It can be treated only if
the whole person with his ultimate mystery, which is called God, is
actively involved, the one human being with his question of salva-

tion and concern for salvation, which he mostly suppresses or leaves aside in the banal variety of his life. Only when the one whole person in his free responsibility for himself as one and whole becomes aware of himself can Christology be properly pursued, since it is meant to be the answer to the one and entire question of human existence. This does not mean that we are concerned here with directly meditative or edifying talking or preaching, that we are to spare ourselves entirely the exertion of conceptual speaking. But what must be clear from the very beginning is the approach to be made by the reader in order to understand these reflections: the approach of a conscious and free responsibility for his existence as one and whole.

Third, access to a modern Christology might be found in a variety of ways. It would be possible to begin with a theology of love of neighbour, with a theology of death, with a theology of the future, and from one of these starting points (which presumably might be still further increased) to show that they lead to a questioning and questing Christology which finds its own answer in the Church's profession of faith in Jesus Christ as the unsurpassable and victorious word of promise of God to man, in which God makes his own self-promise to the world historically tangible and irreversible. By following more explicitly such ways of access to Christology it would certainly be possible to make clearer how today in particular an assent of faith to the Christology of Christianity can be justified. But we must necessarily simplify the matter a little more and, as far as possible, see together the different and as such to be differentiated ways of access to a modern Christology.

Fourth, it cannot be our task in these reflections to present the Church's official Christology as such in its fullness and differentiation in terms of academic theology or even merely in the conventional catechetical form. All that is possible here is to attempt to suggest to a modern person a starting point for such a Christology. The fact that the Church's Christology provides a starting point of this kind, if its content is unfolded and taken seriously, is something that can at best be merely indicated here with the assurance that it is possible to find in this very starting point what the official teaching of Catholic Christianity states about Jesus. Consequently, we do not say right from the beginning that Jesus is God, that Jesus is the Word of the eternal God made flesh who existed from all eternity with the

Father; we are not speaking from the very beginning about the hypostatic union of the divine and human natures in the one person of the divine Logos; we are not starting out from the Christological formulations of the New Testament in Paul and John which themselves represent a highly developed reflection in faith; we are not assuming the impossibility of going behind such a 'late' New Testament Christology to ask about a more original and somewhat more simple experience of faith with the historical Jesus, in his message, his death, and his achieved finality that we describe as his resurrection; we do not think that it must be *a priori* certain and obvious that the orthodox faith in Jesus as the Christ can be expressed only in *those* formulations which have been adopted in the classical Christology of the Western Church, even though they retain a normative significance for our faith for us today and in the future. What is meant by this fourth preliminary observation cannot be explained more precisely here, but it may perhaps be deduced from what is now to be said.

We begin with a reflection that might perhaps be called questing Christology. What is meant by this? Freely tending toward finality, man has to be concerned with himself as one and whole. Admittedly, he can permit himself to be driven through the diversity of his life, occupied now with one, now with another, detail of his life and its possibilities. But he is expected to have in mind and to be responsible in freedom for the oneness and wholeness of his existence; he has to be concerned with *himself,* with his 'salvation'. If he does this, he will find himself in a peculiarly and fundamentally embarrassing situation. Since it is a question of the totality of his existence, it seems that here this very totality alone as one and whole can be important for salvation, it seems that no particularity of his life, of his individual and collective history, can from the outset, from the nature of the case, be crucial for this one and whole. It seems therefore that, however much in other respects he remains unquestionably an historical being, in the question of his salvation man must become unhistorical.

He may attempt in a variety of ways to place the one totality of his existence before himself, regardless of history: becoming aware of himself in a mystical experience in the depths of his being, seeking salvation in the contemplation of this totality; trying to grasp in a metaphysical upswing the eternal truth that hovers constantly over history and assures him of his everlasting nature beyond the many-coloured variety of his history; seeking his real truth, while exposing in a spirit of sceptical resignation all truths as historically and sociologically conditioned. But all this is irrevelant in the last resort, since in all these and other conceivable ways the person thinks he can find himself as one and whole only outside his authentic historical existence; history as such seems to be beyond salvation, merely the outward show that disguises man's true nature in a thousand empty appearances.

If however a person is sure that he can also achieve and experience his salvation only in his history (since he becomes aware of himself and realizes his freedom in contact with his contemporaries and his environment, that is, in history, and cannot even in metaphysics or mysticism really step out of his history), he looks for another human being in whom, by God's free power of course, such salvation has really been achieved and as achieved becomes perceptible to him, in whom then, because of his solidarity with him, for himself, too, not only the abstract possibility of salvation, but salvation also as promise for his hope, becomes concretely apparent. The person who really seeks his salvation and knows that he is responsible for it in his freedom looks in the history of the one humanity to which he belongs for a human being in whom this salvation has not only occurred as promise to himself, but also becomes *tangible* as victoriously achieved by God's power and permits him to hope for it concretely as more than a merely abstract possibility for himself. Whether such an achieved and thus also experienced salvation event is merely *sought* in history or is already actually found there, is not a question that need be considered at this stage in our reflections.

The person at least sought in this way we may call the absolute salvation bringer (although our reflections on this point must be somewhat hasty and spasmodic), since, as we said, it is a question, not merely of the fate of an existing individual solely for his own sake, but of one that promises salvation as a firm hope for *us* and assures us effectively by God's grace of *our* salvation. This of course assumes that the person who is sought and who has reached salvation exists in an absolute solidarity with us and that we can offer and do actually offer to him the same solidarity. In our human situation as it is in fact, this salvation achieved in the persons sought cannot be understood as occurring otherwise than by death, since it is only there that history is completed, freedom becomes definitive, man surrenders himself freely and finally to the mystery of God and thus man's transcendence into God's incomprehensibility and his history reach their definitive unity. But since it is meant to be the effective promise of salvation for us, God's gift of himself to us and not merely the individually isolated fate of this person, this death rescuing the person for salvation, as achieved and saved for us into God, even though in an absolutely once-and-for-all experience, must also become tangible: that is, the death of this person must be capable of being understood as passing into what we describe in traditional Christian terminology as the resurrection of this person. This also implies of course that this person (still being sought) in his life and his self-understanding was such and is historically grasped by us as such that we can believe seriously in this life as redeemed, in his 'resurrection'. But, on these assumptions, such a person, hitherto to some extent projected *a priori* by our question about salvation, can certainly be understood and described as absolute salvation bringer. Seen merely as such a person, he is not himself salvation, for, in view of man's boundless transcendentality beyond any particular good and in view of this transcendence as radicalized by what we describe as grace, this salvation can only be God himself and can be given immediacy and finality only by the self-communication of this God. But this person who is sought is the absolute salvation bringer insofar as his consummation occurring through death and resurrection in the power of God in solidarity with us is for us the irrevocable sign that God has promised himself as the consummation of our salvation.

As we said at the very beginning, we cannot attempt also here to prove expressly and in detail that what is meant, at least implicitly, by the absolute salvation bringer thus depicted and sought is the same as what the classical Christology of the Church means and teaches in talking about incarnation, hypostatic union, God's eternal Word becoming man in the unity of one person and in the unconfused duality of a human and divine reality. But we think that this proof is possible in principle and we presuppose it here as possible and practicable. When *in* the redeemed destiny of one human being and in that destiny experienced *as* redeemed a person grasps God's promise of salvation to himself, he is practising Christology explicitly or implicitly; if in his history he seeks such a human being, he is practising questing Christology explicitly or implicitly. And, since a person can really only culpably suppress the question of his own salvation, such an explicitly or implicitly realized questing Christology involves in every human being today also the presence in transcendence and grace of the prerequisite that he is seeking and will eventually find his own private Christology. The fact is that we do not have to regard classical Christology today merely as an odd and no longer realizable piece of mythology.

It is now time for us to pass from a questing Christology seeking to discover the absolute salvation bringer in history to a Christology which has actually found this salvation bringer in history. In this conviction of having found him lies the real core, the substance, of Christianity. This ecclesial Christianity declares that we have found this absolute salvation bringer in Jesus of Nazareth, the Christ of God, the Son of God purely and simply.

Have we any reason or right to say this even today? Of course, seen merely from the standpoint of the human being, the statement that Jesus of Nazareth in particular is the salvation event achieved and known in faith as achieved, that he is the absolute salvation bringer who guarantees for us in history the concrete hope of our salvation, is a statement loaded with all the difficulties (uniqueness, historical distance, unrepeatability) which are involved in any statement about an historical event. But, for a person who learns in his own individual history that his concrete existence rests not solely on scientifically verifiable propositions, but more crucially on historically unique experiences, despite their permanent uncertainty, for a person who learns that he must stake and does stake always inescapably his existence on such historical experiences (even if it is only an absolute trust in the love of a neighbour), it is impossible to evade the historical experience of this Jesus by adopting a superficially sceptical attitude and claiming that in the last resort everything in history remains obscure, uncertain and ambiguous. He knows that he must transcend the uncertainty of his historical experiences inevitably and courageously in fundamental decisions in regard to other human beings. Why then should this not be possible and legitimate also in regard to Jesus?

In the first place it cannot be maintained that we know nothing with adequate certainty today about the historical Jesus, or at any rate nothing that is relevant to faith or theology. It is true that historico-critical exegesis has shown that even in the earliest New Testament writings about Jesus we are dealing with testimonies of *faith* in him as the Christ and not merely historically neutral accounts of his earthly life; it is true that modern biblical theology reveals a history of a great and dramatic development, even within the New Testament, between the preaching of the historical Jesus on the imminent approach of the kingdom of God and the self-understanding of Jesus implied in this on the one hand, and on the other hand a highly developed Christology in Paul and in John's Gospel, which as a whole borders closely on the classical Christology of the Church. But none of this (which is common property, not only of Protestant theology, but also after some delay of Catholic exegesis and theology) means that today we know of the historical Jesus nothing relevant for our Christology or that the legitimacy of the history of faith from Jesus' historical self-understanding to the Christology in Paul and John and to the Christology of the Church cannot be explained, at any rate if Easter is taken into account. The historically still perceptible proclamation of Jesus and his self-understanding implied there have also a peculiar character and unsurpassability, an incomparability, which permit us to say that in him God's self-promise as our salvation became event historically in a matchless and irreversible way and was then finally sealed by his redeemed death, that in his proclamation and his death Jesus thus became God's definitive word to us in history.

We cannot explain this precisely in detail here or (as we said) still less here and now develop explicitly from this starting point the classical Christology of Scripture and the Church, which is implied in the self-understanding of the historical Jesus. Here we need only say that Jesus does not merely proclaim a liberating image of God as the Father, before whom all—even sinners and the socially and politically downgraded—are equal, a God who forgives and liberates, whose grace reaches and relieves all apparently hopeless human situations. Jesus does all this and, even if there were nothing else, in its purity and absoluteness it would certainly not be negligible. But if this were all that Jesus' proclamation contained, it might be asked whether this liberating knowledge of God as Father could not be gained even without Jesus, whether it really goes essentially beyond the greatest heights of prophetic piety in the Old Testament, whether it could not be grasped in hope even without Jesus and whether therefore in the last resort it could be detached from Jesus and in particular from his proclamation. We need not answer these questions here and now. For Jesus did in fact proclaim more than this, wonderful as it may be on its own account and however much it is experienced as liberating and gladdening today in modern 'Jesus movements' of liberty and fraternity, of unselfish love between human beings. Regarded simply as a matter of historical fact, Jesus had a more radical message which cannot be separated from his person or eliminated from his proclamation.

His proclamation speaks of a new turning of God to man in a form hitherto unknown, a new coming of the kingdom of God, since this coming does not represent merely an *offer* to man's historical freedom, for which it remains open whether and how it will react by assent or refusal in regard in this offer by God of himself, thus leaving open once more the history of this divine offer by God of himself. Jesus proclaims that this offer by God of himself as salvation and not judgment of humanity on God's side and by his power is irreversibly victorious and as irreversibly victorious becomes historically tangible in him, in his proclamation and then finally in his redeemed death, even though the individual human being is not released by the reality and tangibility of God's victory in the history of humanity from the responsibility of his individual freedom, but can grasp for himself this victory of God only in hope.

It may be asked how the man Jesus can be aware of this actual victory of God in his unreconciled and sinful world as present with himself and his message, how he can know that God's offer of himself not only offers man his last opportunity to find God in immediacy, but itself effects the victory of this offer. The answer can only be that on the one hand Jesus is aware of being in an ineffable and indissoluble unity with his God and sustains this in absolute fidelity through all the disasters of his life up to the point of death and on the other hand Jesus has such an absolute solidarity of love for all men that he does not even consider the dilemma of taking the side either of God or of men, but grasps his own salvation as that of humanity. Of course, from Jesus' standpoint it can be said that this salvific will of God was at work creating not only the possibility but unreservedly the reality throughout the entire length and breath of the history of humanity. But it is only when we look towards Jesus in faith that we can say that he is not merely the offer of the opportunity but the reality becoming effective of itself, that as such he became irreversible in his own history and as such historically tangible. This however is essentially what Jesus said in his messages about the new and final coming of God's kingdom in that very message which cannot be separated from his person, and this was definitively sealed in his redeemed death. Thus he is the new, invincible, and unsurpassable word of God's promise to us, even though history goes on and what is established in Jesus' message and fate must still be filled out and continue to appear in the whole course of the history of humanity right to its end.

At this point in our reflections we must speak more explicitly about a matter on which we have touched several times: the resurrection of Jesus, which is the historical seal and manifestation of what is involved in the person and message of Jesus, the historically apparent victory of God's self-promise to humanity. We can grasp in faith what is meant by the resurrection of Jesus only if we keep in mind four factors in their indissoluble unity.

First, we must have a correct understanding of what is meant by resurrection. It amounts to a statement about the person as one and whole; it means the definitive redeemed state of the person and the history of a human being with God; it does not mean a return to our spatio-temporal biological life, it is not a raising of the dead in the form of a return to the bodily existence of the present time as described elsewhere in the New Testament and in the history of the saints; our experience of it, gained through the witnesses of the resurrection, has an absolute singularity which in the last resort cannot be compared with other experiences and consequently is 'historical' in a special way; it is historical because and insofar as in it there is experienced the definitive redemption of a history for its elevation.

Second, man can gain such an experience of a unique character only when and insofar as he brings to it his own hope for *himself* that his own existence will be definitively revealed. If this does not happen, there is nothing for a person to do except to adopt a sceptical attitude toward the account of the resurrection of Jesus and to leave it aside as something belonging to an inexplicable past that really does not concern him at all. But a person can have his own hope of resurrection without destroying himself, and may not (for himself and also in solidarity with the dead) simply permit human existence and history to sink into the empty nothingness of merely having been. Wherever there is real hoping and loving there is faith in one's own resurrection (which need not necessarily be localized at a 'later' point of time in the remote future), even when a person with this hope and love lacks the ability or courage verbally to thematicize and objectify the hope of resurrection implicit in the mere continuance of his existence. But if a person boldly admits his own hope of resurrection, if he sees himself as the one who is called into the definitiveness of his existence, if he encounters *in this way* the message of the resurrection of Jesus and in view of the claim of the life and death of Jesus in absolute love for God and men, then he knows that he is justified in grasping by faith the resurrection of this Jesus. He is faced with the question whether he would not be denying his own hope of resurrection in a final culpable despair if, in view of *this* life and this death of this Jesus, he did not find the courage to believe that the latter is the definitively redeemed, the Risen One.

Third, this hope of ours of our own resurrection and the encounter with the claim that Jesus' fate makes on us then encounter the disciples' message of his resurrection and the faith of two thousand years of the history of hope of Christendom, and we are faced with the question of whether we can rightly refuse our assent to this message and this faith merely because what is definitive and inconceivable extending to the incomprehensibility of God must be believed. Jesus' disciples attest an Easter experience: 'The Lord is truly risen.' For the reason already given, it is only with difficulty that we can elucidate for ourselves the peculiar character of this experience and distinguish it from apparently similar visionary and mystical phenomena, which cannot in the last resort be compared with this resurrection experience. The individual appearance of the risen Jesus, described in the New Testament accounts which cannot in the last resort be harmonized, may certainly be regarded as vividly arranged presentations and in a variety of ways as already current interpretations of the original and authentic resurrection experience of the first disciples. But this by no means disposes of the experience itself; it was perceived and attested to by men plunged into despair by the sight of the disaster of Jesus' life and in no way inclined to believe anything of this kind, men who were certainly in a position and qualified to distinguish this experience from apparently similar visionary and hallucinatory phenomena with which they were familiar. What reason could we have for not believing their testimony, assuming of course that in the absolute hope of our own existence there is an implicit yearning for our own resurrection and that we face the claim of the life and death of Jesus and are not prepared to permit this unique life of unconditional love to sink into an absolute emptiness of merely having been? Certainly we must be aware of our solidarity with the dead and not simply dismiss them as those who have been, who are good for nothing else except to make possible our own history.

Fourth, if our own transcendence to God's immediacy in freedom is alive in what we describe as grace, if it is realized and becomes explicit in history and in the encounter with history, if with our questing Christology we encounter Jesus of Nazareth, then we certainly have the opportunity for our own experience of the Risen One, even though that experience is not entirely independent of the testimony of the first disciples. The experience of our transcendence toward the immediacy of God in history here reaches its unique pinnacle. In grace we experience an ultimate freedom over all powers and forces of history, of law, of sin, of the tyranny of all human relativities; this experience seeks its tangibility and sealing in history; this experience comes in the Easter testimony of the disciples and the Church to Jesus, finds in him the seal being sought and finds it precisely in *this* Risen One, if only because such an offer never took place elsewhere in the religious history of humanity. Experience of freedom in immediacy to God and encounter with this risen one come together in an indissoluble unity and are mutually dependent; we hope absolutely for ourselves, since we encounter this redeemed fate of Jesus as the unsurpassable word of God to us, and we believe in the resurrection, since for ourselves in ultimate freedom we hope for everything, for God in himself. And this unity of experience in mind and history at the same time is certainly an experience of the Risen One in ourselves, even though we can describe it according to the testimony of the first disciples and the Church only with the name of Jesus and this experience would otherwise to some extent remain anonymous.

If the four factors mentioned are clear and seen in faith and hope in their unity, even today we can and may believe in the resurrection of Jesus without on that account getting the impression of being lost in a mythological interpretation of a banal past where in the last resort nothing happened except utopian hope, which perished in a cruel and final emptiness. The Christian has the courage to believe in the resurrection of Jesus, since he seizes on it in a responsibility for the ultimate import of his own existence and ventures hopefully to believe in his own redeemed history.

With these aphoristic observations on our general theme, which leave out and are bound to leave out many important questions (since there is no other way), we may at least draw attention to one particular theme within the whole: to the personal relationship of the individual Christian to Jesus. As risen and exalted, Jesus may, or should at least, not be a mere symbol for a personal relationship of the Christian to the eternal God; particularly as exalted, Jesus should not simply vanish into the nameless mystery that ineffably and incomprehensibly rules over our existence and is called God. He, the person redeemed, with his concrete fate now become definitive, is the guarantor that we can reach God himself in the fullness of his life and his freedom, in his blessed light and his love. But for that very reason this guarantor is eternally effective, the permanent intermediary to the immediacy of God in himself, and consequently as Christians we should have a personal relationship of hope, trust, and love, to this redeemed Jesus in the uniqueness of his human reality. This is something that is possible, something that should be developed and cultivated by Christians.

Why should it not be possible? Even in our own hope of resurrection, in which we anticipate hopefully the redeemed finality of our person and our history, we include the hope that there are such human beings who are redeemed and have become definitive. We have no right to shut out from our world simply and entirely the dead of history and those who have passed from our own circle into the silent eternity of God, those with whom we were united in fidelity and love, and to behave as if they had nothing more to do with us. We shall of course not attempt to set up a relationship with these dead who still live, to get into contact with them with the aid of parapsychology or spiritualism; the Old Testament itself rejected such conjuring up of the dead and practices of this kind are offensive to the majesty of God and to the mysterious redeemed and definitive state of the dead that is beyond our control. But this does not mean that, as Christians who acknowledge the communion of saints in our creed, we could simply abandon our loving fellowship with the dead and behave as if in themselves or at least for us they were no longer living. And if perhaps we did that and allowed the Church's commemoration of all its departed members to be for us an empty ritual, this would not mean that we were acting rightly, but would only show up the incompleteness and partial emptiness of our own existence. But if all this is correct in general, it is true particularly of the relationship that we can have and should have to the living Jesus.

He—the person redeemed in a unique way as guarantor of our own existence—lives in himself and for us. We can hope in him, love him, call to him, we can build on his love and fidelity to us, meditating on his earthly life and death, we can be assured by faith that this life's fate is redeemed and deposited for us with God as the eternal guarantee of our own hope. In his Spirit we can learn that he loves us, each of us in a unique way, that we love him, each of us also in a unique way that is part of the uniqueness of every human existence and history. In such love for the concrete Jesus in God's eternity there occurs the final reconciliation of time and eternity, of history and the preeminence of the eternal God over history. In and with Jesus we grasp the blessed inviolability of God in himself, since in him God gave himself to time and history with his infinity and freedom irrevocably for Jesus and in Jesus for us as our own. But in Jesus and in love for him we also grasp that he and we in him with our individuality and history will not be consumed and will not perish if we approach in immediacy the burning absoluteness of the eternal God, but in this very way will be those who are definitively redeemed and enduring. In him and with him we learn that God and world can exist together in blessed unity, without either one or the other having to perish. He, Jesus, is the unique and irrevocable seal of final reconciliation. Consequently, for the Christian, the loving, always unique relationship of the individual to Jesus is not something that must vanish in the presence of the silent and nameless incomprehensibility of God in immediacy, but is in fact an intrinsic, essential element of this immediacy to God by which it is established and confirmed that we shall remain at the very moment when God becomes all in all and history as redeemed reaches God.

If in faith, hope, and love, we enter into the fate of Jesus, into his unconditional love of neighbour and into his death, if we live with him and die with him in the empty darkness of his death, we shall grasp in his Spirit (in the Spirit that we know as his) that we really can enter into contact with God himself beyond all secular reality, that we can fall into this God of incomprehensible judgments and ineffable mystery without perishing there, in order to find there our final and definitive reality. If we love Jesus, quite personally and directly, if in our love we allow his life and his fate to become the internal form and entelechy of our own life, then we learn that he is the way, the truth, and the life, that he leads us to the Father, that we may and can call the incomprehensible God Father despite his namelessness, that God's namelessness and pathlessness can be our own home, bringing us not extinction, but eternal life. We must love Jesus in the unconditional acceptance of his life's fate as our own norm of existence, in order to experience serenely and joyously our own existence as finally redeemed.

10

FOLLOWING THE CRUCIFIED

The theme of these reflections is 'following the Crucified'. First of all, two brief preliminary observations. Taking the theme as it stands, it would certainly be possible and indeed appropriate to deal with it expressly in the light of the New Testament. For it was in the New Testament and only there that the message of Jesus, as crucified, and of following him, was first given. But a really unobjectionable and exact exegetical treatment of the theme in the light of the New Testament would require more space than is available here and a professional skill that I do not possess. I hope then to be allowed to put forward a few reflections that come within the scope of systematic theology, even though they are bound to seem rather colourless and abstract and even though they are selected somewhat arbitrarily from the whole range of statements which systematic theology might make on the theme, although it must be admitted that systematic textbook theology has not hitherto been particularly interested in the question and that Christian spirituality (without avoiding or wanting to avoid the theme) very easily becomes a mere exercise in edification. The second preliminary observation is that these reflections are simply reflections and nothing more, not a sermon or a prophetic address seeking to rouse in the hearer that existential situation in which man stands before the Crucified and has to decide whether in his own life the message of the cross is accepted as God's power and God's wisdom or rejected with a shrug of the shoulders as folly. These reflections here and now cannot aspire to the function and dignity of such preaching of the cross. As compared with that preaching they remain both tentative and derivative. Moreover our reflections are secondary in the sense that they cannot claim to be systematically constructed or comprehensive, nor will there be any attempt to conceal a certain unsystematic arbitrariness in the choice and sequence of the reflections.

In the exegesis and in the theory of Christian spirituality it is pointed out that 'following' and 'imitation' (despite the iridescent expression 'imitation of Christ' as used in traditional Christian spirituality) are not absolutely synonymous terms, that we must start out from the New Testament idea of following, even though Paul is aware also of the idea of imitation. Certainly we are not really expected to copy and reproduce the life of Jesus as such. We live in historical situations different from those in which Jesus himself lived, we have a different and always unique task which is not the same as that which confronted him in his own historically conditioned and restricted existence; he and we together form the one Christ of the one and unique total history of salvation, in which, for all our crucial dependence on him and on his historical existence in life and death, we do not reproduce him, but (as Paul says) complete his historical individual reality, to become the one Christ in head and members, who is identical with all redeemed humanity, hidden in God and belonging to God himself. In the light of all this, rightly understood, we could say that Christians are followers and not imitators of the Crucified. And yet this is still not the whole truth.

If we were to consider and realize only what has just been said, there would be a danger of turning the imperative of following Jesus in practice into abstract moral principles, perfectly clear in themselves, and reducing Jesus, his life, and his death, to a merely illustrative example of a moral precept which could exist independently of him. But following Jesus, his life, and him as crucified, is in the last resort something different from the realization of a universal ideal, perhaps realized particularly explicitly and purely in Jesus, but in fact simply as an 'instance' of a universal idea that in principle is independent of him. In his life and in his death there must be something that is unique and as such the content and norm of our following of Jesus, so that this following is itself authenticated as such by him and not because his life and death are in their turn authenticated by an ideal, a norm, claiming validity in themselves and independently of him.

If we keep this in mind and do not explain this unique following solely as being driven by his 'Spirit', regarded also as a suprahistorical factor, it becomes understandable and in principle legitimate that the whole history of Christian piety should have brought an element of imitation of the concrete Jesus into his following, should have been oriented to his stay in the wilderness, his fasting, his nightly prayer, his concrete poverty, his renunciation of concrete power and so on, although it cannot be proved or can be proved only with difficulty that following Jesus, seen theoretically and practically, is not possible without these concrete ways of imitating him. This must be remembered when we are talking of the following of Jesus; this following must not *a priori* be absolutely opposed to the imitation of his concrete life, difficult as it may be to say and obscure as it may be in the meantime what exactly can and should be present concretely in the life of Jesus for this imitative following, which can be found in him alone and by which alone this imitative following can be authenticated. If in this question we were to appeal immediately and solely to a *disposition* in which we follow him and thus attempt to evade all questions about a concrete content of this imitative following, then the question would promptly have to be raised about what this disposition really consists in and why it cannot be made intelligible also without direct recourse to Jesus.

We are thus faced with an obscure problem, the difficulty of which becomes apparent in the whole history of Christian piety. In the earliest Christian times the devout person sought to imitate Jesus by following the example of the first witness, by martyrdom. But when martyrdom ceased to be possible, people imitated him in the wilderness, in nightly prayer, in poverty, in renunciation of marriage, but then became somewhat embarrassed when faced with the question of how *those* Christians were to follow Jesus who could not adopt these particular ways of following him, how this following is possible without having to appeal merely to a 'disposition', a following in the 'Spirit'. Today we might perhaps think that we can and must follow Jesus concretely by a solidarity with the poor and downgraded, by a critical attitude to institutionalizations asserted by power in society and Church, by courage for conflict with the powerful. In principle it is certainly possible in this way for what is up to a point a new form of imitative following of Jesus to enter into the Church's sense of faith and from that standpoint also to resist any retreat to a purely internal and private disposition in the following of Jesus. And, since we certainly ought to follow Jesus not only in death but also in life, the emergence of such a new way of following him is certainly of the greatest importance, particularly since the established forms of this concrete following have hitherto been more or less identical with the ways of life of the religious orders, while the 'laity' found such a life-style alien and had no desire to regard themselves as belonging to the following of Jesus only insofar as they remotely or closely imitated the style and mentality of the religious life. But, even if all this is evident and must be regarded as important, the real question that faced us with reference to an imitative following, not to be reduced to a mere disposition, does not yet seem to be solved.

The preference which Jesus showed and lived out for the poor and downgraded in society and which certainly cannot be deduced from an abstract and universal morality, not even from Christian love of neighbour alone, does not present any style of following for the poor and downgraded themselves in society, unless it is to suggest that these poor and downgraded are to follow Jesus by bearing their lot patiently. This is a conclusion drawn only too often and too recklessly in the course of the history of Christianity; but it seems to make religion the opium of the people, it is highly problematic and fails to grasp the difference between voluntarily showing solidarity with the poor and downgraded as a supremely personal act and being caught up in poverty and distress in a way that simply cannot be completely transformed by concrete freedom alone. Moreover, the question will have to be left as it stands, without an absolutely positive answer, whether the preferential treatment of the poor and downgraded on the part of Jesus must be a crucial principle for the style of following on the part of *every* individual Christian or whether this must be said or perhaps desired seriously at most of the community of believers, of the Church as a whole.

This brings us to the question whether there cannot be a particular, concrete, in a sense imitative following of Jesus which must be neither attributed to an internal disposition alone nor merely regarded as taking individual forms and as changing at different periods of Christian history. If we are not to take refuge in an abstract moral idealism, it seems to us that this question can be answered only with the proposition: the Christian, every Christian at all times, follows Jesus by *dying* with him; following Jesus has its ultimate truth and reality and universality in the following of the Crucified. It cannot, I think, be proved that there is any other concrete substance of that following which could hold for *all* Christians taken together and which remains concrete. Our reflections up to now on the following of Jesus thus lead naturally to the reflections on the following of Jesus precisely as crucified.

Before we continue here, there are still some things that must be noted or more clearly stated in advance if the thesis proposed is not to be misunderstood from the very outset. First of all, it is clear of course that the thesis may not be taken to imply a dispensation from following Jesus during life, from a following of his life and not merely of his death. But, if it is not located or diluted in a purely internal attitude or disposition, this following will be very different in the lives of individual Christians and can scarcely be reduced to a common denominator. A socio-critical courage and protest unto death can certainly be a following of Christ, without our having to be able to prove with speculative perspicacity that something of this kind could be found in some sort of homeopathic dilution also in other authentic Christian lives. Life in a Carthusian monastery can certainly be a following of Jesus and in fact also and particularly in what cannot be found in other Christian lives. Jesus' life is reflected diversely and fragmentarily in the lives of Christians. At the same time there is no need to discuss here the question (important for its own sake) whether and how in the life of human beings endowed with grace by the Spirit of God and Christ there can and must be realizations of faith, hope, and love, which as such cannot be found at all actualized in the historically restricted life of Jesus of Nazareth himself and yet are absolutely constitutive of the Christian life of these persons. (Jesus was in fact a man and not a woman, he could not have realized and experienced the burdens and tasks of old age, of a permanent invalid, of a scholar, and so on; and yet these burdens and tasks in their concreteness and not merely in a disposition—which can also be realized elsewhere and otherwise—are part of such Christian lives.) These Christian realities certainly belong to the totality willed by God of the one mystical Christ (with head and members) who is identical with redeemed humanity or the Church. But we shall not pursue further here the question of whether the acceptance of these realities by Christians, by which, according to Paul, they 'complete' Christ's life and suffering, is to be regarded as part of the following of the historical Jesus or not. In any case there are ways of following Jesus which occur in the life of Christians and are not to be regarded as identical with one another, but as particular expressions of that following, which the Spirit of God assigns differently to individuals, as he wills.

There is a further preliminary observation to be made. When we say that the one following of Jesus *common to all* Christians consists particularly in following him in death, this of course does not merely refer to death solely in a medical sense. For death in the sense of dying begins at the very dawn of life, as existential pervades the whole of life in what Gregory the Great described as the *prolixitas mortis*. Consequently, the following of the Crucified as participation in his dying and death goes on of course throughout the whole of life. Christian tradition has always been aware of this in taking the following of Jesus by accepting his cross to mean also patience sustained by faith in the midst of suffering, in the inevitable disappointment and bitterness of life as long as it lasts. This must always remain clear now that we have to examine more closely the meaning of the following of the Crucified.

In what exactly does the following of the Crucified as participation in his death consist and why is this equality of fate, the solidarity of death, something in which we not only resemble him, but depend on him in the proper sense of the term (resemble him not only because like him we also die, but rightly die because we imitate him and by imitating him and inasmuch as his death is the imperatively productive model for our death)? This is evidently the question that faces us. A part of this question is of course, to be more precise, also the question of what is peculiar and unique about the death of Jesus, so that only in the imitation (possibly, of course, merely implicit) of his death can there be a true dying.

At first, the very opposite seems to be the case. Despite its extraordinary concrete peculiarities as a violent death, Jesus in his death shares the lot of all of us; in his death he seems to be following in the way of a dying humanity and not humanity following in his way. There is no need to insist at length that our following of Jesus in dying refers to death as such and not to an historically individual peculiarity of his death, which (at least normally) we cannot share at all. But in this respect is he not following us more than we follow him?

We may safely and must ask about the equality of his death and ours, before we raise more explicitly the question why we are dependent on him in this respect—follow him, that is, in the proper sense—and we and he thus do not simply share as equals the same lot that is assigned to all of us. If we ask first of all only about the equality of our death and his, the question is also of course but by no means solely about death as a physiological event. But we are certainly asking too about this physiological event of a medical exitus, since man not only has a body, but also is body, the entire breadth and depth of human existence up to the most sublime actualizations of that existence is realized corporeally, in a true sense: that is, it is not the body that dies, but the person in his body. But this means that death in a human and Christian sense is thus essentially more than a mere medical exitus, in which the heart stops and the electrical brain currents cease. Death rightly understood is an event involving the whole person and might take place at that crucial point where the act of freedom is finalized, not by any means necessarily in the chronological moment of the medical exitus (even though this is a real factor in the finalization of man's history of freedom), but occurs in a true sense throughout the whole of life and reaches a climax at that moment not ascertainable by our reflection in which man's temporally extended history of freedom reaches its finality. But what does the person do when he thus brings his history of freedom to its finality and irreversibility in death, in what way ultimately and at the hidden core of existence does the one decision of freedom become irreversible, the decision which, although temporally extended, is achieved in the one life of man? We cannot answer the question here by developing precisely and at length an existential ontology and theology of death. It is possible to answer this question only briefly.

It is true that the individual decisions of freedom, which are integrated into the one life's decision, occur during life on a categorial individual material of our life presented to us from our milieu and environment. But these individual decisions are elements of the one life's decision only insofar as (over and above their finite and particular content, even though by their mediation) there occurs in them an assent or a refusal to that infinite horizon and objective of freedom which alone makes possible freedom in the proper sense in regard to the subject and its individual objects and in the final understanding is known as God. If and insofar as the decision of freedom in regard to an individual categorial object of an intramundane character is also a transcending of this object, leaving it behind and in a sense renouncing it, and in this respect and in this way the infinite objective of freedom (called God) is recognized as such and thus as dissociated from the individual object, such a decision is right, affirms God himself as such, although this does not of course require the innermost structure of the true act of freedom to be present as such explicitly and objectified and verbalized. This innermost structure of every real decision of freedom, insofar as it is an internal factor in human death as an existential act, makes itself clearly felt in what we experience empirically as death. In death, empirically seen, the world withdraws from the subject of freedom, and even the latter is lost to itself. Everything perishes; it is, as Scripture says, the night in which no one can work.

How does the subject of freedom encounter this decline, in which it can cling to nothing individual and not even to itself in its explicit factuality? There are two ways in which the subject of freedom can accept this decline. Either the subject in the last resort culpably refuses to accept any freely bestowed love from another person, regarding itself as condemned to an absolute autonomy and autarchy as to absolute futility, against which only a radical protest is possible; or it accepts with resignation and hope this eclipse of all particular realities as the dawn and approach of that silent infinity into which each particular act of freedom has hitherto always risen above its individual object, in order in a sense to be lost into this merely apparently empty infinity. In the first case death is the event of final perdition, in the second the beginning of redeemed finality in God. It is impossible to explain more precisely here why and how this self-surrender to the loving incomprehensibility of God, in the decline of all particular objects of freedom occurring in death, involves what we describe in Christian terminology as the one triplicity of faith, hope, and love, which justifies us and brings us to final salvation, assuming of course (and this has to be assumed as a datum) that this self-surrender of the subject of freedom to the loving incomprehensibility of God, leaving behind and transcending everything individual, is sustained in the present and only real order of salvation by a self-communication of God (described as grace) always and everywhere forestalling our freedom, by which God himself radicalizes our self-surrender toward his immediacy and gives himself as response to it. Nor can it be explained in more detail why and how this decline of all individual realities, making itself felt in empirical death, why and how this decline is initially present as an internal factor within every act of freedom in life and that it so happens that dying proceeds during the whole of life toward a death in which what is or (better) ought to be done in the whole history of freedom of a lifetime becomes apparent and reaches finality: the relinquishment that does not take or hold any particular good as absolute, but lets go of it, in order to entrust itself to the nameless incomprehensibility that we call God.

Perhaps we can now say a little more clearly in what the common feature in Jesus' death and ours consists, what we do when we follow him in his dying, even though this does not yet explain why in the death that we have in common he is the imperative, productive model, why our dying in the proper sense *depends* on his dying and is thus really a following of the Crucified. According to Scripture we may safely say that Jesus in his life was the *believer* (notwithstanding the traditional teaching that at the innermost centre of his existence he had an immediacy to God such as is given to us only in eternal life) and that he was consequently the one who hopes absolutely and in regard to God and men obviously the one who loves absolutely. In the unity of this triplicity of faith, hope, and love, Jesus surrendered himself in his death unconditionally to the absolute mystery that he called his Father, into whose hands he committed his existence, when in the night of his death and God-forsakenness he was deprived of everything that is otherwise regarded as the content of a human existence: life, honour, acceptance in earthly and religious fellowship, and so on. In the concreteness of his death it becomes only too clear that everything fell away from him, even the perceptible security of the closeness of God's love, and in this trackless dark there prevailed silently only the mystery that in itself and in its freedom has no name and to which he nevertheless calmly surrendered himself as to eternal love and not to the hell of futility. In that sense his death is the same as ours, even though the concrete circumstance of dying vary between a gruesome stake at which the cruel madness of human beings tortures another human being to death and a deathbed in a modern hospital where white uniformed doctors do everything possible to prevent the dying person from noticing the state he has reached. Whether we die in one way or another can make a vast difference in many respects, so that we may rightly wish for an easy and gentle death. But in the last resort what happens in death is the same for all: we are deprived of everything, even of ourselves; we all fall, each of us alone, into the dark abyss where there are no further ways. And this death—which in the first place is simply ours—Jesus died; he who came out of God's glory did not merely descend into our human life, but also fell into the abyss of our death, and his dying began when he began to live and came to an end on the cross when he bowed his head and died.

Jesus died as we die. When we say this and visualize up to a point the content of the statement, what we see is Jesus following in our way and not ourselves in his. If and insofar as we continue always to see him as the eternal Word of God, who assumed our human reality, our life, and our death, as his own reality, the statement that Jesus died as we die can of course give ineffable dignity and eternal consolation for our own death. If we believe that our own human reality has been assumed by God, this is true also of course of our death. Since the eternal Logos of the Father suffered it as his own death, this death must be redeemed, sanctified, emptied of final despair and futility, filled with the eternal life of God himself. This can and must be said, if we assume what Christian faith professes about Jesus Christ as the only begotten Son of the Father himself and if in the light of this faith we say that he died as we die, even though we shall not go on from this point to develop its implications for our own death as redeemed.

Can we now say however that we have answered the second question above-mentioned, the question of whether and in what sense we really *follow* in our dying the dying Jesus on the cross, so that Jesus' death truly becomes the productive model of our death, that our death is different from what it would be if we did not die precisely as following him. It would certainly be possible to work out an answer to this question by continuing from the point now reached in our reflections. It could be shown more explicitly how the assumption of our death by the eternal Logos as his own does not merely assimilate him to us, but also transforms our death. But we want to try to answer this second question in the light of a somewhat different consideration, since this makes it more simple and more tangible. Jesus died into his resurrection, his death is the event of gaining the finality of his human reality in the life of God himself. Of course it is impossible here to work out a fundamental theology and dogmatic theology of the resurrection of Jesus. All that we can do is to bring out a few points that are particularly important for our question.

First of all, Jesus' resurrection is not merely an event that could not be expected, attached in a singular way to his death. It is the consequence of his death itself as such, if it is seen at the same time as the death of him in whom the eternal God imparts his own life to the world as its gracious endowment and as the event in which this Jesus accepts finally and irrevocably this self-communication of God through death. However the 'three days' between Jesus' death and the awareness of his resurrection are to be more precisely theologically interpreted, the idea of this temporal interval must not be allowed to obstruct our view of the intrinsic unity of the death and resurrection of Jesus. In his resurrection the very thing that happened in his death is completed and made effective: the incomprehensible God finally accepted this human reality as redeemed, precisely because the latter was surrendered unsupported and unreservedly into the incomprehensibility of God himself. We can really say that (in the sense of an indissoluble essential connection) his death is his resurrection and vice versa, since he entered into definitive life precisely in death and in no other way. But since this is true in the first place only of the only-begotten Son of the Father and in the radical sinlessness of his faith, hope, and love, as distinct from us sinners, his death, despite all its similarity to ours, is in itself quite different from the death that we for our own part and independently of following him can die and must die. If then his death is to become a real determinant of our own death and in that very peculiarity which as such distinguishes his death as death into resurrection from our death as penalty of sin, he must give us a share of his death. But this again implies two things: on the one hand his death must take place for us; he must die in a community of fate and in solidarity with us, and the Spirit of God, in whom he accepted his death purely and simply as the dawn of life, must be offered to us as the opportunity of a death with him. On the other hand, for our part, this opportunity of dying with him as a beginning of life must be accepted in freedom. Since both preconditions exist or can be realized in freedom, it is possible to die with him; the determinant of unity with the resurrection, essential to his death, can also as grace become a determinant of our death, and this death of ours then has a peculiarity which is not merely (like the other determinants of death) common to his death and ours, but belongs to our death only in virtue of his, so that there is present that peculiarity by which a mere similarity between us and Jesus is turned into a real following. In faith in him and his grace our death is transformed from a manifestation of sinful God-forsakenness or an open question that is involved in the mysterious incomprehensibility of God into a death leading to the loving acceptance of our existence by God into his own life, a death into resurrection. There is still something explicitly to be added however to this consideration of the way in which the similarity of death with Jesus and with us becomes a real following of the Crucified in dying.

Our death and Jesus' death, even and more especially as resurrection, occur as a passing into the silent incomprehensibility and unavailability of God. It is for this reason that death is the supreme and most radical act of faith. The following of the Crucified as such is in itself a supreme act of faith, a surrender in hope and love to the incomprehensibility of God which completely takes away from us who are here the result of this act of death, as into a total extinction. We must say this in the first place about our death as following of the Crucified, but that is not all that is to be said about this singular unity of Jesus' death and our death.

It is true that Jesus by his resurrection vanishes from us into the unavailability of God. But his resurrection is at the same time the event of salvation history which, even if grasped only by faith, is part of this history of this world and this humanity and is grasped and acknowledged precisely by faith as such an historical event that truly changes the world. His resurrection took place in this world, even though it is the event that raises this historical world of becoming into the eternity of God. The resurrection has an absolutely peculiar and unique but nevertheless real tangibility in history. This must be remembered also in regard to his death as entry into this resurrection. If in his following we die with him, the question whether we die into the life of God or into sheer annihilation is not answered in a way that is empirically verifiable in regard to our death as such; there is certainly no tangible assurance of a death leading to a resurrection, since (at least normally) we cannot for our own part make any unambiguous judgment about the final destiny of a dying person. But from the clarity of Jesus' death as the way to his resurrection, from the historicity of Jesus' resurrection, a light is thrown on the ambivalence of our own death and this light, too, is part of our dying with Christ. In this matter the situation is the same as in world history in general.

In the history of the world itself as distinct from God's eternal plans, *before* the resurrection of Jesus, the victorious irreversibility of God's self-communication to the world was not firmly established or tangible, the final outcome of world history was not perceptible as salvation in history itself. The drama of world history as a whole was also still unfinished and ambivalent. Things are different after the resurrection: there the peripeteia of the drama of world history to good, to eternal salvation, has already taken place. It is true that we cannot deduce from this any unequivocal conclusion for the individual and his individual destiny of salvation; but even for the individual the situation of hope is different from what it was before Jesus' resurrection. From the one reality already existing the success of other possibilities can be presumed. This is true particularly when an historically and sociologically explicit relationship to Jesus' resurrection is present as promise to the world as a whole. What has been said here in general about the relationship of world history to Jesus' death and resurrection is therefore true also of the relationship of our dying to Jesus' dying, particularly when this relationship is explicitly realized in faith. Our dying admittedly retains an openness and ambivalence, but it is encompassed by the promise that exists for us in the victorious death of Jesus into his resurrection. Paul says: 'Here is a saying you can rely on: if we have died with him, then we shall live with him' (2 Tim. 2:11).

We said earlier that death in a theological sense does not in the last resort coincide chronologically with the medical exitus, but occurs throughout the whole of life and reaches its completion only at the end. Hence, from the nature of the case, it was legitimate for Christian piety in its entire history to seek to realize the following of the *Crucified* in Christian *life,* in the acceptance of everything that Christian usage even up to the present time described as the 'cross': the experiences of human frailty, of sickness, of disappointments, of the nonfulfillment of our expectations, and so on. What occurs in all this is part of man's dying, of the destruction of life's tangible goods. In all these brief moments of dying in installments we are faced with the question of how we are to cope with them: whether we merely protest, merely despair (even for brief moments), become cynical and cling all the more desperately and absolutely to what has not yet been taken from us. *or* whether we abandon with resignation what is taken from us, accept twilight as promise of an eternal Christmas full of light, regard slight breakdowns as events of grace. If in this second way (which cannot by any means be so easily distinguished from the first) we take the cross on ourselves daily, we are accomplishing part of the following of the Crucified, we are practising faith and loving hope in which death is accepted as the advent of eternal life and the following of Jesus, the Crucified, reaches its completion.

PART THREE

Experience of the Spirit

11

EXPERIENCE OF TRANSCENDENCE FROM THE STANDPOINT OF CATHOLIC DOGMATICS

Before attempting to say anything directly on the theme proposed for me, I may be permitted a few preliminary observations. In the first place I am not an Indianologist, but only a teacher of Catholic dogmatics. I must leave it to the Indianologists, the historians of religion, and the historians of the different interpretations of mystical experience to see for themselves whether these reflections of a teaching theologian can provide them with any assistance in dealing with their own problems. Furthermore, when the title speaks of the view of Catholic dogmatics on the problem of the experience of transcendence, the term 'dogmatics' must be understood in a very wide sense. There would be very little to be gained from these reflections if we were restricted to statements which have an absolutely binding character in Catholic dogmatic theology. The Catholic theologian cannot avoid putting forward here also views, theories, and theologoumena which are neither imposed as binding by the Church's magisterium nor supported in textbook theology by a general consensus, but represent his personal opinions which are worth as much as the reasons which can be adduced or suggested in their favour. Of course it is also assumed and claimed that these personal views of an individual Catholic theologian are at least compatible with the Christian faith as it is presented by the Church's magisterium. I think therefore that these reflections may be useful despite a certain lack of binding force from the standpoint of the Church's magisterium. It must also be observed that it is of course no part of our task to show with the aid of an epistemological and existential-ontological reflection that the experience of transcendence (which forms our present theme) actually exists as such in man: to show that, in its transcendental necessity with which it is present as a condition of human knowledge as a whole, it also includes an equally necessary and irreversible dependence of the mind (in knowledge and freedom) on that which or him whom in Christian terminology we call God. All this is simply presupposed here. All that is to be done here about this transcendental experience (which is not really proved nor actually demonstrated in its essence) is to put forward, more or less as supplementary, some theses which seem to me important for a discussion devoted to a comparative study of *those* experiences of transcendence the *interpretation* of which is a matter of dispute between East and West.

The limits of these reflections must then be expressly stated. We are talking about transcendence; we assume that the experience of transcendence is philosophically objectified and verbalized. But how exactly this happens in the religio-philosophical systems of East and West, whether these philosophical interpretations are more correct, better, or more convincing here or there, how the objective of this experience of transcendence is to be correctly described—whether as absolute nothingness or as absolute being or as absolute mystery—and how these different interpretations can be brought together with some prospect of success into dialogue with one another: these are topics which are not actually to be discussed in my reflections. The questions raised here come before and after these questions. What I can say on this proposed theme will be presented more or less in the form of theses, since it would be quite impossible to cope at all with the task assigned to me if the individual theses had to be closely elucidated and substantiated in each case. I must refrain also from any attempt to present these theses in a strictly systematic sequence that is cogent in every respect. I come then to the matter itself.

(1) On the one hand, Christianity refuses to recognize a systematic and more or less technically developed 'mystical' experience of transcendence as the sole and necessary way to man's perfection and, on the other hand, Christian theology, at least in Catholicism, will not cease to regard such mystical experience of transcendence at least as a possible *stage* on the way to perfection and as a paradigmatic elucidation of what happens in faith, hope, and love on the

Christian path to the perfection of salvation wherever salvation in the Christian sense is attained.

This first thesis must be further elucidated in its two aspects.

On the first part of the thesis, Christian teaching and the practice of authentic Christianity cannot admit that the 'mystic' (whatever may be the exact meaning of this term, of the phenomena of immersion, of the formless experience of the absolute, etc.) is the only one who has gone or goes on that path to perfection of which the last stage directly and alone borders on man's perfection (however the term 'perfection' is to be more precisely interpreted). The teaching of the New Testament that the fulfillment of God's commandments in the conscientious observance of routine duties in faith, hope, and love for God and men bring the person through death immediately to perfection and unite him finally with God, the description of the last judgment in the eschatological discourses of Jesus (for instance, in Matthew 25), and many other things in the teaching and practice of Christianity that need not be mentioned here: all this forbids us to regard mysticism and particularly its more or less technically and explicitly developed form exclusively as the necessary and final stretch of the way before attaining perfect salvation or all ordinary practice of the Christian life merely as the *preparatory* phase of the way of salvation which leads to perfection only when it ends up on the higher path of contemplative mysticism. Christianity rejects such an elitist interpretation of life, which can see man's perfection as attained only in the trained mystic. This is particularly important, since Christianity rejects the theory of the transmigration of souls and cannot localize such an explicitly mystical phase for the individual in a subsequent life. This in brief is the content of the first part of our first thesis.

This however does *not* mean simply that mystical experience as such could be or ought to be regarded merely as a single and rare exceptional case in individual human beings and Christians which is granted to the latter either by psycho-technical effort or by a special grace of God as a rare privilege or by both together, without really having any constitutive importance for the actual way to perfect salvation. In the Christian theology of mysticism up to the present time views have been maintained which denied to mysticism in *any* way a constitutive importance for the process of salvation or conceded something of this kind at most in cases where it is a question of a special 'heroic' heightening of perfection, of 'holiness', of gaining a particularly high degree of final glory (which, despite its finality, can, according to textbook theology, have varying degrees). But the first part of our thesis does not necessitate such an interpretation of the really crucial phenomena of mysticism, an interpretation of this mysticism in which the latter has absolutely no constitutive importance in any respect for the event and achievement of final perfection. It seems to me (from the nature of the case we shall return to this point) to be the task of Christian theology as a whole and the Christian theology of mysticism in particular to show and to render intelligible the fact that the real basic phenomenon of mystical experience of transcendence is present as innermost sustaining ground (even though unnoticed) in the simple act itself of Christian living in faith, hope, and love, that such (as we may say) implicit transcendence into the nameless mystery known as God is present by grace in this very believing, hoping, and loving; it seems to us that mysticism in its explicit sense and as expressly practised may signify a higher degree of the Christian ascent to perfection from the standpoint of an objectively reflecting psychology, but not from a properly theological standpoint, and that mysticism in an explicit experience has therefore (conversely) a paradigmatic character, an exemplary function, to make clear to the Christian what really happens and is meant when his faith tells him that God's self-communication is given to him in grace and accepted in freedom whenever he believes, hopes, and loves. The proof of such a *perichoresis* between the normal and routine practice of the Christian life and an ultimate and absolutely radical experience of transcendence into the mystery of God cannot of course be produced here and now in this first thesis. Otherwise a whole theology of the Holy Spirit, of possession by the Spirit, of experience of the Spirit by grace, of the theological virtues (as event of immediacy to God as distinct from the intramundane moral virtues), would have to be developed (which of course is not possible at this point).

(2) A Christian theology is always required to make clear that an irreversible difference exists between an original experience of transcendence (as 'natural' and as radicalized to immediacy by God's gracious self-communication) on the one hand and the objectifying and verbalizing reflection on this experience of transcendence on the other. Christian theology will always maintain that a creaturely 'me-

diation' (which would need to be defined more precisely by a developed theology—which is not possible here—distinguished in its different forms and more closely investigated in regard to its specific function of mediation) does not remove, but under certain conditions can even make possible the immediacy of the mind (at least of the mind endowed with grace) to God. These two statements are connected and may therefore be combined in a thesis, but are not simply identical. They cannot be substantiated in detail here in a theological argument, but they may be elucidated a little.

We come to the first part of our second thesis. The original basic realization of man's transcendence as mind and freedom toward the mystery that we Christians call God on the one hand and the categorial and verbal, reflective objectification on this basic realization on the other are never identical; the result is that on the one hand this basic realization can exist even when there is no such theoreticizing and verbalizing objectification of the basic realization of the mental, grace-endowed, and perhaps really mystical transcendentality, and on the other hand that such a theoreticizing and verbalizing statement about this basic realization (even when the latter is genuine) can be true or false, adequate or inadequate, making use of different conceptual systems and forms of imagery. It follows that even the *genuine* 'mystic' can present a philosophy and theology of his mysticism as original experience which by no means corresponds to that original experience. The first statement of our second thesis implies that there can be and are many theologies of mysticism differing from and even contradicting one another and that nevertheless these differences do not *a priori* exclude the possibility that all these theologies are meant to describe the *same* original experience. Even when the attempt is made in principle to produce in such a theology only a pure description of the original experience of transcendence, a merely descriptive theology of mysticism, this inevitably comes about with the aid of conceptual equipment that is by no means acquired from the original experience itself (for then even the description would be bound to remain completely unintelligible to the outsider), but makes use of images, ideas, and horizons of understanding, which are drawn from different sources and carry with them the relativity of the religious, cultural, historical milieu of the person providing the description.

Contradictions in the theologies of mysticism, even when the latter are meant to be no more than descriptions, can thus be due to the fact that the original experiences (which were to be described and theologically interpreted) were themselves actually different, *or* can occur simply because (for the reasons given) the description of what was originally the same experience is not so apt that it can be made to coincide with other descriptions. Whether the former or the latter explanation is correct is a fundamental question to which an answer must be sought in a dialogue between the different theories of mysticism. It is not possible to discuss here and now the possible methods of such a comparative mystical theology. It seems to me that such a formal methodology has not yet been adequately developed in the discussion between the world religions. But a methodology of this kind in any case could never forget that mystical experience (of whatever character) on the one hand and talk about it on the other hand always remain two different things.

If hitherto we have stressed the difference between man's original, existential, basic experience of transcendentality on the one hand and its conceptual interpretation and terminological theorization on the other and attempted to draw the appropriate conclusions, this should not of course obscure the fact that these very diverse factors also form a unity, are linked with each other and are mutually dependent. If we disregard any possibility of an absolutely imageless and nonconceptual mystical experience, then in any case, *after* this original experience itself, it is present only as combined with an at least rudimentary imaginative and conceptual interpretation and can be (as it evidently should be) important only in this way for the whole life of the mystic. If moreover, despite their distinction, we did not stress also the unity (which does not mean sameness) of these two factors, the meaning of the actual 'teaching' of the conceptually formulated faith in Christianity could not be made intelligible or authenticated. But Christianity is far from regarding such a conceptually articulated teaching in the last resort as a superfluous, merely accidental, and arbitrary phenomenon within the totality of Christianity. In view of the unity of the two factors, despite their permanent diversity, it is of course also quite possible for a person to identify himself with a particular philosophico-theological interpretation of his whole reality with such decisiveness that this identification (if the interpretation is false) substantially removes or destroys also the original phenomenon, as far as this is possible at all in face of the transcendental necessity of certain ultimate structures and realizations of man. A 'theoretical' atheist, for example, can possibly (not necessarily) identify himself so closely with this interpretation of his existence that in the real depth of his existence in freedom he is an atheist and is not merely erroneously interpreting himself as such, even though there persists an ultimate transcendental necessity of his dependence on God, which, however, he denies not only theoretically but existentially. This sort of thing must also be remembered even when it is a question of the unity and difference between originally mystical experience and its theoretical and conceptual interpretation. In any case a theoretical interpretation of a mystical experience can (but need not) change the latter by existential freedom. But this of course should not be obscured by the first part of our second thesis.

The second part of our second thesis is perhaps even more important. Christian faith and theology see the historical reality of Jesus, the Church, the sacrament, and the proclaimed word, as ways of reaching God, not in the sense that all these things are merely elements of a subsequent reflection on the actual salvific relationship of man to God and not constitutive of the relationship itself, but in the sense that they are themselves internal and constitutive elements of this salvific relationship to God. For Christian theology not only is the recipient of the divine self-communication a created finite reality that does not perish and is not consumed in the event of this divine self-communication and is even perfected and validated in its positive and sound finiteness, but for this Christian faith there are also between the absolute God and the finite recipient of his self-communication created realities (of which some of the more essential have already been mentioned) which have a mediatory function in this relationship. Nevertheless (and this is crucial) Christian faith and its theology, if both are absolutely correctly understood, firmly maintain that this mediation does not remove or obstruct an *immediate* relationship of (grace-endowed) man to God, but makes it possible, guarantees it, and attests it in the historical-categorial dimension of man. Christian faith denies that radical immediacy to God, who imparts himself to man as himself in his absolute reality, and creaturely mediation of this self-communication of the absolute are opposed to one another as mutually exclusive alternatives.

For Christian faith the situation is not such that it is possible in principle to receive absolute reality in its divine purity only when this relationship involves the formless disappearance of any finite reality or when a created reality (even though understood as available by the grace of God) is all that is actually present and merely points vicariously to the always distant God. How this conception of a mediation to immediacy can be more precisely understood and theologically substantiated cannot be more closely explained here. For that, it would be necessary to discuss the difference and the unity between created and uncreated grace, the created *lumen gloriae* in the immediate vision of God (a vision itself constituted by God's own reality), the theological virtues as distinct from the moral virtues, the indwelling of God himself by grace in man, the specific nature of Christ's and the Church's causality of salvation on the one hand and the causality of the divine pneuma on the other. *If* and *insofar as* an Eastern mysticism (however theoretically understood) were to seek to reject such a notion of a mediation to immediacy, its attention would have to be drawn to the fact that it would consistently have to leave the finite recipient of such an immediacy to God himself to perish in the event of such a mystical theophany, that it would have to reject the permanent significance of history in its concreteness and the notion of a sound finiteness. Then it would have to be asked whether such a metaphysics and theology are true in themselves and really covered by the original mystical experience. The second point in dispute, the appeal to the mystical experience itself, would then have to be seen in the light of the understanding formulated in the first statement of our second thesis.

As far as the second part of the second thesis is concerned, it must certainly be pointed out that Christian theology also is aware of many modes and degrees of creaturely mediation to the immediacy of God: that is, it does not hold that the forms of mediation are the *same* always and in every case when a person has to deal directly with God himself. The question, for example, of whether mysticism in the present world can include *that* immediacy to God which Christian theology asserts of the immediate vision of God in the hereafter, is a matter of dispute in the Christian theology of mysticism. If and insofar then as mystical theologies outside Christianity teach an absolutely 'formless', purely and simply 'unobjective' experience of God, this is not a reason why a Christian theology must necessarily be opposed to them, but only why it should point out that this sort of formless immediacy to God is always sustained by the grace of God's Holy Spirit who is irreversibly promised in historical tangibility through the historical event of Jesus Christ; a Christian theology would insist that such a mystical experience of a decline of all 'normal' mediation would be a participation in the death of Jesus who in his actual death as absolute decline came to the final dawning of God himself.

(3) The third thesis may be formulated with the reservation that what is put forward and defended here is not universally accepted among theologians. Whenever there is a final radical self-realization of man in mind and freedom and the person thus commits himself to finality, it may be assumed that such a self-realization (which can also, if not solely, take place in a mystical experience of transcendence) in practice is always sustained and radicalized by what is known in Christian theology as Holy Spirit, supernatural grace, self-communication of God, even though this fact of being sustained by grace is not itself as such made an object of reflection or given thematic expression in this occurrence.

In current textbook theology (which, however, carries no absolutely official guarantee of the Church's magisterium) grace (also described as a supernatural elevation of mental acts) is generally understood as an intermittent happening at isolated points in space and time. But if we start out from the Christian teaching of a universal salvific will of God, who offers the concrete opportunity of a supernatural salvation, a salvation, that is, that reaches the immediacy of God himself, always and everywhere in history and thus outside the verbalized message of Christianity and the Church, then we can and indeed must assume that what we Christians describe as Holy Spirit, supernatural grace—at least in the mode of a real offer to man's freedom as radicalizing existential of man's transcendentality—exists as such always and everywhere and therefore also outside institutionalized Christianity, even though of course in the concrete individual this supernatural existential of dynamism toward the immediacy of God can exist *either* in the mode of pure factuality from the outset *or* in the mode of rejection *or* in the mode of free acceptance.

As we said, it is impossible of course here to explain and substantiate more precisely in theological terms the thesis of the universal factuality of grace as God's self-communication. This would require close reflection on the Church's teaching of the universality of God's salvific will, on the possibility as taught today (for example, at the Second Vatican Council) of real supernatural faith always and everywhere and consequently even where the explicit message of Christianity has not yet been heard; it would be necessary to try to show how and why there can be such a universal possibility of faith always and everywhere and even in a person who regards himself as an atheist, without implying a denial of the necessity for salvation of faith in an actual and verbalized revelation; it must be made clear why and how a theology of grace properly understood must interpret the latter as the self-communication of God in his most intimate uncreated reality and how this grace must be understood originally as elevating, radicalizing communication to man's *transcendentality* as such. But all this is impossible here and the thesis can be put forward here only as one that is not supported by a universal consensus, but which can certainly be justified.

If we presuppose this thesis of the universal reality of the offer of grace always and everywhere and primarily to the transcendentality of man as such and if we consider the fact that this grace is present as accepted and justifying if and when this transcendentality of man is accepted and sustained by man's freedom, if moreover we start out from the assumption that such an unconditional acceptance by man's freedom of his own transcendentality can exist also, if not solely, particularly and with a special intensity in mystical experiences of transcendence, then it follows that the mysticism rightly interpreted by Christian theology as a real experience of grace can and must be found even outside institutional Christianity. Nor can this thesis be opposed by the dilemma that mystical experience of transcendence must either be interpreted in an explicitly Christian sense or can at best be only some kind of natural mysticism. It is true that the traditional theology of mysticism in Catholic Christianity has been inclined up to the present time to accept this dilemma as real and inescapable, just as the theology of grace especially from the time of baroque scholasticism has taken it for granted that there are existentially radical mental acts of man (what are known as *actus honesti*) which concretely are not supernatural salutary acts. But if we recall our second thesis and firmly maintain the universality of the factuality of grace from the outset as an existential of man's transcendentality as such, then the possibility of a supernatural, grace-inspired anonymously Christian mysticism outside verbalized and institutionalized Christianity cannot be denied.

The Christian philosopher of religion, therefore, if he is to remain within the limits of Christian orthodoxy, need not assume as a hermeneutical principle of his study the impossibility of discovering outside Christianity any mysticism that can be recognized as substantially the same as Christian mysticism. Whether this philosopher of religion takes into account our second thesis, examining the extra-Christian interpretation of this extra-Christian mysticism in regard to the original mystical phenomenon, and thus in practice succeeds in making such a discovery, or he does not succeed in practice in establishing the discovery with historical and psychological realism and exactitude, is not a question to be answered by the Christian dogmatic theologian as such, but one which must be decided by the philosopher of religion himself. But in any case Christian dogmatics does not forbid the philosopher of religion *a priori* to discover grace-inspired mysticism in the experience of God's self-communication by a transcendentality of man radicalized by the Holy Spirit even outside Christianity. If and when such a discovery is made *a posteriori* without premature blurring of distinctions by passing over the points of difference between Christian and extra-Christian subsequent descriptions of the original mystical experience itself, this is a result that should not be surprising for the Christian dogmatic theologian. It is not surprising if only because he does not interpret mystical experience even within Christianity as something that really goes beyond supernatural faith, supernatural hope, and love, but as *one* possible radicalized form of realization of these three theological virtues and because the same Christian dogmatic theologian, if he does not want to contradict the Second Vatican Council, cannot deny today that supernatural faith in the strict sense of the term can exist everywhere, even outside explicit Christianity, and even in a person who regards himself in his theoretical reflection as an atheist, since the original self-realization and verbalizing reflection on it are never identical and can even contradict one another.

(4) The proclamation of the theological possibility of a grace-inspired, salvific mystical experience of transcendence even outside explicit Christianity admittedly does not settle the problem to which the Christian dogmatic theologian for his own part is expected to contribute. I think that the dogmatic theologian ought to add a self-

critical thesis defining negatively the limits of his competence. We might attempt to formulate it in this way: the Christian theologian does not know and cannot judge whether there may not be experiences possibly outside everyday psychological experiences which on the one hand we can or must qualify as in some sense 'mystical' and which on the other hand cannot be regarded as experiences of supernatural, grace-inspired mysticism as understood in the third thesis.

In this sense the Christian theologian must practice self-effacement and self-restraint, leave the field of nonroutine experiences to the historian of religion, the psychologist of religion, the phenomenologist; he can only invite these experts themselves to examine the question closely and discriminatingly and not to reduce all nonroutine experiences of man too quickly and too hastily to one and the same denominator.

This very negative and abstract statement calls for some clarification. If and insofar as the third thesis which we put forward is correct, it must be said that all mysticism in which man's ultimate transcendentality toward God is experienced and accepted in freedom is also grace-inspired, supernatural, at least anonymously Christian mystical experience, since this third thesis starts out from the impossibility of there being any *actus honesti* in the concreteness of man's actual existence which are not also supernaturally elevated by grace. But this does not mean that an answer is provided to all the questions that can be raised here. The theology which assumes the real unity of personal-radical acts in which man's ultimate dependence on God is accepted in freedom on the one hand and of supernaturally grace-inspired, salvific acts of man on the other, has no reason to claim that there are no other experiences (apart from these mental-natural and grace-inspired mystical experiences of transcendence) which admittedly do not amount to such a natural-supernatural experience of transcendence and yet go beyond the ordinary routine and can therefore in certain circumstances and in regard to certain peculiarities be subsumed up to a point under the heading of 'mystical', if this term is understood in a sufficiently wide sense. The theology assumed here—for which a properly mental act in the strict sense, permitting the experience of transcendence, radically actualizing personal freedom, is in practice always also a supernatural experience of transcendence—does not for that reason need to claim that all experiences are such *actus honesti et salutares*. Man's experience of his corporality, of his biological-physiological condition, of his subconscious and his depth-consciousness, of collective archetypes, of an 'id' in his consciousness, of an embeddedness of his consciousness in a collective reality, etc., are certainly experiences which exist more or less clearly in man, but which are not identical with what theology describes as mental-supernatural experience of transcendence and can also occur apart from such an experience of transcendence. The theologian will naturally and without prejudice allow for this possibility, just as the older moral theology was aware of the existence of what are known as *actus indifferentes,* lying outside the strictly personal sphere of moral decision and of morality properly so-called. Even though the Christian theologian has no real competence in the question raised here, he can nevertheless without prejudice allow for the fact that the experiences indicated on the one hand reach an intensity and radical clarity and peculiarity in certain people, so that they somehow assume a 'mystical' character, and on the other are not part of a really mentally supernatural experience of transcendence which constitutes the essence of properly Christian mysticism.

Quite apart from *a posteriori* empirical evidence, why should not man as subject establish, for instance, by a psychological training a relationship to his corporality that is different from and more perfect than what exists in the 'normal' human being, without this relationship or its attainment belonging to the sphere of man's actual grace-inspired transcendentality? It is, to mention a further example, quite possible that there are experiences of the emptying of consciousness, of absorption, etc., which belong to the sphere that is prior to the actual experience of transcendentality. Whether then *such* phenomena, whatever their exact form, can be brought about by a psycho-technical training or even by a Christian mystic, for whom they are aids or accompanying phenomena to mysticism properly so-called and are interpreted as subsidiary grace, or whether (as is quite conceivable) they are both in one: this is a question which the dogmatic theologian as such is not required to decide. Presumably (purely hypothetically) it would be appropriate to subsume such phenomena under the heading of parapsychological occurrences and not properly under the heading of mysticism, since they can certainly be largely produced by psychological training and can occur also *outside* a religious sphere, without our being able or having to rescue these secular forms of phenomena for a properly religious mysticism by explaining that as such they are events of religious transcendentality to the absolute, to God, interpreted only subsequently as secular and therefore wrongly. But, since such phenomena of a properly parapsychological (that is, here, prereligious and preexistential) character occur also *together* with a properly religious and radical-existential experience of transcendence, it is understandable that these, too, are generally qualified as 'mystical'.

As a matter of fact, traditional Christian theology treats such phenomena as part of its own, albeit secondary object; it speaks of ecstasies, elevations, knowledge of the future, telepathic powers, etc., and in the past has been only too much inclined to interpret these things as extraordinary graces, as if they could occur only within mysticism properly so-called. On the other hand the Christian theology of mysticism (especially as represented by John of the Cross) recognizes that in the last resort these phenomena are not essential and ought really to disappear with the attainment of the highest mystical union with God, even though this creates a special problem for Christian mysticism, which cannot *a priori* reject a mediation to immediacy, as can be seen in the distinction between the mystical theology of Teresa of Ávila and that of John of the Cross. If and insofar as these phenomena, which as such are prior to the actual experience of transcendence toward the absolute mystery, can be a preparation and aid for these properly mystical experiences, exactly as a normal everyday ability to concentrate is a condition and an aid for the average Christian's ordinary meditation, it is understandable that in the practical business of higher spirituality even in Christianity there should emerge more or less spontaneously a psychological training (fasting, solitude, silence, exclusion of the uncoordinated variety of objects of consciousness) directed to experiencing more clearly and appropriating with a more radical freedom even the actual grace-inspired transcendentality of the mind toward God. As we said, the success of such psychological training can be understood without prejudice as subsidiary grace. But, conversely, it follows from our theses that the true grace of the actual experience of transcendence toward the immediacy of God is not present only when and where it is explicitly regarded as grace or (still less) when it is understood as a particular intermittent effect of God, although in reality it is always and everywhere sustained in the mode of an offer by God's self-communication. From the Christian standpoint the actual acceptance in freedom of this self-communication of God is certainly to be understood as a grace of God, since (in Pauline terms) not only the capacity, but also the actual accomplishment, is given by grace and effected by God.

The really important thing about this fourth thesis was simply the understanding that in the concrete realization of the religious relationship to God there can be phenomena (whether regarded as mystical or as parapsychological) which are not really strictly part of the experience of transcendence as elevated by grace and are consequently outside the competence of the theologian. This is the situation even if the theologian thinks that actually any real experience of transcendence in the concrete order of reality is itself an experience of *grace* and therefore that there is no 'natural' mysticism which is not in practice also supernatural mysticism.

In the light of this self-effacement on the part of the theologian, it is possible to find experiences, rules, practices for the creation of more suitable preconditions (perhaps of a parapsychological character) for the better and clearer achievement of mysticism properly so-called: experiences, rules, and practices which exist outside the history of the Christian religion and Christian piety. In principle these can be taken over by Christianity as useful for itself just as readily as it takes over other experiences, rules, and practices of normal everyday psychology and makes use of them in the religious field. This is certainly possible, even if Christian theology is convinced that the reflex interpretation in Christianity of actual experience of transcendence in grace is correct and true (which does not mean that this interpretation and verbalization is adequate, leaving nothing more to be learned).

Christian faith and its theology are persuaded that this mystical experience of transcendence is wrongly or inadequately interpreted when it is objectified and interpreted with a real *denial* of its grace-inspired character as a free personal relationship to a free and personal (or suprapersonal) absolute, with a *denial* of a sound finiteness and of an involvement even of the mystical in a salvifically significant history, with a *denial* (at least implicit) of a universal opportunity of salvation for all human beings even outside an explicit form of mystical absorption. But Christianity must not claim that such a wrong or essentially inadequate interpretation of grace-inspired mysticism (a mysticism which as such it admits to be possible even outside organized Christianity) is what actually occurs always and everywhere outside Christianity. There is no need for Christian theology to make this claim. It will of course say that all mysticism, wherever it exists, has an objective relatedness to Jesus Christ which admittedly is not explicitly grasped in extra-Christian mysticism; this however does not mean conversely that such a mysticism, which has not yet expressly found Jesus Christ, *ipso facto* has no importance for salvation and cannot be salvific faith. Christian theology will in fact consider how and why it can interpret a mysticism of this kind as 'questing' Christology, just as Jesus himself rightly understood an act of love of neighbour done without knowledge of him as in fact done to himself.

12

EXPERIENCE OF THE HOLY SPIRIT

What theme can there be for a meditation at Pentecost other than the Holy Spirit, given to the early Church in the midst of phenomena of enthusiasm, with the promise that he would remain with it always to the very end, with his power, his consolation, and his freedom? In a meditation of this kind we must certainly speak about the Holy Spirit as the gift in which God imparts himself to man.

But what is to be said and how exactly is it to be expressed? Certainly we could look up the Scriptures and read there about the Spirit of the Father, who is given through the Son to all who believe in him; about the Spirit who flows as living water out of the pierced side of the Crucified, as a fount of life, welling up into eternal life and quenching our thirst for eternity; about the Spirit who makes us sons and enables us to say 'Abba', 'Father'; about the Spirit who signifies the coming of the triune God, who gives us a share in God's love, truth, and freedom, in whom we are united with one another and have hope, by whom we are anointed and sealed, who prays in us and with us in ways too deep for speech and in access to the Father gives us assurance of eternal life. These and many other marvelous and sublime things could be found in Scripture, collected for a Pentecost meditation, and offered to the person within us to aid courageous faith and joyful reflection.

To the Christian believer who approaches these words of Scripture with an open mind it is obvious that he can meditate on Pentecost in this way even at the present time. And, even though here and now we are trying to follow a somewhat different way of meditation and want to raise questions about our own experience of the Spirit, it is also obvious, but should be stated expressly, that we always tacitly make use of this teaching of Scripture and that we ourselves could not so clearly grasp our own experience (which is offered to all human beings in the depth of their existence) if it had not been made explicit in the words of Scripture, even before our own efforts.

But, precisely because this Scripture does not speak to us merely doctrinally about this Spirit who is given to us, but at the same time itself appeals to the experience of the Spirit as we know it ourselves (for instance, in the Letter to the Galatians and elsewhere in Paul's letters, in John's writings, and in Scripture as a whole), we may rightly ask when and how such an experience occurs in us.

At the same time we are of course aware from the very outset that this is an experience incommensurable with what we ordinarily describe as 'experience' (especially in a scientific or empirically psychological sense), for the experience of the Spirit begins at the very heart of our existence, at what might be called its subjective pole, and does not signify an encounter with any sort of particular object that happens to come upon us from outside with its effects on us. Apart from experiences explicitly interpreted in a theological way in our consciousness and our reflection, there is an experience in us which is different from and not comparable with the experiences which first come to mind when we hear the word 'experience'.

In the first place the word suggests to us the fact, the impact, of individual realities of our milieu and environment or individual psychological objects in our consciousness: pain, for instance, that can be localized, an individual thought with a particular content, etc. All these individual realities are present to us as individual *within* the total framework of our consciousness; there they fit into some kind of arrangement, they are distinguished from one another and connected with one another.

But, in addition to these individual experiences of certain individual realities, there is a quite different experience, not by any means given thematic expression in the ordinary routine of our experiences: the experience of the one subject as such, that has all these experiences as its own and has to answer for them, that is itself present in its original unity and totality, even though it cannot itself be thematically objectified in detail but takes the form only of an apparent void when it passes into the multiplicity of its everyday experiences and seems to forget itself in the process.

There will be no attempt here in an epistemological or existential-ontological reflection to analyze this singular, original, primordial experience by the subject of itself, always and everywhere present behind all representational experiences. (We shall return later to this 'transcendental' character of man as subject.) All that is intended by this reference is to recall the fact here and now that there is in any case a kind of experience which is not commensurable with the ordinary experiences of individual realities, but which nevertheless is always present, even though it is generally overlooked. The experience of the Spirit which we are considering here is therefore not to be rejected *a priori* as nonexistent, merely because, just like the factuality of the subject as present for its own sake in all individual experiences, it can always be overlooked.

Of course, if we think we cannot really discover in ourselves the experience of the Spirit as understood here, we can accept the testimony of its existence as coming, so to speak, authoritatively from outside, from Scripture and the teaching of the Church. But, however much it must be interpreted in faith and given expression in words with the aid of Scripture, if we did not here and now ask also about the actual experience of the Spirit, there would be a danger of regarding sceptically as ideology or mythology all that Scripture tells us of this Spirit in ourselves and we might wonder with some irritation whether or where everything that Scripture says of the glory of the possession of the Spirit is present in us; we might wonder whether it should not all be set in a dimension (particularly when there is an assent in faith to the teaching of Scripture) which lies outside our consciousness and outside our freely realized piety.

Is there such an experience of the Spirit which on the one hand makes understandable and authenticates the testimony of Scripture to the indwelling of the Spirit in us and on the other hand is confirmed and put into words of truth by Scripture? We say that there is such an experience.

This statement is not refuted by the fact that we can and must *ask* with some hesitation and doubt about such an experience, that consequently this is not an absolutely indisputable experience, of the kind we have, for example, of the external world, without feeling (unless we are philosophers in an ivory tower) any need or necessity to ask whether a person really has such an experience of his milieu and environment. There are in any case also other genuine experiences which *exist in fact* and about which questions nevertheless simply must be asked. If, for example, a German idealist philosopher or even a modern Christian philosopher asks about the transcendental subject of knowledge and freedom and about its structures, if the modern depth psychologist tries to track down deeply repressed attitudes, they are all rightly convinced that there can be real experiences in man which are felt only unthematically, which are not verbalized, which are perhaps suppressed and not brought to man's free attention. Experience as such and objectified, representational and verbalized experiences are not simply the same thing, although it might seem so to consciousness lost in the objective reality of ordinary life and worried only about what goes on there. There can therefore be an experience that amounts simultaneously to a genuine question.

The *question* then about the *experience* of the Spirit cannot be dismissed *a priori* as contradictory. But how can it be answered?

Today, as often also in the Church's past, it is perhaps appropriate to recall the fact that there have always been mysticism and enthusiastic occurrences, experiences and movements in the Church which, even though in the most diverse forms and interpretations, have been understood as experiences of the Holy Spirit.

There has been and there is mysticism. Here, those who have been so privileged said and continue to say that either in a sudden awakening or in a long and gradual ascent they experience grace, God's immediate proximity, union with him in the Spirit, in a holy night or in blessed light, in a void silently filled by God, and, at least at the moment of the mystical event itself, cannot doubt their experience of the immediate proximity of the self-communicating God as effect and reality of God's sanctifying grace in the depth of their existence: in other words, as 'experience of the Holy Spirit'.

How this experience has been described in the course of the history of mysticism in Christianity factually or in theological terms; how this objectifying and verbalizing interpretation has taken the most diverse forms, dependent on the background of the history of ideas, the history of civilization, of philosophy and theology; how the question is to be answered about the relationship of this Christian mysticism or mysticism interpreted in Christian terms to similar mystical phenomena outside Christianity, particularly in the East and especially in Islam and Buddhism; how such an experience can co-exist with ecclesial-social and sacramental-ritual piety: all these are questions which need not occupy us here and now.

The mystics tell us of an experience of the Spirit and in principle there is nothing to prevent us from regarding their testimony on the whole as credible, particularly if on the one hand we justifiably allow for the fact that the original experience is the one thing and the philosophical and theological interpretation of it another and that consequently diversity and inconsistency in the interpretations need not discredit the original experience, and if on the other hand we remember that among these mystics there have been persons of the utmost sobriety and with acute powers of observation up to the present time, including Carl Albrecht, the mystic who was also an outstanding doctor, psychologist, philosopher, and natural scientist. The fact remains that there are people who have the courage to provide us with credible testimony to the experience of the Spirit.

Admittedly in the theology of Christian mysticism there has been considerable insistence on the extraordinary and elitist character of such mystical phenomena; on the one hand because people (rightly) wanted to stress the grace-inspired character of these phenomena and at the same time were guided by the tacit opinion that what is effected by grace and unmerited must by its very nature be rare and on the other hand because such clearly mystical phenomena are generally accompanied by circumstances of an ecstatic, almost para-psychological nature, which really are rare. Hence it is understand-able up to a point that the normal Christian is inclined to leave aside such mysticism as a matter which has nothing to do with him.

But if we were to distinguish (which is not possible here) the really *central* mystical experience more clearly from these rare marginal phenomena such as ecstasy, absorption, etc., then it would be easier to understand that such mystical experiences are certainly not oc-currences lying completely outside the experience of an ordinary Christian; that what the mystics talk about is an experience which any Christian (and indeed any human being) can have and can seek, but which is easily overlooked or suppressed. But in any case it is true that mysticism exists and it is not as remote from us as we are at first tempted to assume.

In addition there are enthusiastic phenomena and movements in non-Catholic and Catholic Christianity. Whether these things also involve a mystical closeness to God and union with him in the sense of classical, more or less individual and individualistic mysticism, or whether and how mysticism and (former or present-day) enthusiasm of a more social character must be distinguished phenomenologically and theologically, this is a question into which we cannot directly enter here. It is not really necessary to do so, particularly since the classical theology of mysticism recognizes very diverse forms and degrees of mystical experience and consequently allows for the possibility of arranging enthusiastical experiences in a series of steps on the mystical ascent, without making them coincide with the peak of mysticism, the final unification by grace with God in the mystical union.

Enthusiastic movements exist anyway in Christendom at the present time. People are looking for the experience of the Spirit and his power. Lengthy charismatic religious services take place in a community, where people think they perceive the presence of the Spirit and particularly in ecstatic speaking in tongues and marvelous cures of the sick. At these times of prayer there are not a few who think that they are experiencing what they describe as 'baptism of the Spirit', being filled once and for all with the Spirit of God.

Even a solidly rational theology does not need to reject such enthusiastic experiences out of hand and in all cases or to regard them completely sceptically. This is true even though the fire of God often produces a lot of human smoke, even though many of the phenomena of American enthusiasm may not appeal to us, even though many features of these phenomena can be explained (if not theologically interpreted) with the aid of very secular psychology and take exactly the same form outside a religious context.

Even though in such enthusiastic movements the person who is still on pilgrimage in time and history may never assume that he is perfect, that he has received and experienced an absolutely certain and even final promise of the Spirit (something that traditional theology would describe as 'confirmation in grace' and would count among the most sublime mystical experiences), it need not be disputed that there can be particularly impressive liberating experiences of grace here transforming the person and providing quite new horizons of life, which mark for a long time the innermost attitude of the Christian and can certainly be described (if desired) as 'baptism of the Spirit' and also (particularly within such community prayer meetings) experienced as effect of the Spirit given to the congregation.

II

But—and here we really come to our proper theme—where do we stand, who do not venture to describe ourselves as mystics and who, perhaps for the most diverse reasons, can find no personal approach to such enthusiastic movements and practices? Have we no experience of the Spirit? Can we merely bow respectfully before these experiences of others regarded by ourselves as elitist? Do these people merely give us an account of a country that we ourselves have never entered, whose existence we admit as we admit that of Australia which (perhaps) we have never seen.

We say that as Christians, supported by the testimony of Scripture, we *confess* that we can have such an experience of the Spirit and even *necessarily* have it as an offer to our freedom. It is an experience that exists, even though in the routine of ordinary life we mostly overlook it, perhaps suppress it, and do not want to admit it.

If in what follows we try to draw attention to such an experience, it seems impossible to avoid prefacing these concrete references to our own experiences with some more or less theoretical considerations on the intrinsic nature of human knowledge and freedom, even though they can only be brief and to some may seem very abstract. It is only in this way that the actual structure and peculiar nature of our experiences of the Spirit can be made clear and understood, why in our explicit and verbalized representational consciousness we can easily overlook them and thus be led to think that they do not exist at all. We must therefore ask particularly for attention and patience for these theoretical preliminary considerations.

We may consider together man's knowledge and freedom, since, despite their radical difference from each other, in the last resort they have a common structure. In knowledge and freedom man is inescapably the being of transcendence. This term may sound pompus, irritating, and redolent of ideology. But it is difficult to avoid, referring as it does to an ultimate, inescapable, essential structure of man, whether the ordinary person or even the empirical scientist is inclined to take note of it or not. In knowledge and freedom man is always both involved with the individual object (nameable and distinguishable from others) of his ordinary experience or of his particular fields of study *and* at the same time carried beyond it, even though he leaves this always implicit trend unconsidered and unnamed. The movement of the mind to the individual object, with which it is occupied, always goes toward the particular object *precisely* by going beyond it. What is objectively known and named as individual is always grasped in a wider unnamed, implicitly present horizon of possible knowledge and freedom as a whole, even though it is always with difficulty and only subsequently that reflection succeeds in making this implicitly present awareness into something like an individual object of consciousness and giving it objective expression in words.

The movement of the mind and freedom, the horizon of this movement, is boundless. Every object of our consciousness which confronts us, making itself felt in our milieu and environment, is only a stage, a continually new starting point of this movement, which passes into the infinite and unnamed. What is present in our ordinary and academic consciousness is no more than a tiny island (even though it is large enough in itself and continually and increasingly enlarged by our objectifying knowledge and action) in a boundless ocean of the nameless mystery which grows and becomes clearer the more precisely we know and will in detail. And if we want to set a limit to this apparently empty horizon of consciousness, we would by that very fact have again transgressed this limit.

In the midst of our everyday consciousness we are saved or damned (as we will) for nameless unencompassable infinity. The concepts and terms that we use subsequently of this infinity to which we are continually referred do not represent the original form of our experience of the nameless mystery that surrounds the island of our ordinary consciousness, but the small signs and images that we set up and must set up to remind us continually of the original, unthematic experience—silently present and silencing its presence—of the strangeness of the mystery in which we live, despite the clarity of ordinary consciousness, as in a night and in a pathless desert, reminding us of the abyss in which we are unfathomably rooted.

Anyone who wants to do so can of course angrily claim that too much is required of him and leave all this aside and continually press on to what is new; he can attempt to disregard the night which alone makes visible our little lights and gives them their brightness. But a person who takes up this attitude is really acting contrary to his fundamental nature, since this experience of being referred to the boundless mystery, seen more closely, is not a superfluous mental luxury, but the condition of the possibility of ordinary knowing and willing, even though in the routine of ordinary life and in academic activity this is generally disregarded and not considered.

If we wanted to describe as 'mysticism' this experience of transcendence in which man in the midst of ordinary life is always beyond himself and beyond the particular object with which he is concerned, we might say that mysticism always occurs, concealed and namelessly, in the midst of ordinary life and is the condition of the possibility for the most down-to-earth and most secular experience of ordinary life.

He whom we call God dwells in this nameless and pathless expanse of our consciousness. The mystery purely and simply that we call God is not a particular, especially peculiar, objective piece of reality which we add to the realities named and systematized in our experience and fit in with the latter; he is the encompassing, never encompassed ground and precondition of our experience and its objects. He is known in this strange experience of transcendence, even though it is not possible here to define metaphysically more precisely the unity and difference between the experience of transcendence on the part of the intellectual subject in knowledge and freedom on the one hand and the experience of God himself on the other hand that is present in the experience of transcendence. Such a definition would be a difficult philosophical undertaking at this stage and it is not necessary here.

The fact remains that the boundless expanse of our mind in knowledge and freedom, which is inescapably always present unthematically in all ordinary knowledge, permits us to learn what is meant by God as the ground opening up and filling that expanse of the mind and its limitless movement. However and wherever it is brought about by a concrete, categorial object, transcendental experience is always also experience of God in the midst of ordinary life.

At this point an observation must be made, of which the philosophical and theological senses are linked in a peculiar relationship of mutual dependence. The unlimited transcendental movement of the mind toward God has actually a radicalness that makes it tend toward God, not merely as an asymptotic goal, itself remaining always at an infinite distance, but as that which itself forms in immediacy the attainable goal of this movement.

Philosophically we can think of and hope for this radicalness by which God himself becomes in himself the goal of this movement, at least as a possibility that cannot be excluded; *theologically* we grasp this possibility as in fact given by God and describe as grace this actually available radicalness of the transcendental movement toward God's immediacy in himself up to the point one day of the immediate vision of God, for it is in this that the actual and ultimate nature consists of what we call grace, self-communication of God in the Spirit, and of what finds its ultimate fulfillment in the immediate loving intuition of God; *existentially* we freely grasp this radicalness of our movement toward God in immediacy, sustained by God's Spirit, when we surrender ourselves unreservedly and unconditionally to this movement of the Spirit as it actually ranges of itself, when in our freedom we set no limits to it, but let it in a sense swing out in its own boundlessness up to the immediacy of God himself.

If grace is so understood, as it must be grasped philosophically as possibility, seen theologically as reality, and existentially realized (thematically or unthematically) in hope, then, in the actual order of reality, experience of transcendence (which is experience of God) is always also experience of grace, since the radicalness of the experience of transcendence and its dynamism are sustained in the innermost core of our existence by God's self-communication making all this possible, by the self-communication of God as goal and as strength of the movement toward him that we describe as grace, as the Holy Spirit (at least as offer to man's freedom). The experience of transcendence permitting God to be present (because of God's salvific will in regard to all human beings, by which man is oriented to God's immediacy) is in fact always experience of the Holy Spirit, whether a person can or cannot interpret explicitly in this way his inescapable experience of the unknown God, whether or not he has at his disposal theological expressions such as those we have just been using.

There is something more to be added to what has just been said. It is true that all this applies to the average person in the ordinary activity of knowledge and freedom, at least where (but always where) we find really intellectual knowledge and freedom, in which a human being as real subject is aware of himself and definitively disposes of himself. But this transcendental experience of God in the Holy Spirit is present in the ordinary course of human life only unthematically, covered and concealed by preoccupation with the concrete realities with which we are involved in our milieu and environment. In everyday life this transcendental experience of God in the Holy Spirit remains anonymous, implicit, unthematic, like the widely and diffusely spread light of a sun which we do not directly see, while we turn only to the individual objects visible in this light in our sense-experience.

But even if we disregard the question whether this transcendental experience of God in the Holy Spirit can occur quite independently (for instance, in phenomena of a formless absorption, in an attitude of consciousness emptied of objects of an individual character, in mystical experience), there are in any case concrete experiences in our existential history in which this transcendental experience of the Spirit always present as such is thrust more clearly to the fore in our consciousness: experiences in which (conversely) the individual objects of knowledge and freedom that concern us in ordinary life, by their singularity, bring to our notice more clearly and more urgently the accompanying transcendental experience of the Spirit; in which these objects of themselves silently refer more clearly than otherwise happens in our ordinary and banal daily life to that incomprehensible mystery of our existence which always surrounds us and also sustains our ordinary consciousness. Everyday reality then becomes itself a pointer to this transcendental experience of the Spirit, which is always present silently and apparently facelessly.

This reference—which our everyday reality grasped in knowledge and freedom as such always carries with it and announces more forcefully in certain situations—can also be implied by the positiveness of this categorial reality in which the greatness and glory, goodness, beauty, and transparency of the individual reality of our experience point with promise to eternal light and eternal life. But it is also understandable without more ado that a pointer of this kind is perceived most clearly where the definable limits of our everyday realities break down and are dissolved, where the decline of these realities is perceived, when lights shining over the tiny island of our ordinary life are extinguished and the question becomes inescapable, whether the night that surrounds us is the void of absurdity and death that engulfs us or the blessed holy night already shining within us is the promise of eternal day. If then in what follows attention is drawn particularly to such experiences which bring to the fore in this second way the transcendental experience of God in the Holy Spirit, this does not mean that the human being and the Christian are forbidden to allow this experience of God to occur also in the first way indicated and to accept it. In the last resort the *via eminentiae* and the *via negationis* are not two ways or two successive stages of the one way, but two aspects of one and the same experience, even though (as we said) it is right for the sake of clarity to stress particularly the *via negationis*.

We may now at last begin to point to concrete experiences of life which, whether we are explicitly aware of it or not, are experiences of the Spirit, assuming only that we cope with them in the right way. In regard to these references to the concrete experience of the Spirit in the midst of the ordinary routine of life there can be no question of analyzing them in detail to their ultimate depth, which is in fact the Spirit. In this connection what was said in a formal preliminary outline of the real nature of all these experiences in general must suffice. Nor can the attempt be made here to offer a systematic chart of such experiences. All that is possible is to give a few arbitrarily and unsystematically selected examples.

Here is someone who cannot get his life's accounts to come out right, who cannot balance the entries in these accounts, consisting of good will, mistakes, sin and disasters, even if he tries (impossible as it may seem) to add repentance to these entries. The accounts simply do not add up and he does not know how he can insert God as an individual entry in order to strike a balance between debit and credit. And this person, unable to balance his life's accounts, surrenders himself to God or, to put it both more and less precisely, to the hope of an incalculable final reconciliation of his existence, marked by the presence of him whom we call God; trusting and hoping, he gets away from his unfathomed and uncalculated existence and does not himself know how this miracle occurs, bringing no advantage to himself and not to be regarded as his own possession.

Here is someone who can manage to forgive, although he gains no reward for it and the silent pardon is taken for granted by the other party.

Here is someone who is trying to love God, although there appears to be no response of love from God's silent incomprehensibility, although he is not sustained by any feeling of enthusiasm, although he cannot confuse himself and his desire for life with God, although he thinks he will die of this love which seems to him like death and absolute rejection, which apparently calls him into the void and the wholly unknown: a love that looks like a terrifying leap into unfathomable depths, since everything seems to become intangible and utterly futile.

Here is someone who does his duty even when it seems that he can do it only with a burning sense of really denying and annihilating himself, when he can do it only by doing something terribly stupid for which no one will thank him.

Here is a person who is really good to someone from whom there is no sign of appreciation or gratitude, while the good person does not even have the feeling of satisfaction that he has been 'selfless', decent, and so on.

Here is someone who is silent, although he could defend himself, although he is unjustly treated; who is silent without being able to profit by his silence as evidence of his supreme irreproachability.

Here is someone who has to make a decision purely in the light of an innermost dictate of his conscience, a decision that cannot be made clear to anyone, in which he is quite alone and knows that it is a decision of which he cannot be relieved, for which he has to answer always and eternally.

Here is someone who obeys, not because he must or because he must otherwise put up with some inconvenience, but merely because of that mysterious, silent, impalpable reality that we call God and his will.

Here is a person who renounces something without thanks, recognition, or even any feeling of inward satisfaction.

Here is someone who is utterly lonely, for whom life is drained of all its colour, for whom everything tangible on which he could rely fades into an infinite distance, but who does not run away from this loneliness which is felt as the last moment before drowning, but endures it with resignation in an ultimate hope.

Here is someone who sees that his clearest ideas and the most intellectual operations of his thought are disintegrating, that in the breakdown of all systems the unity of consciousness and what is known consists only in the pain of not being able to cope with the immense variety of questions and yet of not being allowed and not being able to cling to what is clearly known from individual experiences and from learning.

Here is someone who suddenly notices how the small rivulet of his life winds through the desert of banal existence, apparently aimlessly and with the terrifying possibility of completely drying up. And yet he hopes, without knowing how, that this rivulet will find its way to the infinite expanse of the ocean, even though this is concealed from him by the dark sand dunes apparently stretched out endlessly before him.

It would be possible to continue in this way for a long time and even then not to have visualized in particular that experience which for a certain individual is the experience in his life of the Spirit, of freedom, and of grace. For every human being approaches it in the particular historical and individual situation of his own unique life. Every human being? But he must admit it, dig it out, so to speak, from under the refuse of the ordinary business of life, and, when it becomes faintly visible, not irritably turn away from it, as if it only created uncertainty and disturbed the obvious course of his daily routine and his scientific clarities.

Permit me to say it once more, although I am merely repeating the same thing with almost the same words:

When, over and above all individual hopes, there is the one and entire hope that gently embraces all upsurges and also all downfalls in silent promise,

when responsibility is undertaken and sustained, even though no evidence of success or advantage can be produced,

when someone experiences and accepts his ultimate freedom, of which no earthly constraints can deprive him,

when the fall into the darkness of death is accepted with resignation as the dawn of incomprehensible promise,

when the sum total of all life's accounts, which we cannot work out ourselves, is seen as good by an incomprehensible 'other', although this cannot be 'proved',

when the fragmentary experience of love, beauty, and joy is felt and accepted as promise of love, beauty, and joy purely and simply, and not regarded with deep cynicism and scepticism as facile consolation in face of ultimate bleakness,

when the bitter, disappointing, and fleeting monotony of ordinary life is borne with serene resignation up to its accepted end out of a strength whose ultimate source cannot be grasped and so cannot be brought under our control,

when we venture to pray into a silent darkness and know that in any case we are heard, although there seems to be no response from there about which it would be possible to reason and argue,

when we get away from ourselves unconditionally and experience this capitulation as the true victory,

when falling becomes standing firm,

when despair is accepted and mysteriously experienced as assurance without any easy consolation,

when man entrusts all his knowledge and all his questions to the silent and all-sheltering mystery which is loved more than all our individual perceptions that turn us into petty lords,

when we practise our death in the course of ordinary life and then attempt to live in the way that we wish to approach death, calmly and with resignation,

when . . . (as we said, it would be possible to go on for a long time),

then God is present with his liberating grace. Then we experience what we Christians describe as the Holy Spirit of God; then an experience occurs that is inescapable in life (even if it is suppressed) and is offered to our freedom with the question of whether we want to accept it or to barricade ourselves against it in a hell of freedom to which we condemn ourselves. The mysticism of everyday life is there, God is found in all things; here is that sober intoxication of the Spirit of which the Church Fathers and the early liturgy spoke, which we may not reject or despise simply because it is sober.

Let us look ourselves for such an experience of our life, let us look for our own experiences in which something of this kind happens precisely to us. If we find them, we have had what we mean by experience of the Spirit. The experience of eternity, the experience that the Spirit is more than a part of this temporal world, the experience that the meaning of man is not absorbed in the meaning and happiness of this world, the experience of risk and of overwhelming trust which really has no demonstrable justification based on success in this world.

From this standpoint we can understand what is the secret passion alive in those people who really belong to the Spirit and in the saints.

They want this experience. In a secret fear of being stuck in the world, they want to be continually assured that they are beginning to live in the Spirit. They have acquired the taste for the Spirit. While ordinary people regard experiences of this kind as unwelcome if not entirely avoidable interruptions of normal life with the Spirit merely providing the flavour and the trimmings of another and not wholly real life, the people of the Spirit and the saints have acquired the taste for the Spirit purely and simply. Spirit is in a sense drunk pure by them and not merely as a flavouring of earthly existence. Hence their odd life, their poverty, their desire for humility, their longing for death, their readiness to suffer, their secret yearning for martyrdom. This does not mean that they are not also weak. It does not mean that they do not also need constantly to return to the ordinary routine. It does not mean that they are unaware of the fact that grace can bless also ordinary life and rational behaviour and can turn all this into an approach to God. Nor does it mean that they do not know that here and now we are not and are not expected to be angels. But they know that man as spirit in his actual existence and not merely as a matter of speculation is meant to live really on the frontier between God and the world, time and eternity, and they are constantly trying to reassure themselves that this in fact is what they are doing, that spirit in them is more than a way of giving a human character to life.

When we have this experience of spirit, then (at least if we are Christians living by faith) it becomes *ipso facto* the experience of the *supernatural*. Perhaps very anonymously and inexplicitly. Probably even in such a way that we may not and cannot at the same time turn to catch sight of the supernatural itself. We know however, when we lose ourselves in this experience of spirit, when the tangible, the demonstrable and available, is lost to sight, when all that is heard is a deathly silence, when everything acquires the flavour of death and corruption, or when everything vanishes as in an ineffable, strangely white, colourless and incomprehensible bliss, we know then that what is active within us is not only spirit but truly the Holy Spirit. This is the moment of his grace. Then the seemingly unfamiliar unfathomability of our existence as we feel it is the unfathomability of God, imparting himself to us, the advent of his infinity that is pathless and appears to us as nothingness, precisely because it is infinity. When we have freed ourselves and no longer belong to ourselves, when we have denied ourselves and no longer dispose of ourselves, when everything (including ourselves) has moved away from us into an infinite distance, then we begin to live in the world of God himself, the God of grace and eternal life.

At first all this may seem bizarre and terrifying and we shall constantly be tempted to take refuge in our more familiar and intimate world, in fact we must and may often do this. Nevertheless, we should gradually get used to the taste of the pure wine of the Spirit, filled with the Holy Spirit, at least to the extent that we do not thrust back the chalice when it is offered to us by his guidance and providence.

At this point the question might be raised as to whether we have not hitherto extolled a mysticism of ordinary life which is by no means properly Christian and not related to Jesus Christ, crucified and risen, but which can exist even apart from any explicit religious or theological interpretation. It is admittedly a question that cannot be answered adequately here, but for which some few hints of an answer will be given.

First of all, if and insofar as the experience of the Spirit mentioned above is present in a mysticism of ordinary life, even outside a verbalized and institutionalized Christianity, and is discovered there by the Christian in the life he shares with his non-Christian brothers and sisters or in his study of the history of religion, this observation need not upset the Christian. It merely makes clear to him the fact that his God, the God of Jesus Christ, wills the salvation of *all* human beings, offers to *all* his grace as liberation for the incomprehensible mystery, that the grace of Christ is effective in a mysterious way beyond the limits of verbalized and institutionalized Christianity and gives a share in the paschal mystery of Jesus even when someone who is faithful to his conscience has not yet been confronted by a convincing presentation of the explicit message of Christianity and has not yet been marked by the Christian sacraments.

An observation of this kind is not only not forbidden to the Christian when and where he can make it; he must also expect it, since his faith requires him to believe in the universal salvific will of God, which reaches its limit only at the personal mortal sin of an individual and even offers the grace of Christ again and again to every human being in his whole life. The grace of God (which the history of the Crucified and Risen One made effective and irreversible in the history of humanity) is consequently the grace of Jesus Christ even when it is not yet explicitly and reflectively grasped and interpreted as such. This is not merely an opinion which a Christian may hold; it is part of his faith, which acknowledges the universal and supernatural salvific will of God for all human beings and forbids him to hold the opinion that this salvific will of God in Jesus Christ effects a person's salvation only when the latter has explicitly become a Christian.

If we also recall what we said about man's experience (radicalized by God's grace) of transcendence into the ineffable mystery of God, it becomes clear that this experience has something to do with the death of Jesus, whether this is explicitly considered or not.

The real experience of transcendence in the Holy Spirit accepted in freedom is primarily and ultimately not a matter of theoretical reason, but something that involves the *whole* person in the *concrete* history of his life and his freedom. In the last resort then it occurs at the point where it is impossible to stop at any individual reality of life as if it were final and absolute, where a final, autonomous self-defence is abandoned in free and liberated hope unsecured by anything else: in a word, at the point where dying is a passing into the incomprehensibility of God.

For the Christian who cannot and will not shut his historical existence out of his relationship with the absolute God, the moment of his mystical union with God and the climax of his experience of the Spirit is present, in the last resort, not in a sublime experience of mystical absorption as such, but in his death, even though the latter event must not necessarily take place at the very moment of his medical exitus and even though (conversely) truly existential dying as the final self-forsaking which is actual death may possibly (but necessarily) occur also in a mystical experience of absorption (assuming only that this experience is not regarded as secure and final before death in the ordinary sense of the term occurs).

It can be seen therefore that there is an identity between experience of the Spirit and participation in the victorious death of Jesus, in which alone the real success of our death is experienced and experienced within a believing community. In this life the chalice of the Holy Spirit is identical with the chalice of Christ. But it is drunk only by someone who has slowly learned up to a point to taste fullness in the void, dawn in doom, discovery in renunciation. A person who learns this experiences the Spirit, the pure Spirit, and this is the experience of the Holy Spirit of grace. For this liberation of the Spirit comes about as a whole and permanently only in faith by the grace of Christ. But when he liberates this Spirit, he liberates him by supernatural grace into the life of God himself.

III

Before closing these reflections, two observations may be put forward, both of which lead us back expressly to the point from which our reflections started and from which, it is to be hoped, they never became entirely remote. What we mean is the connection between experience of the Spirit and the ordinary routine of life.

As always understood here, experience of the Spirit in the first place has nothing to do with an elitist sense on the part of the chosen, claiming to be the only ones so dedicated and setting themselves apart from the great mass of Christians and ordinary people. If what has been said hitherto is really rightly understood, experience of the Spirit in the sense meant here as such occurs always and everywhere in the life of someone who has awakened to personal self-possession and to the act of freedom in which he disposes of himself as a whole. But in most cases in human life this does not come about expressly in meditation, in experiences of absorption, etc., but on the material of normal life: that is, when responsibility, fidelity, love, etc., are realized absolutely, while even in the very last resort it remains a secondary question whether this activity is accompanied by an explicitly religious interpretation, although (conversely) it is not denied that a religious interpretation of this kind is right and also important as such. Meditation and similar spiritual 'exercises' are not thereby depreciated. They may be rehearsals, so to speak, for admitting and accepting in radical freedom fundamental experiences of the Spirit whenever they occur in life; these exercises can *also* (but not solely) be the point at which such experiences of the Spirit become clearer and more explicit and are grasped by man's ultimate basic freedom in such a way that they amount to a decision embracing the whole of existence and leading to salvation.

Christianity however is not elitist. The New Testament is aware also of sublime experiences of the Spirit in the most varied forms, which can be summed up under the heading of 'mysticism'; but it also assures to all who love their neighbour unselfishly and thus experience God that final salvation in God's judgment which is not surpassed even by the highest ascent or the deepest absorption of the mystic. The New Testament then (even without expressly considering the matter) is certain that this unsurpassable salvation in the self-communicating Holy Spirit of God can take place even when apparently all that happens is the observance of the harsh duty of ordinary life and the resigned acceptance of death. The fact that such a fundamental experience of the Spirit (contrary to all elitist pride on the part of 'pneumatic' enthusiasts) can happen in the midst of ordinary life and how this can be regarded as possible: these things are just what our reflections as a whole were meant to show.

Admittedly, when there is a genuine concern for salvation, when God is loved, when a person learns increasingly clearly that he may never finally come to a stop on the way of freedom to himself (and thus to God), when he faces the terrifying and blessed excessive demands of the Sermon on the Mount, then neither will he ever refuse to follow at least those explicit ways of meditation and spirituality which are in fact opened up to him in the ultimately uncontrollable history of his life.

In the course of reading the letters of the apostle Paul, we come across his teaching on the charisms. These are not simply identical with a possession of the Spirit and an experience of the Spirit on the part of the person justified by faith; but they are intrinsically connected with this possession of the Spirit and the experience of it. They are regarded by Paul as diverse powers and commissions for building up the Christian community, continually assigned in different ways to individuals, never in their entirety to a single individual. They may (for instance, powers of healing and speaking in tongues) have an extraordinary, almost spectacular character; but they can also certainly be present in the form of more or less secular, everyday abilities, including, for example, ability to manage the funds of a community. Here for the time being the significance of these charisms for the building up of the *community* can be ignored. We can safely say that all powers and possibilities of Christian action, as authorized, sustained, and animated in the last resort by the Holy Spirit of God, are charisms, gifts of the Spirit.

If at the same time we do not forget that the manifold and diversely assigned charisms are distinct from the possession of the Spirit which is one and the same in all those who are justified, it may perhaps be possible to elucidate up to a point the connection and distinction between possession of the Spirit and the charisms. Charisms, seen quite prosaically, are primarily individual commissions, individual abilities and individual offers, which the ordinary routine of a person and of his varied life puts before him. These possibilities are always more than an individual with his limited powers and time can actually realize. He must choose, distinguish. If he makes this selection rightly (that is, in the Spirit and in virtue of it) he can regard what is chosen really as 'charism', as 'God's will'.

How is a choice of this kind made correctly? The masters of the spiritual life reflected and experimented considerably on the rules of such a discernment of spirits, of finding the will of God in the concreteness of life, particularly since they were sure that finding what is here and now concretely right is not *merely* a matter of rational consideration and theoretical moral theology. We cannot repeat here this teaching of the masters of the spiritual life. But, in the light of all that has been said up to now, we can perhaps very briefly add something of fundamental importance which combines once more the ultimate experience of the Spirit and these ultimately 'charismatic' individual decisions continually demanded by life. When such a choice of an individual object by freedom in the course of ordinary life is not only (this is an obvious assumption) justified rationally and according to the principles of a Christian morality, but also (which is not obvious) does not obstruct and does not obscure an ultimate openness to the real experience of the Spirit in unlimited freedom; when a Christian is aware of the presence of an ultimate synthesis (not to be produced at will, not open to rational analysis, but simply there as a fact) between the basic experience of the Spirit and the will for a particular individual object of his everyday freedom: then he is acting, not only reasonably and morally, but also charismatically. Of course a great deal of practice and spiritual experience is needed to see more clearly when a will for an individual object offered by ordinary life does not obstruct this fundamental experience of the Spirit passing into the apparently empty freedom of God and beyond all individual realities, but precisely as material and starting point of this experience of the Spirit offers it to an effective synthesis between experience of the Spirit and everyday duty. But the experience of such a synthesis, in which a person abandons everything to admit the boundless mystery of God *and* makes the courageous decision for a concrete reality of life and the 'world', is possible and alone constitutes the totality of Christian life. In that life man forsakes everything with the dying Jesus in order to reach the inescapable and formless freedom of God *and* accepts lovingly the individual reality of this world intended for him in ordinary life in order to take it up into this Spirit of God.

Let us look in the very consideration of our life for the experience of the Spirit and of grace. Not to say: 'There it is; I have it'. We cannot find it in order to claim it triumphantly as our property and possession. We can seek it only by forgetting ourselves; we can find it only by seeking God and surrendering ourselves to him in self-forgetting love, without returning to ourselves. But we ought to ask from time to time whether anything like this deadening and reviving experience is alive in us, in order to judge how far the way still is, and how far away from the experience of the Holy Spirit we are still living in what we describe as our spiritual life.

Grandis nobis restat via. Venite et gustate, quam suavis sit Dominus! ('A long road still lies ahead of us. Come and taste, the Lord is sweet!')

13

FAITH AS COURAGE

The theme 'faith as courage' was suggested to me by others. However unusual and surprising the suggestion to say something on this subject may sound at first hearing, I gladly accepted it. It gives me an opportunity to explain that Christian faith (and this is what we are talking about), contrary to popular impressions, is really a very simple affair and difficult only because it is the concreteness of something that we can describe as 'courage'. All this assumes that this kind of 'courage' is understood in all its radicalness in relation to the totality of human existence.

Without claiming the competence of a linguistic philosopher, I think nevertheless that it is perhaps possible to distinguish between two groups of substantive terms. In the one group the terms have a quite firmly outlined sense, which can be defined even more closely by the exact sciences: a sense that unambiguously distinguishes them from other terms. Hydrogen, beetle, house, etc., may serve as examples of these terms. They define and distinguish an absolutely definite individual reality in the variety of our empirical experience of the world.

There is however a second group of terms which are quite different, although they cannot be denied sense and reality because of a demand for clear and exact speech. They are terms which have a particular starting point within human existence and nevertheless are not restrictive or conclusive, but—if the radicalness of their meaning is admitted—are open to the totality of human existence and reality as such. They are terms of a specifically human character and always involve the whole person. They involve the human person who as mind and freedom always reaches out beyond the individuality and definability of particular realities within his empirical experience and thus in the last resort is always lost in that mysterious darkness which permeates and encompasses the whole of human existence.

The rationalistic positivist may say that terms like this are unscientific and should not be allowed to occur in science or in sober philosophy, which eschews poetry; what cannot be said clearly (that is, cannot be unambiguously determined in its meaning) must be passed over in silence. But is it possible to be a human person and to exist in a human way, while seeking to avoid terms like freedom, love, fidelity, joy, responsibility, fear, etc.? It is not possible. Terms like this however are lost into the totality of human existence, albeit from a particular starting point, and consequently cannot be defined in the same way as individual realities which have a quite definite place within human existence and its milieu. For this whole existence of man as one and whole is always imposed on the person; in his discouragement or irritation, he cannot therefore simply leave them aside as 'incomprehensible' or as 'not clearly expressible'. When he asks and knows that 'he' is doing this, when he decides freely and responsibly and can no longer shift this responsibility on to others, then in fact he is always involved in this totality of his existence, no matter whether he is explicitly aware of it or 'forgets' or suppresses it in his preoccupation with a particular individual object which is clear or can be 'scientifically' made clear.

When he is very busy a person can in fact allow himself to be driven by the variety of the individual things in his life and by the detailed knowledge of these things and the particular moods they create; he can forget *himself* in all the thousand details of what he is doing and what he has: he can then *try* to make every effort to restrict himself to the area of language of the first group of terms. But even in this way he will never really get away from himself. The totality, the oneness of his existence, that he is trying to suppress and forget in the routine of his everyday life will emerge constantly out of its dark roots and present him and his freedom with the one and final question about his attitude to this oneness, what he wants to do with that and not merely with the thousand details of his life. In his concrete life of freedom and responsibility therefore no human being can live only with the first group of terms, which are those of what are known as the exact sciences. If he asks again what science, truth, etc., are themselves, he is landed once more unavoidably in the field of this mysterious second group of words, which are inescapable even when he denies them the character of scientific clarity and unambiguity.

The term 'courage' is also one of those unavoidable terms which point to the mysterious totality of human existence. It is this term which will be considered now. What is to be shown is that this courage, if it is understood in its necessity and radicalness, is precisely what Christian theology describes as faith.

First, however, a brief preliminary observation to prevent the stated intention of these reflections from being misunderstood from the very outset. As we said, the terms of this second group refer to the totality of human existence. If a person speaks of freedom, he is primarily thinking of something different from what he means when he speaks of responsibility. Joy and fear, despair and hope, and so on, look at man's totality from different angles, describe different ways in which man's basic freedom approaches the one totality of existence. But since each of these terms always refers to the one human being in his unity and the boundlessness of his questioning and action, they always merge into one another, draw into themselves (by affirmation or denial) the meaning of the other terms; this means that they are not merely synonymous, but neither are they absolutely clearly distinguished from each other. This strange relationship between such terms (which can be barely indicated here) involves also the possibility of a variety of 'key terms' which become detached up to a point in the course of the history of ideas and faith of humanity. These key terms are meant on each occasion to throw light on the mysterious totality of human existence, but do so every time from a different starting point, are different and yet, if they are understood radically, merge into one another. Consequently, without on each occasion being involved in their ultimate task of giving meaning to the totality of human existence, they can either exist alongside one another or become separated in the course of the history of ideas.

The Christian is familiar with at least three such key terms: faith, hope, and love. All three are found in the New Testament, but the emphasis is different in its individual writings, so that *one* key term can also lead to the understanding of *another*. In Catholic theology (especially at Trent) the attempt has been made to distinguish these three terms, describing the human and Christian basic realization of existence, as clearly as possible from each other and to see them as successive phases in which the one basic realization increasingly enters into consciousness. This effort may be regarded as wholly legitimate. But in the last resort it can be seen again and again that all three terms and each of them apart look to the one whole basic realization of Christian existence. Each of these three terms acquires its radical and full meaning only when it is 'elevated' into the other two.

There are, of course, in the New Testament other similar key terms, all of which belong to our second group: freedom, logos, light, truth, possession of spirit and grace, atonement, peace, righteousness, etc. All these terms (which in themselves are all or can all be key terms of this kind) have had a varied lot in the course of the history of Christian ideas, since of course the peculiar character of the age did not always permit them the same effectiveness in throwing light on the totality of human existence. Hence, in the course of this Christian history of ideas up to the present time terms arising mainly from the dimension of man's knowledge or from his individual concern for salvation—like logos, truth, intuitive vision of God, love, justification—had a function of this kind only for that particular epoch.

Today, however, in the age of creative freedom, of openness toward the future, terms like universal justice, emancipation, and hope can be more effective in this way as key terms. These new key terms do not simply abolish the old, but themselves, rightly and radically understood, in turn throw light on the old. If, for instance, someone really and radically hopes, he also believes and loves, since hope has always also an element of knowledge of faith as a constituent of itself and only reaches its own plenitude when hoping means love for the other or when loving is hope for the other.

If today perhaps hope is the 'principle', the key term, the term preferred among those belonging to the second group of which we spoke at the beginning, the term 'courage' promptly springs to mind. For courage in the last resort is hope and hope is not hope if it is not courageous. If then we consider the term 'courage', that is not to confer on it precisely the quality of an epochal key term for Christian existence, for each and everyone. But in the light of the term 'courage' the term 'hope' can be understood better and more radically. It can become clearer that hope is not (as it is always in danger of seeming to be) a way of escape, feeble consolation, or, still less, 'opium of the people.' It can become clearer that hope is decision, deed, venture, all of which are typical of the courageous person. And, as we said, we shall try to show that such courageous hope and hopeful courage, if only they are sufficiently radical, are *eo ipso* the very thing that a Christian theology describes as faith in the strict sense of the term. This is not by any means to deny that the faith present from the outset in this courage must be developed and made concrete as actual Christian faith, if it is to reach its own fullness of being.

It is difficult to say what courage is. Not because we do not know, but because as a peculiar realization of the existence of the whole person it cannot be defined as a particular occurrence distinguished from many others, in the sense of the first group of terms of which we spoke; because it is related to the totality of human existence, because it is no more open to an adequate reflection or definition than is this existence itself; because the courage that we really mean here is not courage for one thing or another that we can do, but courage for ourselves in the one totality of the human reality.

Nevertheless, it is possible to provide many hints of the meaning of courage and in this way to bring it before man's reflex consciousness. Courage has something to do with uncertainty, with the danger of missing the reality to be actualized and sought by freedom, with decision. Certainly courage can and even should be co-existent with planning, calculation of opportunities. But courage is really required when rational reflection is faced by an obvious distance between the calculation of the possibilities of success and the deed as actually posited, a deed of whose success it is impossible to be certain before it actually occurs. The deficit between the precalculation of the goal and its prospect of success is made up in a deed precisely by what we call hopeful courage or the courage of hope. The distance between the deed as not adequately calculable in advance and the real deed is bridged by what we call courage.

The rational human being today has indeed entirely the right and the duty, in his undertakings and actions, to calculate in advance as accurately as possible and to try to achieve certainty. In advance of the deed, he must reduce the distance as much as possible up to the point at which in practice courage ceases to be necessary for the deed. So, for example, the structural engineer knows with almost absolute certainty before the completion of a bridge that the bridge will hold and that consequently no courage is required to walk across it. But in a thousand human actions the distance remains, the effect to be realized cannot be adequately calculated in advance, no adequately comprehensive knowledge of all the factors of an action is possible, and if action has to be taken courage remains indispensable. This is true even in ordinary life with its thousands and thousands of particular undertakings. It is particularly true when there is a question of *that* deed and *that* courage for the deed which are related to the *totality* of the one human existence. In what follows we shall be speaking only of this courage.

That there is and inevitably must be such a radical and total courage assumes of course that man as subject of freedom has to do, not only with one thing or another, with the thousand particular objective realities of his existence, with this partner, with that professional task, with this vocation and that individual difficulty, etc., but with himself as one and whole. The assumption we make for the notion of courage as it is meant here cannot now be justified more precisely. We assume that man as subject has to do not merely with an enormous mass of details of his life, by which he is driven or permits himself to be driven; in and through all these detailed realizations of his life he is *himself* absorbed as one and *whole,* whether he knows it explicitly or not. In real freedom man as oriented to finality is himself subject and object in one. He has not only to be concerned with a great deal and with a great variety of things in his life, he is concerned for himself as one: a task that we describe in a theological language as concern for salvation. In the varied business of his life he can forget or suppress this one and ultimate task. From being an 'I' he can become a 'one'. This being absorbed in ourselves, being condemned to freedom, being ultimately always responsible for ourselves, is however present even as suppressed and forgotten, and comes clearly to the fore in moments of solitude and final decisions, in the invocation of a final responsibility applauded by no one, etc.

If we may assume here what has just been merely indicated, it becomes clearer what is meant by that total and radical courage of which we want to speak. Man is imposed on himself in his freedom as one and whole, he is himself his one and ultimate task. But at the same time he knows that the fulfillment of this one and entire task depends on a thousand conditions and causes that he cannot wholly understand and that are not within his own power. And over and above all this he experiences his own freedom as already posited and threatened in itself, he experiences what is most properly his own in his character as subject as mysteriously alien to himself.

For both reasons there exists here in the most radical and irremovable fashion that distance between the acting subject with its capacity, its power, its means which can be calculated in advance, on the one hand, and, on the other, what has to be done in this one life's deed: the ultimate and definitive self-determination in a fulfillment of the boundless possibilities initially present in man as mind and freedom, the ultimate self-understanding that a person does not merely passively accept, but gives himself creatively in freedom. He experiences this distance, since he experiences himself at the same time as the being with with unlimited claims, as the person who can never definitively stop at a restricted goal, *and* as one who is powerless, the person doomed to death, who is always fragmentary, an unhappy consciousness. This distance is bridged only by absolute hope, by the anticipation of a fulfillment which is not one's own achievement, by a hope of an absolute future as possibly and actually offered, that we call God and know originally and properly only *in* this hope.

The decision for such hope implies however also that courage with which we are concerned here. In this courage the totality of human existence is hoped for as achieved; the ground of this hope is not an empirical detail which could be completely understood and possessed; this hope is founded on the incomprehensible God, and on this God as free. Man must then entrust himself to another's freedom and accept this, not as imperiling, but as redeeming. This hope has not really anything outside itself which could serve independently as its ground and security, since the ground of hope, called God, is experienced only in hope itself. But such hope is for that reason courage purely and simply.

Before we can prove that this hopeful courage is faith in the strictly theological sense, something important must first be mentioned. We can of course objectify and verbalize the nature, content, and ground of this hopeful courage (just as we have done here and as every religion does with the aid of the most varied formulations) and realize a free act of courageous hope in regard to this reality as so verbalized. In other words it is possible to attempt expressly to hope courageously in an explicitly religious act. But however good such an act may be (and, under certain preconditions, even required) it is not simply to be identified with what we mean by this courageous hope. For in the first place it is by no means certain for man's reflective consciousness whether such an explicit individual religious act comes from that deepest centre of the acting subject from which the totality of human existence is really hazarded and surrendered, as redeeming and reconciling, to the ultimate mystery, called God. Not every religious act, however clear and well-meant, really itself disposes of the whole of existence for finality. Even if someone says sincerely, 'God, I hope in you, I love you,' it is far from certain that what is thought and said here really happens, that the person's whole existence moves toward God in a free decision from its innermost centre.

What is still more important, however, is that this hopeful courage can be realized very unthematically and without much reflection in the most varied free acts of life, without any attempt verbally to thematicize its nature in explicitly religious terms. If someone remains faithful to his conscience to the very last, even without reward; if someone succeeds in loving so unselflishly that in reality there is no question of a mere balance or harmony of egoisms; if someone quite calmly and without any final protest allows himself to be taken in the night of death; if the one life of a human being, despite all unceasing evil experiences and sad disappointments, opts for light and goodness; if someone, perhaps in apparently total hopelessness and despair, nevertheless hopes that he is hoping (since even hope itself cannot be established for certain as a solid fact on which further calculations could be securely based, but that very hope must be hoped for), and so on, then that courageous hope is always realized, even if it is not explicitly thematicized in religious terms. At this point man's freedom is at once identified with that hope which is the basic structure of human existence and continually offered to man's freedom throughout all the individual occurrences of life. In that very hope there is experienced and known what is really meant by 'God', even if this expression is not part of the vocabulary ordinarily used by such a person.

What is courageous and final about this free hope in courage is spread up to a point anonymously over the whole course of the history of human freedom. That, of course, is not to say that explicit realizations, verbalized in religious terms, of courageous hope are superfluous or worthless. On the contrary, they can be so many ways in which this generally anonymous hope becomes fully conscious. They represent the practice of this basic hope in freedom at the heart of existence. They protect the person as much as possible from the danger of failing to make the final act of hope in the decisive moments of his history of darkness and menacing despair.

This courageous hope however is itself faith in the properly theological sense of the term. Many theologians will readily admit that this hopeful courage has the character of a 'trusting belief', of a kind of provisional human form of faith properly so-called, but shrink from describing this courageous hope as itself faith, faith in revelation. They will say that this courage of absolute hope, essential as it is for a person's existence, is not yet to be described as faith, since faith in the strictly theological sense of the term is an assent to God's personal revelation, but this is not present in such a human hope as it were 'from below' and thus cannot be accepted in faith.

Conversely however the theological 'lay person' will perhaps be too quickly inclined to regard this hope as salvific faith, on the assumption that a person who seeks God in hope must certainly find him. This is true, but it does not answer the question raised by the theologian when he declares that faith, properly so-called, in revelation is necessary for salvation, appealing to Scripture, Christian tradition, and (when he thinks he cannot really see how this hope, this total courage, can itself be the response of faith) to God personally revealing himself.

But it can certainly be said (and it can be admitted that the merely apparently naive lay person is right in this) that such hope is in fact faith in revelation, even though only in a rudimentary form that needs to develop into its full nature. Why? First of all, it must be remembered that freedom is always also an acceptance of what is concealed, unconsidered, in a decision of freedom. Freedom is always acceptance of a 'risk', always takes on more than it explicitly and reflectively intends. This is true especially of *that* act of courageous hope which is being considered here. For here man's one whole and never completely explicable existence is staked on God's incomprehensibility and freedom. Hope is centred on the uttermost reality, on everything, in fact on God himself, transcending all particular individual realities and individual goods which man encounters in the course of his history. That it is possible to hope in this way not merely for a great deal or for one individual reality after another; that hope is of God in himself; that the movement of mind and freedom, transcending all individual realities that can be grasped successively, does not in the last resort peter out into the void or need eventually to come to a stop at any individual reality, however significant, as the sole really possible fulfillment, at a 'creaturely' good, but will reach God himself, the original fullness and creative ground of all individual realities; that God himself is the absolute future of our hope: these things do not amount simply to an obvious possibility of our own, but to a gift that might be refused, purely and simply grace. God himself is the innermost dynamism of this boundless movement of hope toward himself.

The very fact that God himself thus becomes by grace the dynamism and goal of our hope means that revelation has taken place. Grace, given to spirit as such, the possibility of hope founded on grace, anticipating God himself as its goal, this is revelation. It need not be explicitly grasped *as such* or explicitly distinguished from the rest of the experience of the spiritual subject of freedom, nor need it be expressly understood as distinguishable on each occasion from an isolated individual event. But this in no way alters the fact that it is a question of really personal divine revelation. It does not in fact take the form directly of the communication of certain propositions, but starts at the innermost core of the free spirit-person, opens up the latter in his dynamism toward the immediacy of God and thus gives him courage to hope for everything, that is, for God himself. When this innermost dynamism of man is accepted in freedom, when it is not diverted as a result of false modesty (implying a deep-seated secret fear of life) to a particular good as its ultimate goal, then what is described theologically as faith is *ipso facto* present.

Again, this acceptance in freedom of boundless and absolute hope must not be understood primarily as a single explicitly religious individual occurrence. When a person is faithful without any reservations to the dictate of his conscience, when in a final decision (despite all disappointments and adversities of his earthly experience) he does not reject an ultimate and absolute hope, then he surrenders in hope to the unrestricted, not wholly calculable movement of his spirit. At that point there is revelation and faith. From the Christian standpoint, what is present there is the Holy Spirit, whether this can be explained in express terms or not. This courageously hopeful acceptance of one's own existence (which is released into the salvific incomprehensibility of God and his freedom) can take place in the midst of the dull ordinary routine of the average person, since even this ordinary average person cannot avoid such final decisions, even though they generally occur very unobtrusively. Consequently such a faith in courageous absolute hope is certainly something that can occur even where religion does not occur or scarcely occurs in thematic form. Such a faith can be present even when a person, for whatever reasons, hesitates to give a name to the incomprehensible and ineffable character of his existence. Courageous hope, which is real faith, is required everywhere and is found even among those who are merely anonymous Christians. Actual faith in the full sense of the term is possible only in free hope, which is absolute courage; and, conversely, such absolute courage of unconditional hope is itself faith in the Christian sense.

We must however also consider the courage of hope (which is faith) from quite a different aspect. We must think about the courage for explicitly Christian faith, for explicitly Christian hope. We might then get the impression that Christian faith with its almost incalculably great quantity of doctrinal propositions, dogmas, etc., in all Christian denominations, despite all denominational differences of opinion, is something quite different from the faith in hope of which we have hitherto been speaking. It might be thought that the courage required for the hopeful acceptance of existence as one and whole, oriented to the incomprehensibility of God, is something quite different from, more simple and more obvious than, the courage to cope in faith with the complicated doctrinal fabric of Christianity with its detailed theology.

Of course the one courage and the other are not simply identical. Not only from the evidence of solid everyday experience, but also in the light of the conviction of Christianity itself, it is certainly possible for a person to have that innermost faith in courageous hope for the totality of his existence as oriented to God, to realize it freely in the commonplace routine of his duty and love and yet *inculpably* to be unable to produce *that* courage which is required in principle from the Christian for faith in regard to Christian teaching as a whole. In the vast confusion of religious and ideological opinions which are part of his life's situation, in view of the intellectual difficulties involved in the understanding of the Christian faith as subtly formulated and so articulated as to be almost incomprehensible, it is certainly possible for a person to abandon that faith without any real fault of his own and to take up toward Christian teaching the attitude of indifference and scepticism widespread today among both educated and uneducated people. But in principle it must be said that the courage for Christian faith properly speaking is nothing but the concreteness of the courageous hope of which we have been speaking up to now. In the last resort then it is a question of the same courage and the two forms of courage, which can certainly be distinguished, differ in fact only more or less as the seed differs from the flower.

In order to appreciate this, we must now ask what exactly Christianity teaches in its message, if the latter is grasped at its deepest level. Our answer can be given in two parts.

First, Christianity declares explicitly precisely what we have indicated up to now as the 'content' of the courageously hopeful faith on which we reflected here as best we could. It states then that we may hope that futility, darkness, and death by no means have the last word, that we may hope absolutely and boundlessly, that we are hoping for God himself and experience him in the unrestrictedness and absoluteness of this hope. It states that we may and must have the courage still to hope even if we have offered to this hope a desperate refusal in what is described in Christian terms as guilt and sin. It tells us that in this hope we may accept forgiveness particularly when our sin is hopeless and insurmountable as far as we ourselves are concerned. This courage, which, sustained by God himself, constantly breaks through the banality of our ordinary life and the weary scepticism of our mind, may be difficult and may call on the very last resources of our heart, resources which in fact are no longer our own. But in this respect the courage for hope that is in our existence and the courage of Christian faith are in the last resort the same thing. It may also be true that the religious explicitness of this hopeful courage within Christianity (as distinct from anonymous faith existing in the secular world outside Christianity) not only, as is certainly true, incites and fosters that anonymous courage for life of an absolute character which is faith, but also up to a point creates a new difficulty for it, akin to the difficulties which an explicit theory of action can create for the spontaneous carrying out of this action instinctively and without reflection.

Second, in addition to this statement to the effect that the one and the other form of the courage of faith are really the same thing, distinguished only as an unthematic and a considered realization of existence, there is in Christianity a second fundamental statement: the statement about Jesus Christ. But what does this statement about Jesus crucified and risen really say? Properly speaking, only that here in this man doomed to death the absolute hope which was his and is ours was really achieved, reached its goal; that the consummation of the hope that is also ours became palpable and historical also for us in what we grasp in faith as Jesus' resurrection; that the fulfillment of our hope, which is the heart of our existence, has been promised to us by God in Jesus as also historically irrevocable. This is not the place to make clear that what has just been said about Jesus itself contains the rudiments of the classical orthodox Christology of all Christian churches. That ought of course to be explained in greater detail than is possible here.

If however we start out from the thesis, simply assumed here, which certainly relieves the dogmatic conscience of the ordinary Christian who is not a professional theologian, then the situation of the Christian today in regard to faith, his courage for faith, is relatively simple. He takes hold on Jesus, crucified and risen, on him who is plunged into the radical powerlessness of death and as saved is known in the faith of his disciples and of all Christendom; he grasps him then precisely as the historical happening of what he grasps for himself by hope in that courage of which we spoke in the first part of our reflections as the ultimate achievement of our existence.

Ultimate courage for existence and explicitly Christian faith in Jesus, crucified and risen, are not therefore two areas of the one Christian faith brought together externally as lying alongside each other. What really happens is that Christian faith grasps as fulfilled and achieved in Jesus and there also promised by God to *us* what the Christian (and, in fact, any human being) hopes for himself when he accepts in hope his own existence at the very point at which it is plunged into the incomprehensibility of both God and his own death. Despite the possibility and necessity of a thematic distinction between fundamental courage for life and explicit faith in Jesus Christ, in the last resort these two factors are one. In the Christian they enter into a relationship of mutual dependence; since in his fundamental courage for life he believes in *his* 'resurrection' (that is, in being redeemed in his own death), he believes in the resurrection of Jesus, which for him is not then a miraculous coincidence within the field of his purely external historical experience, but the historical manifestation of the structure of his own innermost existence grasped in hope. Since he is human, he gives his assent in faith and hope to the Son of Man, crucified and risen in Jesus. But likewise, conversely: since with the disciples of Jesus and a worldwide history of faith of Christendom in past and present he finds courage for faith that Jesus in his death fell into God's redeeming freedom and not into the empty void, the Christian has also the courage expressly to profess his own hope, which he always realizes (if not perhaps explicitly) in his existence, so far as he does not surrender himself in a final culpable despair. Since the Christian believes in the *God*-man, he has also the courage to believe in hope in himself and in his supreme possibility, the possibility of reaching the absolute God as his own most intimate life.

Of course, over and above its innermost core, which is related to its ultimate realization of existence in the courage of hope purely and simply, the Christian faith contains many individual statements, especially about the community of those who believe in Jesus as God's historically palpable self-promise to us (that is, about the Church), about the sacraments as the concrete realization of the Church in the life of the individual, about Christian life and, thus, about Christian morality. But all these further dogmatic and moral theological statements, so far as they become relevant and binding in the light of particular situations in the life of the individual, can always be differentiated at a variety of levels and thus related to and derived from this ultimate faith in the risen Jesus, a faith in Jesus himself which for the Christian is his fundamental courage for life. Hence there is no need to speak here about all these varied explications of Christian faith.

It can happen in the light of his concrete possibilities and situations in life that the individual Christian in his fundamental courage for life does not succeed in actively linking the derivations and references in particular statements of faith to the centre of his faith in Jesus, the Risen One. He should not then deny these individual statements, for he has neither the right nor the obligation to do so in view of the faith of Christendom as a whole; but for the time being he may patiently leave them aside and simply entrust the further explication of his own actively realized faith in the explicit totality of the Church's faith to the further development of his own sense of faith, a development to which he remains open in principle.

It is by no means so certain that we really have an ultimate and total courage for life centred on our existence as definitively achieved. For such courage is always the act of our freedom in the depth of our life. But a person can fail to accomplish this act, however firmly or defiantly he stands up to the thousand details and individual tasks of his life. But when there is such a courage for total hope in the success of our one whole existence, in the success which itself is grace and rooted in the incalculable freedom of another—of God—and precisely in this way hoped for in the ultimate courage of existence, then faith in the Christian sense is present and achieved in freedom. But when a person looking to Jesus, crucified and risen, accepts as historically palpable and as confirming his ultimate courage for life the answer to the question raised by his hopeful courage, then Christian faith is present in its explicit and proper form. This kind of human and explicitly Christian courage of absolute hope is both difficult and easy.

14

CHRISTIAN DYING

I. PROLIXITAS MORTIS

1. Introductory Preliminary Remarks

Reflections on Christian dying are prior to eschatology properly speaking, although they are on its borderline. This means on the one hand that theological reflection on dying must refer to those phenomena of human life which are not really part of man's definitive mode of existence in his consummation, but belong to the life of history in the present world and to a freedom not yet fulfilled, and can consequently be experienced in principle in the way in which human experience, enlightened by revelation, is related to other factors of human life and its history of freedom. But on the other hand, despite all experience of dying, we can speak appropriately of Christian dying in the light of the event of death and the dawn of eternal life only by looking to death itself as such and to the permanence of the eschatological consummation which it involves. The experience of dying can thus always be lived and understood in a Christian way only in the light of the knowledge of faith in regard to the condition of being dead and to the final consummation. How these two elements of dying can be coordinated with each other in a Christian death and what hermeneutical principles result from this mutual relationship are questions which would have to be discussed at the beginning of eschatology properly speaking. In this reflection then death will be discussed as the advent of consummation only insofar as this is indispensable for the understanding of Christian dying. If and insofar as we must say of Christian death substantially what is usually said about death in dogmatic theology, this is unavoidable from the nature of the case and creates no special difficulties, as long as it takes into account a preliminary glance at general and individual eschatology. But the fact remains that our theme here properly speaking is Christian dying. And to that extent it is possible to discuss here particular themes which are not usually discussed in a dogmatic theology of death.

For a great variety of reasons arising from the nature of the case and from traditional habits the theme of *dying and death* is never treated completely and comprehensively at any one point in a Christian dogmatic theology, even though this as such would not be impossible, if it is appropriate to conceive a Christian doctrine of faith as an 'anthropology' of salvation history in the comprehensive sense of the term and thus perhaps to concentrate all the themes related to dying and death at one point. However that may be, it is possible to find in different parts of this dogmatic theology important statements on dying and death which must be presupposed here and cannot really be repeated in all their breadth and depth. We may refer particularly to the treatise on man as sinner and to the treatise on the cross, dying, death, and descent of Christ into the underworld. In these two treatises especially, what is essential about dying and death is said, since both are understood in a Christian sense only if they are seen and realized as both the manifestation of the sin of the world and of the sinful condition even of the Christian and also a dying with the redeeming death of Christ. This means that on the one hand not everything mentioned in these two treatises can be entirely omitted here, but on the other hand these things may and must be repeated only in a kind of formal abstractness referring back to their full content in the original treatises. But conversely a number of things must be discussed in regard to the theme of dying and death which could certainly find a place in other parts of a dogmatic theology. For, fundamentally, there is no element of a Christian anthropology which, if it is really to be understood in a Christian sense, need not be confronted with the doctrine of death in a Christian understanding, whether this happens or is overlooked in a traditional theology. The orientation of human existence as a whole to death is in reality, as a co-determining factor, part of any treatise on a dimension of human existence, of a theology of mind and knowledge, of a theology of freedom, of a theology of human fellowship and love, of a Christian description of the basic realizations of human existence (fear, hope, joy, despair, trust, etc.), and so on, since this 'being for death' co-determines everything in human life and imparts to the latter its uncertainty, its openness to mystery and its ultimate seriousness. This more or less transcendental occurrence of death in the totality of human life, the whole of anthropology as theology of death, can of course be put forward here only in a very rudimentary fashion and in a somewhat arbitrary selection. Otherwise the whole of dogmatic theology would have to be repeated here.

2. Fundamental Option and Clinical Death

The point of the theme of Christian dying to be discussed here would be missed from the very outset if death were seen only in the generally accepted sense, as consisting in those biological and medical occurrences which directly and immediately closely in time lead to death, to being dead. Specifically, Christian dying (insofar as it is supposed to be not sheer suffering, but a Christian deed in freedom) cannot simply and certainly be located in the last hours of a human being, since as human and Christian he may perhaps be no longer capable of such an act of dying and yet the latter may not simply happen (even though this act may be conceived under certain conditions as produced without much reflection and 'anonymously', depending on the individual's disposability even within the history of his freedom). For this reason dying must be recognized as an event that is taking place throughout the whole of life, even though at all times with varying intensity and with a fresh application of the freedom that accepts death in life or protests against it. This *prolixitas mortis* (as Gregory the Great describes it) must be borne in mind. In this connection we must at once issue a warning against a possible misunderstanding: we should not ascribe to death as an event coming at the *end* of life and only there peculiarities (apart from those to be mentioned later) which we deny in principle to other moments of time within the life of a human being.

At the moment (immediately before or in or 'after') of death everything possible can 'happen' that we regard as conceivable, that we may presume, for which we can appeal to accounts given to us by those who have endured more or less the agony of dying and nevertheless escaped. But in principle to ascribe to the moment of medical decease a theological significance that cannot belong to any moment in the rest of life, to assert that in the moment of clinical death and only at that point there occurs man's real and comprehensive act of freedom in the total disposal of his existence for or against God, since this passing alone offers an adequate situation and opportunity for it: this is an assertion which is not probable in the light of empirical psychology and biology,[1] can be supported only with the aid of ideas savouring of mythology, and which theologically is neither probable nor necessary. If and insofar as the total disposal of freedom in regard to our own existence before God (for or against him) has to be understood as localized at all as such at a definite point or at definite points in time, although in our reflection we can never or (apart from a mystical 'confirmation in grace', traditionally accepted in mystical theology as possible, even though considerable misgiving must be expressed in this connection because of man's continuing and always threatened history of freedom) rarely determine with certainty where exactly such a moment lies within the temporal course of our life's history; that moment need not in any case simply coincide with the moment of clinical death, since, as we said, empirically this is extremely unlikely in the majority of cases and theologically in no way necessary. It is the same even if we take an optimis-

---

[1] Medical and psychological scrutiny of dying people and those who have been 'rescued' after 'death' from heart failure may yield interesting factual conclusions. These facts permit us to hope that in very many cases of a slow passing there occurs a phase in which the individual's physical condition makes his personal surrender to his destiny of death easier and consequently that the basic act of the history of human freedom is possible also at the time of clinical death. But this in no way alters the fact that there is no return to the present life after a real death (from the very nature of actual death as the definitive end of the history of freedom) and that all accounts of dying are accounts of experiences before death and that there is no guarantee that what sometimes happens on these occasions must always happen.

The question whether individuals have been 'raised from the dead' in the sense that they really died and yet returned to this earthly life (Lazarus, etc.) is one that cannot be examined here. It would be impossible to clarify the many preliminary questions. Certainly those who were resuscitated in this way had not died in a theological sense of death as the finality of a personal life's decision. But it is impossible to explain here what this 'not dying' means in the concrete, not even on the assumption that the stories of raising from the dead in Scripture and in the lives of the saints can claim historical validity.

tic view of salvation for as many as possible or for all human beings (and this is the hidden motivation for this false hypothesis) and assume that they are saved despite the empirical appearance of their sinful life. For on the one hand our general thesis to the contrary does not exclude the possibility in individual cases of a more or less exact coincidence in time of the final basic option for God and clinical death, and on the other hand it is possible to think of a sufficient number of other ways of an explicit or of an unthematic character in which this fundamental option could occur within the course of life. The assumption behind this understanding of a totally free decision for or against God that does not need to happen mysteriously at the very moment of physical death (as, for example, Ladislaus Boros seems to think) lies in the fact that we understand and take seriously the *prolixitas mortis* in life itself as the permanent and inescapable even though unthematic confrontation of freedom with death in the whole course of its history.

3. Experiences of Oncoming Death

We are not yet going to provide the ultimate existential-ontological and theological justification of this idea of *prolixitas mortis* throughout the whole of life in the light of the nature of human freedom. (This will be attempted in section 2 of the second part of this chapter.) At this point it is a question only of straightforward indications of various experiences which herald the coming of death and do so from very different aspects.

(*a*) There is something like an experience of death even when there is no question of suffering and sickness in the proper and ordinary sense of the terms. The transcendental constitution of man, who in all his mental achievements of knowledge, freedom, production and in all other intellectual-personal achievements aims at a particular categorial object and at the same time (even though generally only unthematically) surpasses it, produces to a continually increasing extent the experience of the finiteness of his milieu and environment and thus, too, of himself and consequently that 'disappointment' as a basic mood of our existence which the Preacher in the Old Testament described in radical terms at an early stage. This very experience itself is a presence of death in which all the 'disappointing' individual realities of life perish and thus the finiteness of the subject itself becomes a matter of radical experience. Here there is an experience of dying inwardly that is not an individual occurrence here and there in the course of life, but a basic mood permeating all things, whether the latter is accepted in freedom and resolution or not.

(*b*) This basic mood makes itself felt as warning and herald of death whenever suffering, failure, and the like are experienced, as something that even an average, everyday consciousness regards as what ought not to be. All this (which need not be presented here in detail in its thousand shapes) is every time a partial death, no matter what attitude a person takes toward it. Something perishes that the person judges to be possible, realizable, and desirable, and yet he is deprived of it. Hence the theodicy relevant to suffering in the world, possible only in the hope inspired by faith, is an element in the theodicy of death, and vice versa. At the same time we should be under no illusion that bravery, rationality, and so on could *so* remold and transform all these disappointing experiences, that the 'maturity' of a person could be so effective and assured and thus the success of 'heroically' coping with death could be established. Consequently there will be no attempt at this point to produce (once again) a theodicy of death in terms only of an unconditional surrender of man to the incomprehensibility of God in what in the last resort is a self-evident hope; it would in fact be nothing but the understanding of faith, hope, and love in regard to God's incomprehensibility in face of death, before which alone the meaning of these basic Christian achievements can be made radically clear. This is true then also of that *prolixitas mortis* which consists in suffering of every kind in individual and social life.

(*c*) This infiltration of death is felt most clearly in real (that is, dangerous) illness, for it is the danger of biological death as directly perceptible. That is why in the Old Testament also death through sickness as distinct from a smooth fading out of life at an advanced age was regarded as particularly hard and problematical and liberation from sickness as a special mark of God's favour. Even apart from all the discoveries of modern psychosomatic medicine, sickness is distinguished as a total human phenomenon and not merely as a disturbance of man's biological dimension, because in the light of our very ordinary experience (even though not clearly verifiable

in every individual case) it threatens and reduces even man's intellectual and free subjectivity, diminishes or withdraws from man the
possibility of reacting to it, so that this helplessness of the subject
itself is an element in a really human and not merely biological
sense. But in this way and not as a purely biological disturbance
sickness points and tends toward that endpoint of life in which man
as a whole is deprived of himself and his sovereignty, and which we
call death. The experience of a sickness rendering the whole person
helpless up to a point itself shows that human death is not to be
identified simply with clinical death understood in terms of natural
science with its immediate causes. By its individual peculiarities
also sickness proves to be as such preeminently *prolixitas mortis*.
The impossibility of completely foreseeing and manipulating sickness; the helplessness into which it thrusts us; the special, remote
relationship to society into which it forces us; the solitude and the
curtailment of possibilities of communication; the weakening of the
capacity for active self-direction; the permanent uncertainty of any
interpretation of its 'sense' and its causes within the total structure
of a human life; the burden it imposes on the people around the sick
person; the withdrawal from an efficiency-oriented society; the sick
person's experience of being useless to others; the impossibility of
integrating sickness meaningfully into a plan of life, and many other
peculiarities of sickness make it a herald of death.

4. Memento mori

In the light of this constant presence of death in the whole course of
life Christian wisdom has always been aware of a *memento mori*. If
and insofar as dying and death amount not only to a purely passively
endured happening at the end of life, but also to an active deed of
man (as will be explained more precisely in the second part of this
chapter) and if this act, as we said, cannot be located simply at the
moment of the advent of death in the medical sense, then for the
Christian, coming death cannot be something which does not concern him 'for the time being', something that he might now suppress
as much as possible. Within life he has to live with death. This
happens primarily and fundamentally through all those accomplish-
ments of freedom in which a person accepts with resignation the

finiteness of his milieu and environment and of himself in hope of the incomprehensible and thus abandons the attempt to regard as absolute anything that can be experienced in itself; this sort of thing happens also when someone simply accepts as unanswerable the question of his ultimate identity and his relationship to God as sinner and (as he hopes) justified before God. This ultimate acquiescence, too, is an anticipation of that 'night in which no man can work'. But, in addition to these basic, even though unthematic realizations of a *memento mori,* in Christian life and in the life of the Church there is rightly an explicit remembrance of the prospect of death. There is no need to describe here in detail these ways of keeping death in mind, of explicit preparation for death, of organizing life with an eye on death, etc. Despite their derivative character, they are of great importance, since in the light of man's nature the reflex thematicizing and practising of basic realizations, which, whether accepted or rejected, are in any case inescapably present in human life, is of great importance for the very reason that it renders more secure retrospectively the true and radical acceptance of these basic realizations by fundamental freedom and because man is bound in principle (of course, only insofar as it is possible) to make these things secure.

5. *Styles of Dying*

In the history of the Christian life and also in the history of the life of mankind as a whole there can be found obviously varying styles of dying. The method and custom of a particular society presents to its individual members a definite style of dying, to be preferred as right and proper, at least for the 'normal' case. In Christendom, too, there are such 'rules for dying' and they have not always simply remained the same. In particular a certain style of dying was expected from those holding important positions in the Church, a style in which their rank, their responsibility for others, their Christian faith, could be presented as an example. Formerly, a Christian died within his family circle, said goodbye there, blessed them, had a few last words to say, asserted his orthodox faith and his Christian hope, etc. It is very different today, when, as a result of thrusting the sick into the impersonal atmosphere of public hospitals, dying has largely become styleless. This may be deplorable and need not simply be accepted as inevitable; but it is part of that lack of style (that is, shapelessness) which we accept as belonging to death and thus also to dying, which in the last resort is beyond our control. The individual styles of dying possible to a Christian and up to a point being successively eliminated in the course of history need not be described here in detail. Their alteration and the continually changing concrete circumstances of dying, which determine this style on each occasion, are also part of that radical uncontrollability that is proper to death. Thus all that remains to be noted here in theological terms—as distinct from those of a (perhaps ecclesial) cultural history of dying—is that the Christian is bound to the Christian Church's style of dying in the 'normal case', that is, when the concrete possibilities are available and can be realized without recourse to extraordinary measures, insofar as he is 'bound' to die in an explicitly Christian way. Concretely, this means that he is expected to receive the 'last sacraments'. An attitude of this kind, in which there is also realized an indispensable readiness to accept death, is present (to put it circumspectly) according to general Christian feeling also when the dying person can regard himself as being at peace with God, as justified, and thus the 'last sacraments' are not for him the obligatory mode of sacramental reconciliation with God and the Church. The exact form of this obligation to an ecclesial 'style of dying' can be examined in a work of moral theology.

6. Advent of Death

The question of the advent of death, that is, the criteria according to which a person is already dead or is still living although unconscious, is in itself primarily a question of a natural empirical anthropology. But it has theological consequences for the Church's practice: for example, for the decision as to whether a Christian can still be given the anointing of the sick. Since and insofar as death in a theological sense is the end of an historically personal life in freedom, it can be said today that death has come at the point where the functions of the brain as the foundation of this life have irreparably ceased, no matter whether other 'organs' of the person continue to 'live' or not.

II. DYING SEEN IN THE LIGHT OF DEATH

1. *Official Statements of the Church*

We come at once to the official statements of the Church on death. The reason for this is simply that the Christian tradition on death cannot really be set out in all its fullness at a later stage, so that it is possible only to put forward the essentials of this tradition in a certain formal abstractness.

(*a*) What strikes us first all in these official statements is that not all aspects of death or, consequently, of dying find adequate expression in this teaching. Of course Jesus' death as the crucial salvation event is frequently mentioned, but at the same time the real nature of this death is not clearly considered nor is there any attempt to deduce from it statements of the magisterium about human death as such. It is also shown there that death is the consequence, the 'penalty', of original sin, but its positive significance for salvation is scarcely given clear expression in the statements of the magisterium. In addition to this hamartiological aspect of death, little more is stressed than the fact that 'all' human beings must 'die' and with death the mental-personal history of man passes directly into the definitive permanence of the subject and its history before God; in other words, the idea of a migration of souls, of reincarnation, etc., is incompatible with a Christian understanding of man and his death. In view of these gaps in the teaching of the magisterium on death, it is not very important how we are to arrange these somewhat amorphous statements. Some observations on the meaning and limits of these statements of the magisterium are here directly linked with the presentation of this teaching.

(*b*) Death is seen as penalty (*poena*) of original sin (DS 146, 222, 231, 372, 1511–1512, 1521, 2617). This teaching need not be described here in detail. It is sufficient to refer to the treatise on sin. Insofar as 'original sin' as compared with grave personal sin can be called 'sin' only analogously, can certainly be understood as an historical and universal condition of man's freedom and must be regarded as an element in the 'sin of the world' (while, admittedly, the lack of grace resulting from sin must be seen as part of this situation in the sense that there would be this lack of grace from the dawn of history if it had not been surpassed by the redemption of Christ), death, too, is a penalty only in an analogous sense, a penalty really surpassed by the death of Christ and thus turned as such into a redemptive event. The *relativity* of the hamartiological interpretation of death (insofar as it comes from 'Adam') is not explicitly brought out in the texts of the magisterium on death as penalty for sin, but it may be assumed as implicit in them if the other statements of Scripture and tradition on the positive meaning of the death of Christ (and of Mary) and on death as dying with Christ (cf. DS 72, 485, 3901) are given their full force. Neither is this 'penalty' to be understood as an additional element, as God's reaction attached as it were to sin extrinsically, but as a consequence of the intrinsic nature of sin itself. Nor can the penal character of death consist in the appointed ending of man's history of freedom *as such*. For it is part of the nature of a creaturely history of freedom to reach a definitive consummation in a unity of restraint and freedom, a consummation which might as such also be called 'death' and which is prior to the distinction between guilt and innocence. It will be explained at a later stage what exactly is the element that enters into this 'death' in the concrete history of man and makes this 'death' into death in the traditional sense as penalty for sin (as understood in the doctrine of original sin). Then it must also be seen how the character of death as penalty for sin can be compatible with the teaching against Baius and others (DS 1955, 1978, 2617) that death is a 'natural' characteristic of man.

(*c*) With death comes the *finality of man's basic option*, which permeates his history and in which he disposes of himself in confrontation with God, set before him by world and history (DS 410, 839, 858, 926, 1002, 1306, 1488).[2] With this official teaching of the Church, which, with certain qualifications still to be indicated, must be understood as the teaching of faith, a number of theories are rejected as incompatible with the Christian understanding of man and the seriousness of a unique history. These include the theory of an apocatastasis (at least and certainly also merely as a firm, theoretical statement, as distinct from a hope, that respects God's sovereign and unknown disposition and the openness of every history of

---

[2] Cf. also *Collectio Lacensis* VII, 567; Pius XII: AAS 47 (1955) 64–65.

freedom known to us)[3] or the theory of a migration of souls (metempsychosis, reincarnation). From both aspects however it can be said with some caution that this doctrine of the uniqueness and permanent validity of every personal history secured by death is certainly true when such a history of freedom has actually occurred. Every human being and Christian has to admit that in his own life he must allow concretely for such an absolute and definitive history of freedom has actually occurred. Every human being and Christian has to admit that in his own life he must allow concretely for such an absolute and definitive history of freedom and can never discard the burden of such a responsibility, that he must presume such a history of freedom in every other human being when he encounters rational life in freedom in the course of his secular experience. But, despite the declaration of the Fifth Lateran Council (DS 1440, cf. 2766, 3771, 3998) and the ordinary understanding of faith in the Church, it can be said that in the last resort we do not know how or whether this doctrine of the always unique history of freedom passing through death into finality is to be applied to those who die *before* the moment at which, on the basis of ordinary experience, we would be inclined to ascribe to them an actual decision of freedom in the radical sense; nor do we know whether in fact everyone who is 'adult' in the sense generally understood really makes *that* decision of freedom of which the official teaching of the Church says that it is raised by death into finality. From the Christian standpoint, all that we can really say must be about the 'normal case' of humans and Christian life, we must take this seriously on each occasion for ourselves, read official teachings of the Church which seem to go beyond this normal case more or less as broad, general statements, not intended in the last resort to express anything purely and simply about marginal, if very numerous, cases; for the rest, we must admit an ignorance which in the last resort is obvious from the nature of the case.

[3] At the same time of course we are disregarding our profession of faith on the eternal redeemed state of Christ and of Mary and the teaching of theologians that the saints solemnly canonized by the Church have certainly gained eternal happiness. But it must be remembered that the good news of salvation and of God's victorious salvific will certainly does not permit us unconditionally to expect that the possibilities of life on the one hand and of death on the other form part of the content of the Christian message in precisely the same way.

The Church's official teaching says nothing about whether death as biological demise (understood of course within the totality of the one person) implies as such the finality of personal history or whether the coincidence of biological death and the end of personal history arises simply from an independent decree of God, who could also have decreed otherwise without destroying the unity of man's body-soul nature. This question has been disputed in theology up to the present time. But, as will be repeated later, it will be appropriate to opt, with Aquinas, for the first alternative and also read the official statements of the Church in the light of this assumption.

(*d*) The Church's official statements on death include also its *universality* (DS 1512), which extends as widely as the universality of original sin. In view of the literary genre of these ancient narratives, the old question as to whether Enoch and Elijah were exempted by a special privilege from this universal law has ceased to be relevant today. The same certainly holds for the question of whether, according to Scripture and tradition, those human beings whom we think of as existing at the end of the whole course of history will die or enter 'alive' into the consummation of history. In any case they will experience 'death' in the sense that it is the consummation decreed by God of their history of freedom. And, beyond this, there is no more to be said except that all, living or dead, come in the end to the consummating immediacy of God in judgment. Insofar as Paul, too, speaks in the light of the hypothesis of his eschatological imagination (1 Cor. 15:51), it is impossible to deduce from his work any dogmatic decision on this question.

2. Death as Close of the History of Freedom in the Presence of the Pardoning God

(*a*) The doctrine of Sheol, as found at least in the older strata of the Old Testament, speaks of a shadowy continued existence of the dead. But if in the first place we read these texts 'literally' (which is not the same as 'correctly') they suggest that these dead are remote after death from God, deprived of his power and care, of no account. But if this doctrine is not to create great difficulties for us in regard to the inerrancy of the inspired Scripture of the Old Testament, this imagery must actually be an expression of the devout person's con-

viction in Old Testament times that with death an absolute definitiveness and a real end is reached. Despite its vivid imagery, the
doctrine of Sheol does not really provide a view of a world beyond
death, is not meant to indicate the substance of a 'hereafter' as such,
but refers purely and simply to death as such, in order to see it in the
radicalness in which death brings to an end the life of man as one and
whole. If the later parts of the Old Testament (in the doctrine of the
resurrection and in a differentiation of the lot of individuals hereafter
according to moral standards) and the New Testament (in developing further belief in the resurrection of the just and in view of Jesus'
resurrection and the indissoluble union of the believer with the
Lord) offer the dying person a hope, this hope, arising from the basic
experience of the Old Testament of the radicalness of death, cannot
consist in the fact that the dying person is promised a 'further' life
that on the one hand might be understood as 'living on' with different means but in the last resort in the same style, and that on the
other hand would be bound to raise the question of why in this
further life there might not be new moral decisions, conversion, etc.
Only on the ground of the radicalness with which the earlier strata of
the Old Testament bring the life of the whole person to an end at
death can the later hope of an eternal life hereafter be rightly understood.

This life is not a continuation of earthly life; on the contrary, it is
only by this afterlife that the impossibility becomes clear of escaping
the radical importance and the inalienable seriousness of the responsibility of freedom even by a flight into the void, since this eternal
life is nothing but the finality (as redemption or perdition) of this
earthly life and its subject possessing it in freedom. If we think in
terms of biblical theology and at the same time evaluate positively
the Old Testament's radical experience of death and yet (in the same
light however) go on to the New Testament hope, it cannot be a
question of the conception of an immaterial intellectual subject sur-
viving and 'going on' as soul after the biological death of the body,
but of seeing the one human being radically affected by death and
nevertheless inescapably burdened and hoping with an absolute responsibility of freedom. That is not to say that a positive appreciation of a Platonic theory of the 'immortality' of the spiritual soul is
not at all possible, particularly since even the Western Christian
tradition understands the fundamental definition of man within the

scheme of a distinction between body and soul and death accordingly as separation of body and soul (cf. DS 991, *animae separatae;* and DS 1000, *ante resumptionem suorum corporum,* etc.).

From the original starting point of Scripture, however, it is understandable that the one fate of the one human being should be seen as a resurrection of the dead, a resurrection that does not come subsequently as the lot of the body as additional to that of the soul; that the doctrine of the judgment (in the last resort impossible to systematize) sometimes places that judgment as an event occurring at the death of the individual and sometimes as what happens for all at the same time at the end of world history. If all this is considered without tacitly assuming a positivistic understanding of revelation, then it must be said that for the theology of Scripture death sets an essential internal limit as a *consummation of freedom* from within and not merely an end of the history of moral freedom assigned arbitrarily by God 'on the occasion' of biological death. Otherwise the ancient doctrine of Sheol could have no *positive* meaning for us, but would raise the unanswerable question as to why it had not been simply erroneous even in its earlier form. The later teaching in the Old Testament and particularly in the New on an eternal life of a positive character could not be understood as a radicalization of what was really meant by the doctrine of Sheol, but would be merely additional, leaving it still obscure why a supplementary teaching had not developed only out of the experience of Jesus' resurrection, but had also been present at an earlier stage. If it were to be said here that this teaching had developed out of the conviction of Yahweh's irrevocable fidelity to the people of the covenant and from the feeling that a history leading pointlessly to breakdowns must have a meaning in the sight of this God of fidelity, this would be merely another way of saying what had hitherto been meant: there is only this one earthly history, which is ended by death as its internal limit, and this history has an irremoveable finality and permanency before God.

It is from this standpoint alone that the fundamental meaning of particular texts, especially of the New Testament, is really to be appreciated. The final sentence of the judge of the world with its irrevocable consequences is related to man's deeds accomplished in his earthly life and to nothing else (Matt. 25:34–46, etc.). The time of earthly life is the day that is followed by the night when no one can work (John 9:4). We must work 'in the body', 'while we have the chance', and this alone is the standard of the final judgment (Gal. 6:10; 2 Cor. 5:10; Rev. 2:10). The free sovereignty of God frequently stressed by Scripture, with which he decides on the death of a person, need not mean that the restriction of the opportunity of merit is based on a divine decree external and additional to the nature of death, but is assured simply by the fact that man's death as such by its very nature has in itself a passive, incalculable element not completely at man's disposal.

If we disregard the always sparse remaining supporters of an apocatastasis doctrine from Origen onward or interpret this doctrine as the expression of a universal *hope* impossible to work out in theory and consequently permissible, then it can certainly be said that the Christian sense of faith was always and unambiguously sure that death is the end of the history of human freedom, in which that history is raised up into an enduring finality. As we said, it remained and still remains a matter of dispute in this Christian tradition whether the finality of history arises from the nature of death as a biological event (affecting however the totality of man) or whether this death and the end of personal history are linked with each other by a supplementary decree of God. It has also been said that the first alternative is accepted here, because otherwise it is quite impossible in the last resort to see that this connection can be revealed or how it can be revealed. (If someone wanted to say that this link, despite the lack of an essential connection between death and the end of the history of Jesus, arose with his death as *such* and consequently this link had to be accepted also with all other human beings, then it must be recalled that the actual experience of Jesus' resurrection—however much it must be understood as something new and fundamental—is also and indissolubly associated with the belief in a future resurrection of the just: a conviction existing even before Jesus' time, which must have been formed legitimately, and, as indicated above, could have emerged only on the assumption of an essential connection between death and the end of history, even though Scripture never explicitly considers the reasons for this connection.)

(*b*) The understanding of death as the elevation of the history of freedom into its finality must take into account three factors simultaneously: the intrinsic nature of freedom; the unity of the self-realization of the corporeal-historical and spiritual-personal human being;

the precise nature of the consummation which is made possible for freedom and required of it. As a result at least of the third factor, the doctrine with which we are concerned here belongs properly to the field of the mysteries of faith and is not merely part of a philosophical anthropology. If the doctrine in question here is derived from these three factors, that is not to deny that a clear and certain understanding of the factors can equally well be conceived up to a point in the light of the conviction of this doctrine, of a conviction attained unthematically but firmly rooted in life. In its fundamental nature freedom is not the ability to do or to omit one thing or another of a categorial nature, but the basic condition of the subject in its transcendentality, in which it disposes of *itself* for finality.

Freedom thus opens up history, but this history is by no means the opportunity of being able permanently to go on into the void, to be occupied with what is irrelevant (since it is always open to revision), but is precisely the opportunity of establishing something really definitive. The inalienable responsibility imposed on the subject in its freedom, which alone makes the subject what it is as such, would not exist if the self-disposal of the subject could at any time be revised, so that each particular decision would become irrelevant since it could always be revised and replaced by another; the subject could always relieve itself of itself and its freedom, continuing into a future of empty opportunity. Freedom would possess an infinite potential which would make it, not more significant, but irrelevant in everything it really brought about. The fundamental nature of freedom is therefore the opportunity of a 'once and for all' disposal by the subject of itself, a definitive self-disposal. This uniqueness of a self-disposal, which aims at being definitive and irrevocable, in man of course has a temporal extension and dispersal throughout the multiplicity of single moments that make up the corporeally historical life of man. The uniqueness of this free self-disposal is not something lying behind man's spatio-temporal life, the latter being merely the ultimately superfluous projection of a fundamental option, timeless in itself, on the part of the subject of freedom on to the conveyor belt of time; this uniqueness occurs within time itself, but is not annulled by the multiplicity of the individual moments of time. For this very reason however the uniqueness of the one total self-disposal by the subject of freedom of itself as one and whole cannot be regarded as bypassing spatio-temporal historical life. It is pointless to think of this corporeal history of freedom as continued beyond death as the end of man's historical corporality; otherwise this self-disposal of man would be placed from the very outset and always somewhere outside his spatio-temporal history, but in such a way that this history itself would be understood as no more than an appearance spread around true freedom and concealing it. If the history of freedom continues in death after the end of corporeal history, then history properly so-called was never actually present as such in this spatio-temporal life. But a person who is down-to-earth and Christian is aware of only one history, which is true history of freedom before God and thus possesses unfathomable depth and absolute radicalness, but occurs in the course of the ordinary routine of life.

If we introduce into this context the third factor mentioned above, this both renders more acute and clarifies the problems involved in the conviction that man achieves the uniqueness of a final self-disposal in an earthly history spread over space and time and only there. If this self-determination decides on an ultimate and definitive relationship to God, who makes himself in his most intimate reality and in immediacy the ultimate content of this history of freedom and thus in particular of the finality of this history, this certainly imposes an enormous and ultimately incomprehensible burden on the problem of this unique history of freedom of a spatio-temporal subject of freedom. How can a subject of this kind, with the creaturely finiteness of his freedom and in the poverty of his spatio-temporal history, really and definitively and once and for all decide for or against this infinity of his real life, which is purely and simply God himself? But if we regard this as possible and as Christians *must* so regard it, this possibility also provides some relief to the problem with which we are concerned. A preexistence or migration of souls, the disclosure of opportunities of freedom that lie before or after or behind this corporeal history of ours, even apart from the fact that they are not comprehensible in the light of sober experience, provide no help toward a solution of the actual problems involved here. If it is a question of a decision of freedom, involving radically the infinity and permanent incomprehensibility of God in himself, then this opportunity is not made any easier to understand if we say that man can cope with it if he has a few more opportunities of freedom available to him behind, before, or after his earthly life.

The theory of a migration of souls can be attractive only if we have in mind the particular categorial contents purely of moral life: then the impression may be given that man needs more and better material on which to achieve his moral decisions than he is granted in the course of a short and miserable life. But if we consider the nature of freedom as the one self-disposal into immediacy before the incomprehensible infinity of God, an increase (that always remains finite) of the historical material provided is no answer to the basic question presented by the nature of freedom as self-disposal toward God. Even additional material always remains incommensurable with this basic nature of freedom. If we wanted to avoid this incomprehensibility of a decision for or against God as such, produced by a finite material, then no idea of a migration of souls or anything of that kind would help; all that would remain would be the possibility of a never completed realization of freedom and the denial of the Christian teaching that freedom can really have something to do with God pure and simple. But *such* a freedom would contradict the basic Christian sense that, at least by grace, we have to do with God himself and in the last resort would become irrelevant and irresponsible, since it could only continually choose options open to improvement. What has been said does not of course decide the question touched on above, whether there are not phenomena of human life that do not in fact involve any history of freedom in a Christian sense (ending of life at an embryonic stage, biological life that never comes to 'the use of reason', etc.) and whether in such a case the attainment of an eternal consummation must or can be conceived.

(*c*) The history of freedom of the subject's decision in regard to itself in its relationship to God as self-communicating grace, ending with biological death, is *in a dialectical relationship to man's disposability* which finds its radical manifestation in death. Only in the dialectic between freedom and disposability, completely radicalized in death and in such a way that the concreteness of this dialectic is still absolutely hidden from man, is the real nature of 'infralapsarian' death present, that makes it possible for death in this hidden dialectic (beyond our understanding) to be the manifestation of sin and redemption and liberation. As present in knowledge, human freedom has an infinite horizon, particularly since on the one hand in the concrete order of salvation this freedom has to do with God himself in immediacy and on the other hand this freedom is not related solely to those finite realities which it can produce or achieve in a popular sense, but at least in the form of free renunciation or unselfish recognition can be related to everything. But this infinite freedom is nevertheless finite in its concrete realization; it is faced from the outset by certain finite preconditions and restrictions of its possibility; it always has its own place. But if freedom properly so-called is not placed behind or before or after its encounter with the concrete realities which draw this freedom to themselves, then it must be said that, although it is related to the infinite God as such, this freedom retains in itself as realized the finite categorial constituents which draw it to themselves and thus always remains finite and controlled freedom. Only in this way can the consummation of freedom be the permanent finality of man's history. Over and above this, freedom is aware of being finite and under control, since it is aware of itself as set up, as initiated by an infinity which is not itself, just as the boundless transcendentality of man's knowledge does not make the latter an absolute subject, but makes him aware of his beginning as appointed by absolute being and thus of his createdness.

This disposability of finite freedom, both by its nature and also in virtue of the material of its environment and milieu drawing this freedom to itself, is experienced radically and irrepressibly in dying and death, no matter where precisely this radical experience (which must not necessarily occur at the very moment of clinical death) has possibly to be located in life. Wherever the experience is made as an act of freedom accepting its radical finiteness within the one and unique act of freedom of life, it reaches in dying and death its complete realization and manifestation. For at that point man is drawn away from himself and rendered powerless. Because he is deprived of everything of which he can dispose and the subject of freedom is withdrawn from itself, freedom is seen in the last resort as something granted and assigned. Insofar as freedom is aware of itself as finite as it is actually situated, man's radical disposability in death cannot be understood as something external to the one and unique act of freedom by which a person disposes of himself for finality; this disposability of man in death is in fact an *intrinsic* element of the one act of freedom consummated in death by which a person disposes of himself before God. Death is both man's final self-determination *and* final, irrevocable disposability,[4] even if we try to appreciate better the active-passive finalization of man and his freedom by identifying the moment at which he is rendered utterly powerless with the point in time at which clinical death occurs, while assuming the man's free self-disposal of himself takes place at some other moment within the course of life. Even then the unity of the history of freedom, to which the factor of disposability is intrinsic, would keep together these two factors in the unity of a specifically human death. This unity is also involved particularly as a result of the fact that the absolutely proper 'object' of freedom is the very acceptance or rejection of this disposability, that is, of finite creatureliness, which enters into our experience precisely through the infinite horizon of freedom.

At the same time of course this passive disposability of man conceals the nature of freedom as self-disposal. In death it seems as if man no longer has anything on which self-disposal can be achieved as the means of its self-realization or as if all former results of his individual free acts as elements of the one and entire self-disposal had been annihilated. And conversely the act of freedom in the boundless range of its possibilities can always spread the impression of an absolute autonomy and conceal the disposability of freedom, so that eventually biological death would present itself as something that really does not touch the person properly speaking and his freedom. But since the appearance exists on both sides and all appearances are deceptive, since moreover in his fatal impotence man cannot break down this impression, nor can he judge or effect the dialectical relationship between absolute powerlessness and absolute deed from a higher standpoint, particularly also since (because of the impossibility of adequate reflection) the act of freedom as such cannot be judged in its concrete reality with certainty in the light of explicit knowledge: for all these reasons death has the character of hiddenness and of an insoluble question. No one knows

[4] It is no different with suicide, which has only the semblance of a self-disposal greater than that which is present in normal death. In this respect, too, freedom acts in the light of existing factualities, not determined by ourselves, and tends toward powerlessness. The theme of suicide, incidentally, must be left to moral theology, however much it needs to be considered as a whole by an anthropology and however often it is there made to seem too easy and too simple.

concretely what sort of death he will face. He must see it as the event of active finalization of the one act of freedom of his life; he experiences the same death as the height of his powerlessness; he knows that his freedom must accept this powerlessness while hoping to the very end; he cannot tell explicitly and with certainty where and how, in living or dying, the opportunity of such an acceptance by an act of freedom has been given to him in his powerlessness and whether he has actually accepted it. Insofar as this death involves the approach of God's incomprehensible mystery, embracing both the incomprehensibility of his nature and also that of his freedom in regard to man, the incomprehensibility of death becomes definitive in its hiddenness.

3. Death as Manifestation of Sin

(*a*) Attention has already been drawn to the texts of the Church's official teaching which speak of death as the penalty for original sin. But it was also pointed out that statements of the Church's magisterium nevertheless describe death as 'natural', as a consequence of man's natural essential constitution. As the teaching of the Church and of tradition is that in the first justification (at least as achieved in baptism) not only are original sin and personal sins remitted, but also all punishment due to sin, so the traditional theological formulation was that death for the justified person had the character only of a *poenalitas* and not of a *poena,* although and even because death comes also to those who are justified. In the first place the term *poenalitas* is one that conceals rather than illuminates the problem facing us. For it is not clear how the empirically existing factuality, at least apparently permanent for all (justified and sinners) can be at one time a punishment and at another merely a *poenalitas*. Nor does the explanation that the punishment due to original sin is turned by justification into a mere *poenalitas* bring out the positive importance for salvation of the death of the justified person, an importance that cannot be denied to this death as dying with Christ and in view of Jesus' salvific death.

As far as the first problem is concerned, it can of course be said that death can be a pure *poenalitas* also because it is itself natural and a consequence of man's natural being as a biological organism.

But then the question again arises as to how death can be conceived and experienced as punishment, if it is a natural essential consequence in human existence. Certainly in human life there are particular occurrences and injuries which are contrary to man's natural being and thus can be seen and experienced under certain conditions as 'punishment'. But if such a penal character is to be assigned to death as a *universal* natural phenomenon, this penal character and the experience of it cannot be seen as related to man's natural being. But if something that ought not to be (without which 'punishment' cannot be conceived) is present in death, this can be understood only as relative to the claims which man as a being committed to a supernatural goal and endowed with the offer of God's self-communication by grace rightly raises and simply cannot fail to raise. In order to understand the penal character of death, it must also be made clearer what there is in man that ought not to be (purely relative to his supernatural destiny, since the character of death as the consummation bringing to an end the history of freedom in deed and endurance evidently cannot be seen as something that ought not to be) but under any circumstances belongs to man's nature.

(*b*) The penal character attributed to death can therefore consist only in what was described as the *hiddenness of death,* insofar as this is or can be experienced as something that ought not to be, relative to man's supernatural elevation, at least as a retarding factor that must be overcome in the development of man's life under the influence of grace. In the first place it is at least not unthinkable that a history of freedom can clearly grasp, in the increasing radicalness of the fundamental option gradually integrating all plural elements of human existence, the success of this process of integration and thus the outcome of the history of freedom. This cannot be unthinkable, since man actually has at least partial experiences of this kind of maturing, of the growth of his 'identity', of at least a partial 'integrity' which overcomes (up to a point, at any rate) 'concupiscence' as the nonintegratedness of many of man's realities into his free fundamental option. From this standpoint in the first place it is at least not positively contrary to man's nature as subject of freedom, even though not completely attainable by his natural being, that in his history of freedom, which finds its consummation in the finality of his self-disposal (described in a metaphysical sense as 'death'), he should experience the complete success of this process of integration, which means that the hiddenness of death ceases when it becomes an act of freedom by the endurance of a helpless passivity in which the subject and the outcome of his act of freedom are withdrawn and concealed from him in life. For there are styles of dying and death in which (at any rate, as it appears to us) a death in 'integrity' is attained at least asymptotically, where someone can die 'old and weary of life', where death is freely accepted in complete peace and final composure, in possession of the intrinsic results of a life brought to its fullness.

It should not be claimed that (apart from Jesus) such a death in pure integrity, where what is really meant by 'concupiscence' has been overcome, is ever fully realized. But it can be seen from such approximations that a 'death' in integrity without this hiddenness of death, depriving the subject of freedom of the clear and palpable outcome of a life, is not under all circumstances contrary to man's nature. If then the official teaching of the Church and the teaching of the New Testament explain death as 'payment' for sin and the experience of man (which can or must be seen as affected by grace) in which a protest is made against the darkness of death and its concealing powerlessness is regarded in this teaching as justified and 'encouraging', then it can easily be understood that the real punishment of sin consists in this hiddenness of death; it can be understood that this situation corresponds to man's natural being, but need not be present in human existence under the influence of grace, that this hiddenness of freedom in concupiscence and death would not have appeared if there had been grace at the beginning of the history of mankind and increasingly at the end, and consequently this hiddenness of death is seen in the light of this grace and the experience of it as something that ought not to be, as a punishment of sin.

(c) Contrary to a widely held opinion, it must now also be said expressly that death in its hiddenness is not merely an expression and manifestation of that remoteness of God which humanity brought on itself by sin at the beginning, in 'Adam'. Closer consideration of the New Testament statements on death (Rom. 1:32, 6:16, 21, 23; 7:5, 9, 10; 8:2; James 1:15; similarly in John) shows that it is regarded there as also the *consequence of serious (unremitted) personal sins* and (as with original sin) as intrinsic, essential expression and manifestation of these personal sins also in the total corporeal reality of man. Death then is the manifestation of the one 'sin of the world', beginning with 'original sin', built up from the sin of mankind as a whole, and manifested not only in the internal and external situation creating suffering for the individual or in the bad social conditions that can never be completely removed but also in concupiscent death, death as hiddenness.

With the principle that death is the expression and consequence also of personal sins the teaching of Paul can be connected without more ado, that there is a link between *death* and a *law of God* that is not under grace. If the law of God apart from the grace of Christ in fact (even though contrary to its own original and intrinsic intention) becomes the dynamism of sin (1 Cor. 15:56), it is understandable that mere law, by rousing man's sinful protest against itself, produces death as the consequence of this sin, not only death of the soul, but also death purely and simply, including also man's bodily ending in the peculiar form in which we actually experience it, that is, in its hiddenness (2 Cor. 3:6; Rom. 7:5, 10, 13).

(*d*) In this connection attention must be drawn also to the link attested in Scripture and the Church's official teaching between *death resulting from sin and the devil* (Heb. 2:14; John 8:44; Wisd. 2:24; Gen. 3:13, 19; DS 1511). As death is the consequence of sin, so, too, it appears in Scripture as expression of the devil's sphere of power as ruler of the world. If and insofar as the 'sin of the world' is connected with the 'authorities and powers' that we sum up and interpret in the term 'devil' and that are part of the situation in which and in the light of which the sin of the world takes place, the relationship between sin that means death and the devil already exists in principle. To describe this relationship more closely would lead us into an angelology and a demonology that cannot be discussed here.

(*e*) Death is the most universal of all realities and everyone admits that it is natural and a matter of course for us to die. And yet in everyone there is a concealed protest at this end and an irresolvable horror of it. A metaphysical anthropology alone cannot explain this fact. If it recognizes that man as a spiritual being is 'immortal', that his death is 'natural' to a biological nature, and that by the very nature of freedom he cannot want merely to live on endlessly, it is really impossible to see why he is so afraid of death, unless that fear is no more than the expression of frustration of a purely vital drive for self-assertion, the very thing that fades out at death: thus the problem of the fear of death is distorted.

At this point the testimony of Christianity comes in. Man rightly has a *fear of death*. For he was and is expected in the act of his life (carrying with it an element of passivity that admittedly can be integrated as such into his freedom) to raise up his history of freedom into finality and in this sense to 'die'; but he ought not to have to suffer this darkness of death, since even now he has within himself that vitality of divine life which, if it had been able to find pure expression from the beginning in this world of ours, would have outdone death from the outset. The fact that man dies and is not simply brought to fulfillment is the consequence of sin at the dawn of the history of humanity as a whole and of all those sins in which man makes the sin at the beginning and the situation it created his own. This consequence is not a punishment inflicted by God, breaking in upon man from outside, without having any intrinsic material connection with the punishable offence, even though of course death as suffering and as a rupture inflicted from outside, as the 'thief in the night' which it always is, is concretely under God's free decree and thus always carries with it the character of the intervention of a judgment of God. But what especially comes to the fore in death is sin.

Emptiness, hopelessness, surcease, insubstantiality, the indissoluble conjunction of supreme deed and sheer instinctive submission, of utter clarity and fundamental dubiousness: all these peculiarities of the death that we actually die are nothing but manifestations of sin, to which the same peculiarities belong analogously in a higher and more hidden dimension of the subject of freedom. But since the creature belonging to God, by its very nature as elevated by grace, shrinks from the ultimate mystery of emptiness and helplessness and nothingness, from the mystery of wickedness, and since—holy or sinful—as long as it lives it is always driven also by the power of the divine life that calls it and is active within it, this creature feels a secret dread (not self-explanatory) of death as the rising to the surface of visible life of that which alone is death properly speaking. If it wanted really existentially to conceal this horror of death by simply interpreting it as a fact of life, whether by taking refuge in superficiality, by taking refuge in despair or in a tragic heroism, then it really would turn this death into that aspect of it which rouses an unadmitted terror: the advent of eternal death.

4. Death as Dying with Jesus and as Event of Grace

(a) It was pointed out earlier that death as dying with Christ, so far as a person dies in grace and from it, does not find any clear expression in the Church's official teaching or in textbook theology. Textbook theology only says, with reference to the Council of Trent (DS 1515), that the death of the justified person is not really a punishment for sin, but only, like concupiscence, a mere consequence of sin, *poenalitas* and not *poena,* which God permits for the testing, purifying, and probation for the justified person, something to be wrestled with. We spoke about this at an earlier stage. But the New Testament has more to say about the death of the justified person. There is a 'dying in the Lord' (Rev. 14:13; 1 Thess. 4:16; 1 Cor. 15:18), a dying that is not really death, since anyone who lives and believes in Christ will never die (John 11:26), a dying with Christ that gives life (2 Tim. 2:11; Rom. 6:8). According to the New Testament, the acceptance in principle of the death of the death of Christ takes place of course by faith and baptism, so that dying with Christ and the gaining of new life even now secretly permeates our present life (Rom. 6:6, 11; 7:4–6; 8:2, 6–12, etc.).

Apart however from the fact that these statements of the New Testament assume that real death must be understood as an axiological factor permeating the whole of life and also as an act of freedom, if dying 'during' an earthly Christ-like life shaped by faith and the justification that comes from faith is not to be dissolved into an ethical-idealistic conception and to lose any connection with the reality of death, we must conclude from these very statements of the New Testament that for the justified person actual dying, too, determined of course by life, considered as the end-event, is a dying in Christ. But this means that death itself in the person endowed with grace is to be regarded as a salvific event, while of course this death must also be seen as an act of freedom recapitulating that person's life; it can then remain an open question at what point in time this act as such occurs in life, to what extent it coincides in time with the biological cessation of life or is distinct from the latter. Those who die in faith are 'dead in Christ', not only because they lived their earthly life in Christ, but also because their dying itself was in Christ. If and insofar as death as an act of man is the event that gathers together the whole personal act of man's life into the one consummation, and if in 'death' there occurs 'pragmatically', as Eutyches said, what had occurred 'mystically' at the sacramental high points of Christian life in baptism and the eucharist (that is, assimilation to the Lord), then death must be regarded as the culmination of the work of salvation and its final acceptance.

(b) What has just been said refers only to a fact attested in Scripture, but it has not yet really been made clear how this *dying with Christ* in our death is to be conceived. This further question as such would best be answered by referring to the theology of Jesus' dying and death, since this death as a once and for all event was not only effective of 'objective' redemption, but, in view of Jesus' consubstantiality with us as man in grace, it is also of the same nature as our death, and since Scripture says more and speaks more clearly about this dying of Jesus than about our own death as such. But at this point we cannot refer again expressly to Jesus' dying and death. All that can be done is to draw attention once more quite briefly to the fact that Jesus did not redeem us 'on the occasion' of his death in a moral achievement of obedience, love, etc., which would have had nothing to do with death as such, but that this redemption came about by the very fact that death as manifestation of sin, as the visibility of the emptiness and hopelessness of this sin, as domain of eternal darkness and God-forsakenness, was accepted in faith, hope, and love, and transformed in the midst of desolation and loneliness into the manifestation of the obedient surrender of the whole person to the incomprehensibility of the holy God. All this must always be kept in mind, if the dying of the justified person with Christ in grace is to be rightly understood.

(c) We are attempting therefore to gain an understanding of death as dying with Christ in the light of the *nature of grace,* while assuming always that this grace is the grace of Christ, which is given by him and for him and incorporates our life into his life and conforms us to him. We must then briefly recall what is the real nature of grace and then show that dying and death constitute a situation corresponding to its nature and excellent for the free realization of grace.

Grace consists fundamentally in God's self-communication to enable man in freedom by faith, hope, and love to accept the immediacy to God that is offered to him. Since and insofar as grace makes God purely and simply the immediate goal, content, and condition of the possibility of an immediate relationship to God, grace and its free acceptance always imply a self-abandonment, a self-transcendence above all finite realities (among which the human subject of freedom itself must primarily be counted) toward the incomprehensibility of God as blessed fulfillment, attainable only 'ecstatically'. In that sense, in every act sustained by grace toward God's immediacy there is an element of self-surrendering, 'renouncing', becoming free, which is also explained in Scripture by the assertion that faith, hope, and love 'remain' (1 Cor. 13:13), that is, they are also elements of the eschatological consummation, among which particularly in hope (but also in the vision of God's incomprehensibility and in love) the peculiar character of a self-abandoning getting away from self is plainly evident.

This character of a 'renunciation' does not of course remove the possibility of a blessed consummation, since man as creature (which he remains even in a supernatural consummation) finds himself only when he radically submits to God's disposal, seized and overpowered by God and not an autonomous subject; when, in other words, he summons up courage (again by God's act of grace), embracing and surrendering his whole existence to believe, hope, and love, that he finds himself only when he loses himself to God. But as long as freedom continues in the present world and this realization of its nature has not yet become blessed and obvious factuality, but still remains an overtaxing task which may not be accomplished, as long as freedom still coming to be is situational, there are undoubtedly situations in which the element of renunciation in every realization of grace becomes clearly present as task, manifestation, and import of this realization of grace. Certainly we may not adopt a more or less tragic attitude, assuming that grace and its realization are present only when and insofar as 'renunciation' (to the point of extinction) is imposed on man. This is contradicted by the fact that the bliss of eternal life is the supreme act of the grace of Christ, that the positivity of the finite and not only its negativity has a positive relationship to God, that a positive relationship to reality distinct as such from God can certainly be an internal element of man's relationship by grace to God. But man's experience and the event of the cross of Christ as redemption in death as such show that at least in practice the situation in which the element of renunciation (present as such in every act directed toward God as grace-given goal) appears in a particularly harsh form and to immediate experience as exclusive, is the situation preferred for the event of grace in the present order of salvation. Insofar as Christian teaching sees the peculiarity of this situation of renunciation as 'infralapsarian', as consequence of sin and thus of the freedom of sinful man and of God as 'permitting' sin, the situation is not made absolute, as if we knew and could say that it could not be otherwise and that, to use gnostic terminology, it arises solely from the mysteriousness of God himself; but on the other hand this situation of renunciation is explained and maintained as the universal and inescapable situation of our self-realization toward the immediacy of God.

This renunciation as present in the very nature of grace and inescapably required of us in our infralapsarian situation reaches in death its unsurpassable culmination. Since in death as an event affecting all humanity man is deprived of everything and thus even of himself, since in death the actual success of the act of freedom in which as a justified person he accepts and approves this self-withdrawal in death remains hidden, in our infralapsarian situation (in which the subject cannot realize itself in integrity and cannot grasp the effect of this realization in final bliss) death is the culmination of the grace of Christ crucified and thus a dying with Christ. At the same time it cannot be overlooked that part of this renunciation in death is to accept in self-denying freedom the fact that this concealed and concealing death in particular need not have been, that 'essentially' things could have been different, so that death now contains within itself the acceptance of its own not derivable and not 'ideologizable' facticity.

(*d*) None of this of course means that dying and death are the mode of realization only of an 'abstract' renunciation. This self-abandonment radicalized in death is in fact an aspect of the realization of grace as faith, hope, and love. Dying can be an act of *faith,* since it thwarts any recourse by man to a categorial justification of faith or (if that is perhaps an exaggeration) since this justification of faith in terms of fundamental theology in the light of man's intramundane rationality proves to be something that simply cannot produce faith as such. Dying is *love* of God insofar as this renunciation in freedom required in death is brought about as the effect of a love in which God himself is loved for his own sake and consequently the person never recovers himself. The acceptance of death can certainly be seen also as an act of love of *neighbour,* insofar as the historical subject then leaves the mundane sphere of freedom and the stage of history free for others. This of course does not mean that man's dying can be seen only in *this* respect as an act of love of neighbour. If we are obliged in love to bear witness to our neighbour by our whole life of grace, of God's freedom and the hope of eternal life, this is true also of the witness of love that we must bear by our dying. 'Both during his whole life and also and even more at the time of his death,' says Ignatius of Loyola, 'each one . . . ought to strive earnestly that through him God our Lord may be glorified and served and his fellowmen may be edified, at least by the example of his patience and fortitude along with his living faith, hope, and love of the eternal goods which Christ our Lord merited and acquired for us by those altogether incomparable sufferings of his temporal life and death'.*

(*e*) Christian tradition, beginning with Scripture, has always seen *martyrdom,* a death freely endured and accepted to bear witness to the faith as the most perfect way in which a Christian can die with Christ. And rightly so. For in a martyr's death the universal essential constituents of Christian death are most clearly manifested: the indisposability of death, death as free act, death as testimony of faith for others. The secret yearning for martyrdom, which is constantly attested in the course of the history of Christianity, is rooted in the hope that dying with Christ, which is part of every death in grace, is assured most securely by this kind of death.

* This translation is taken from *The Constitutions of the Society of Jesus,* translated and with a commentary by George E. Ganss, (St. Louis, Mo.: Institute of Jesuit Sources, 1970): 595.—Translator.

PART FOUR

Grace and World

15

JUSTIFICATION AND WORLD DEVELOPMENT FROM A CATHOLIC VIEWPOINT

I agreed to the theme of 'justification and world development from a Catholic viewpoint' because it surprised me on the one hand but interested me on the other. In regard to this task, it is true, I feel like a schoolboy unexpectedly presented with a difficult and unusual mathematical problem. But this is the very reason why the theme attracts me, for it is odd in some ways. As far as I know, it is not a familiar theme in Catholic theology. Of course there must be connections between justification and world development. But at the point where justification is explicitly discussed in Catholic theology the theologian considers only the isolated subject in its relationship to God alone and there is no mention of the task of world development. World development may be a theme that certainly receives attention in a variety of theological treatises, particularly in moral theology and Christian sociology. It may have become clearer in 'political theology' and in the 'theology of liberation;' it is now considered much more than formerly and became a conciliar theme in *Gaudium et Spes* at the Second Vatican Council. But this is still far from clearly explaining the connection between the theme of world development and the Catholic doctrine of justification. That, in fact, is to be our theme. In this state of theological reflection it is obvious that there can be no question here of any more than a modest attempt to discover connections between the two ideas, an attempt that is more or less entirely the responsibility of the author alone and which cannot be covered here by explicit declarations of the Church's magisterium (or, at any rate, it is not possible to attempt so much here and now).

It also seems obvious to me that in this essay we are not dealing with a theme that properly belongs to controversial theology, although the title speaks of a 'Catholic viewpoint'. All that is meant by this qualification is that these reflections make use of a terminology familiar in Catholic theology and that our starting point is the Catholic doctrine of justification without any explicit consideration of the Protestant doctrine of justification. But this does not mean at all or at any rate does not certainly mean that we are engaged in controversial theology. For one thing it is no longer possible today to claim that the Catholic doctrine of justification in the sense in which it is absolutely binding on the Catholic as the Church's official teaching is completely opposed to Protestant teaching on justification; more importantly, a Christian theory of world development, of the Christian's world task in history and society, is itself expressed in different ways among Christians of all denominations, different ways that cut right across the denominations, so that none of them (apart from the most extreme cases) can be unambiguously attributed to a particular denomination. In fact and insofar as a theory of the Christian's world task by and large is perhaps common property, it can be approached in the light of different ideas of justification. For it is doubtful whether subtle distinctions of controversial theology in regard to justification need to affect our understanding of world development or whether (when it is a question of concrete and practical precepts for this world task) they can be overcome by a more global and common understanding of Christian existence. It seems to me that our theme has nothing to do with controversial theology properly speaking, particularly since the Protestant theory of the relationship between law and Gospel, of the two kingdoms, etc., and the Catholic theory of natural law, of the relationship between nature and grace, etc., are so diversely interpreted even by each denomination on its own account that there is no basis there for a controversy which would mean exactly the same to both parties.

After these preliminary observations, we may come to the actual theme. The reflections put forward here will have to find their way and their method for themselves, without the possibility of assuming a formal structure in advance and as unambiguous from the nature of the case.

These reflections therefore begin, with a certain arbitrariness (which is readily admitted), with the traditional Catholic teaching that the event and effect of justification consist in the realization and free acceptance of the three theological virtues of faith, hope, and love. For the Council of Trent, justification as being justified consists in the possession of these three habitual theological virtues as 'infused' and justification as event in a responsible person consists in the actual realization of these three virtues. The Council of Trent leaves the question open as to whether what is known as 'sanctifying grace' is identical with these three theological virtues or merely inseparably united with them. In any case then, if we want to know what is the grace of justification, we may turn without more ado to the consideration of these three theological virtues. In our context, too, the problem is irrelevant as to how precisely the doctrine of the 'infusedness' and the character of a habitus of grace—that is, an ontically objective conceptuality—can be reconciled with the Reformation teaching on grace, with its more descriptive and existential conceptuality; we assume merely that this is not impossible in principle. Here we can also safely leave aside the fact that the Tridentine doctrine of justification, based on the medieval theology of grace, arbitrarily and tacitly assumes that these three theological virtues are realized in a temporal succession and acquired habitually and therefore that it is possible in principle for the habitus of faith and also of hope to be present without the habitus of love.

If we recall with the Council of Trent that the real and sole justification comes about only by the realization and possession of the three theological virtues together (that is, in *fides spe et caritate formata*) and if we also recall that the council does not forbid us to think existentially and concretely of these three theological virtues as jointly realized and present in this unity, even though, because of their conceptual distinction, they can be seen abstractly as developing in a temporal succession to one another and, in view of the intrinsic temporality of the one realization of the one existence, this is not *a priori* pointless, then we can safely regard the three theological virtues here as one factor. We may see these three terms, faith, hope, and love, as three aspects of the one realization of Christian existence, as three key terms for this realization of existence as one and whole, which inevitably merge into one another conceptually and objectively, even though in the history of the Church's sense of faith and in the history of theology at any particular time one or the other of these three key terms came to the fore and represented the one totality of the Christian understanding of existence (as perhaps today 'hope' is the key term mainly emphasized). For our question about the relationship between justification and world development we may therefore consider without prejudice all three factors of justification and ask what they contribute taken together and as distinct from each other to the understanding of the Christian's world task.

We are asking then whether in this one triplicity of the three theological virtues in their unity there is involved a particular relationship of the Christian to the world, insofar as this world as finite and created on the one hand is distinct from the God to whom in justification man acquires a positive, salvific, and comprehensive relationship and, on the other hand, as historical, presents a task for man's active freedom. If we can answer this question up to a point comprehensively and appropriately, we shall have found the answer to the question which is the theme of these reflections. At the same time it is obvious that an answer sought in this way can in any case turn out to be only very formal and abstract. For concrete history as act of man's freedom and as free endurance of the history of nature, in which man is rooted from the outset and never adequately available for his freedom, is and remains precisely history: a history that is never concretely derivable for men from the concepts of justification (which always remain somewhat abstract) or from the incomprehensible mystery called God, to which man is related in justification. With this reservation, however, we are attempting to gain from the Christian teaching about the triplicity of the theological virtues a few insights into man's relationship to the world, into a Christian world development. In this connection we are starting out from statements referring either to the triplicity as a whole or to one particular theological virtue.

In the light of a view that is legitimate, although not universally accepted and binding in Catholic theology, it can be said that this triplicity as a possibility effected by God at least in the mode of an offer to man's freedom is always and everywhere present in the individual human being and in mankind, that this triplicity as a possibility of man's historical freedom effected by God is not merely an event occurring at a definite point in space and time, but an existential (although the effect of God's grace) that always co-determines man's existence and history. At least according to the teaching of the Second Vatican Council there is a universal salvific will of God everywhere offering justification; real faith, real hope, and love, imparting God himself and justifying man, are possible spatially and temporally in the whole history of mankind and consequently even outside verbally expressed, sacramental, and sociologically institutionalized Christianity to include also a theoretical verbal atheism. It is not the place here and now to consider how this opportunity of justification in faith, hope, and love, offered by God's salvific will always and everywhere, can be seen to be possible even where man has not been touched by the explicit message of salvation of Christianity. This, too, is something that cannot be discussed here.

We may however assume what may be called this radically optimistic view (contrary to an Augustinian conception of history); we may assume therefore that the possibility of justification as a permanent existential is offered to man always and everywhere and can therefore be accepted by man's freedom even outside explicit Christianity (an acceptance of course, if it actually occurs, which is itself again a grace of God); we may further assume that on the one hand (as will be shown later) this acceptance of justification has also an essential importance for man's relationship to his world and on the other is also actually realized by man's freedom. Assuming all this, we can and must say that man's relationship to the world, his development of the world, is always and everywhere and consequently even outside institutionalized Christianity characterized at least anonymously by what we Christians call justification, that is, by man's liberatedness for the immediacy of God. But from this there results an important insight: much of what we encounter in the history of humanity as interpretation of the world in practice and theory outside and inside explicit Christianity can by no means be taken *a priori* as an interpretation that is without grace outside Christianity and in this sense is unchristian or achristian *or* has something to do with justification only within explicit Christianity. Christian interpretation of the world in theory and more especially in practice can be Christian even outside explicit Christianity and indeed, according to Vatican II, in its realization in practical life is actually Christian (that is, sustained by grace) where a person does not seriously and culpably reject the dictate of his conscience, even though this practical development of the world is not interpreted in explicitly Christian terms and perhaps co-exists with theoretical interpretations of the world and man that Christianity rejects as false, even though such a concrete interpretation of the world in practice occasionally occurs in a way that explicit Christianity has not yet expressly and clearly realized in its own historical and sociological situation.

In the Catholic understanding the triplicity of the theological virtues means an immediacy of man to God in a form which would be absolutely impossible without the gift of these theological virtues as God's grace; but, if and insofar as it is accepted in freedom as justifying, this immediacy to God involves a particular relationship to the world that consequently would also be utterly impossible without this justifying grace and conversely is both required and brought about by this justifying grace. This is the second point to be made and elucidated to some extent about the relationship between justification and world development. According to traditional Catholic teaching the triplicity of the three theological virtues does not mean merely the restoration and the factuality of some kind of good and right relationship of man to God as Lord and Creator, merely forgiveness of man's sins, merely a purification of man's moral relationship to God in a form that could be recognized as binding even independently of a divine verbal revelation. Since and insofar as the ultimate salvific relationship to God (as made possible by God and on this assumption required by God) is from the very outset God's free grace, is 'supernatural', it is on the one hand the supreme and most radical realization of man's nature and on the other hand a grace that is in no way due to man, not only as sinner, but to man as such. This is implicit in the Catholic teaching on the distinction between nature and supernatural grace. This supernaturality of grace and the relationship to God that it makes possible and sustains can be explained by the fact that this grace gives man a relationship of radical immediacy to God, not only existentially, but also ontologically; by this grace God is not merely the creative precondition of a creaturely reality that as such in its self-realization would merely remain entangled in its own finiteness and would have God only as its creative ground and only as the always remote mover of its self-realization always remaining within the finite. The truth is that by grace there is present a real and veritable self-communication of God in his own absolute reality to the intellectual creature, so that the latter is moved toward God strictly in himself. For a Catholic doctrine of grace the principle is really inescapable: *finitum capax infiniti*.

This is implied (which can only be briefly indicated here) in the doctrine of uncreated grace, of the communication of the Holy Spirit who is God himself, of the immediate vision of God in eternal life, which is not mediated by any created reality. This doctrine of grace as the most intimate self-communication of God in himself to the intellectual creature has an effect then on the traditional doctrine of the triplicity of the theological virtues. These must be strictly distinguished from the moral virtues, even if the latter require a particular religious relationship to God as Creator and Lord of the creature. All 'moral' virtues have a finite reality, a finite moral value, a creaturely formal object, even though these realities of course always carry within themselves a reference to God as to their ultimate precondition. But in this triplicity of the three theological virtues and only there we have to do with God in himself in immediacy. This of course assumes that the acts in which man is related to God immediately and not mediated by a created reality representing him are themselves sustained by God's self-communication, that God himself is not merely an asymptotic goal of a purely creaturely movement toward him, but with his own reality is himself an internal constitutive element (albeit by grace) of the spiritual movement of the creature toward God himself. In faith God himself is heard and not merely in a finite word 'about' him; what is received and heard is the divine Word who is God himself; in hope God himself is hoped for and not merely a creaturely reality created by him as salvific, because he himself sustains this movement of hope toward its consummation by himself, moves the creature in the goal toward the goal; love for God is itself sustained by God's love for us, in which he gives himself and not merely a gift representing and mediating him and his love. None of this may be understood as a purely verbal emphatic enhancement of the importance of a banal reality, in which the finite creature still remains stuck in its finiteness and God is attained only in the sense that he, the absolute Other, unattainable in himself, enables us to grasp and admit our own finiteness.

If and insofar as there is in God such an immediacy to God, either in the mode of an offer to man's freedom or in the mode of free acceptance (then called 'justification', which of course implies for-giveness of sin), then there exists that freedom over all powers and authorities of the world of which Scripture speaks and which consti-tutes the real nature of the relationship of the justified person to the world and thus characterizes the development of the world which is proper to him. This person justified by grace (whether inside or outside institutional Christianity) is not really turned away by justi-fying grace from the world and his task in the world (something will be said about this very shortly), he remains turned to his world and thus participates in God's self-communication to the world, a self-communication that establishes God in the world as its most proper goal and innermost dynamism; but for that very reason the justified person is not merely a piece of the world, its servant, its element determined solely by the world, neither collective nor individual, he realizes his relationship to the world in the light of God himself, who is not a part of the world, not even its supreme part. Unfortunately it is not possible here to explain more closely how this relationship to the world, transcending the world, on the part of the Christian, is to be considered and experienced more precisely. It would be possible, for example, to refer to the doctrine current in Christian spirituality of resignation, of indifference, which, rightly understood, is an es-sential and constant modality of the triplicity and in the last resort can be justified only by the latter; we could also safely refer to a mysticism in East and West of a formless experience of God, which can explain by its radicality such a relationship to the world, even though (as will be pointed out later) it is not the sole form of this Christian relationship to the world. But in any case the attitude to the world produced by the triplicity means a radical, more or less demythologizing relativizing of all secular, finite, immediately present values and tasks in the world, a destruction of all idols (that is, of all absolutizing of intramundane values and tasks), and an ultimate reservation in regard to all these things, a reservation which is really possible, since God in his own self-communication (if only this is grasped) has made himself man's final standpoint.

In this way there is actually a realization of man's existence—in which life and death, rise and decline, historical success and failure, experience of meaning and meaninglessness, and so on, are all caught up together—toward the absolute God, who really permits himself to be attained through the possibility given by himself in his self-communication of an immediate relationship to him in the triplicity of the theological virtues. In other words, the traditional teaching on this triplicity can and must be seen as the doctrine of an ultimate absolute freedom of man in regard to the world (to which, of course, he himself belongs with his essentially finite subjectivity and historical relativity) since in fact in this triplicity, in which God in himself is attained, man experiences also his liberatedness in regard to himself. There is no need to explain further that all this is 'fundamental' also to the Christian character of the task of world development.

To this first statement about the relationship to the world established in the triplicity of the theological virtues (that is, in justification) we must immediately add a second statement which has a certain dialectic relationship with the first. In order to elucidate the radicalness of the immediacy to God involved in this triplicity and thus man's preeminence over the world in his world task, successful or unsuccessful, we referred briefly to formless mysticism in East and West. But that was meant only as a clarification and by no means implies that man has immediacy to God as such primarily or solely in this way. On the contrary. Presumably as essentially distinct from Eastern mysticism, Christianity is assured (paradoxical as it may sound) that there is at least normally a necessary and possible mediation to this immediacy to God.

This is evident from the very fact that Christianity, when and because it seeks to be the event of immediacy to God and thus to an ultimate preeminence over the world, nevertheless regards itself as founded on a revelation of God that finds objective expression in human words, as Church of the word and sacrament as a historical and sociological institution. It is evident on the other hand from the fact that Christianity believes that man can reject an elitist esotericism and find complete salvation in the straightforward fulfillment of God's commandments (admittedly by faith, hope, and love) in the midst of ordinary life. As this Christianity cannot of course regard the ordinary routine of fulfilling the commandments of God in fidelity to conscience as a substitute for 'mystical' immediacy to God, as ordinary routine fulfillment of duty which only *after* death will be rewarded by something quite different (that is, by this immediacy to God), and as Christian teaching insists that this normal fulfillment of everyday duties as the way of salvation must spring and can spring from the triplicity of the three theological virtues as immediacy to God, so Christianity's understanding of existence implies the conviction that categorial involvement with the world, when it occurs in ultimate freedom, is also the realization of the theological virtues toward the immediacy of God; that this is the categorial mediation, take-off point, and historical concreteness precisely of that absolute transcendentality in grace in which man reaches God himself as such. Man does not realize primarily and still less solely his immediate relationship to God in a formless mysticism in which the world fades out and is dismissed as unreal. The categorial factor, the historical and concrete world task of man, when it is effected under the influence of the triplicity of the theological virtues (and this in fact is both possible and necessary), is mediation to the immediacy of God. The world is rightly grasped and faced precisely when this happens in virtue of that freedom and superiority over the world which God offers to man in his threefold grace and in which he is himself immediately God.

If we disregard the question of an absolutely unworldly mysticism (a question that remains open in Catholic theology and, even if it is answered in the affirmative, raises a new question in regard to the condition of the finite subject itself in such mysticism, the subject which Christianity could not regard as perishing even in this form of mysticism), it must in any case be said that according to the Christian conception of man his immediacy to God and consequently his God-given status over the world and over himself is, must be and can be mediated by his world achievement and world task in his history of freedom. Unfortunately it is not possible here to explain precisely how and why such a mediation to immediacy to God does not contain a contradiction, but is rooted in the fundamental structures of the intellectual subject, whose transcendentality toward the absolute has always been the condition of categorial knowledge and freedom and yet is not totally exhausted in this function, but has a possibility of being radicalized by grace toward God's immediacy without thereby losing its function as condition of the possibility of intramundane categorial knowledge and freedom. Assuming all this however, it can be said that the realization of man's world task at least normally can be and (when this world task is objectively and subjectively rightly accomplished) actually is also the realization of his immediacy to God in the three theological virtues.

In regard to this statement of course it ought to be made clearer than is possible here that such a categorial mediation to God's immediacy can exist not merely where this categoriality is of an explicitly religious character, is explicit faith verbalized in Christian terms and sacramental, but also where it is 'merely' fidelity to one's own conscience and consequently objective and subjective fulfillment of the world task (assuming, of course, that such a secularity of the categorial mediation to God's immediacy does not imply a culpable rejection of those categorial mediations which are explicitly religious and Christian and appear making their demands in the collective or individual history of man and offer themselves as such mediations). But at any rate, if what has been said is correct, there is a very differentiated mutual relationship between justifying grace and the Christian's world task. Justification offers man as equipped for absolute freedom for his world task a standpoint over the world from which in ultimate freedom he both accomplishes and endures this task, and this world task itself even to the very limit of its apparent secularity is the mediation for the free acceptance of this immediacy to God which is given to him as the grace offered always and everywhere as supreme possibility and absolute salvific task. Grace, we might also say, has always and everywhere an incarnatory structure; it descends into the world, does not make this world unreal, but gives this world as it is realized in persistence and breakdown the immediacy to God in which the world accepts God himself as such as its consummation.

If there were more space available, what has just been said might be explained very simply and perhaps more understandably by appealing to the traditional Catholic teaching on the unity of love of God and love of neighbour. For traditional textbook theology basing itself on the New Testament, love of neighbour is not merely the fulfillment of another commandment derived from the love of God. If only it attains to its own radical nature, this love of neighbour is understood *as* love of God itself. As textbook theology expresses it, the formal object of love of God and love of neighbour is one and the same (in fact, God himself) without the concrete individual neighbour being reduced in his importance and claim on us to a merely external occasion for loving God himself alone. According to this teaching therefore, love of neighbour at its root is itself the realization of God's love, even if it is not expressly thematicized in this realization; it is the event of the transcendence of the person toward God's immediacy, the assent to God's offer in which God imparts himself to man in the miracle of his own love. When it reaches its own fullness of being unreservedly, when the loving subject really breaks out of the prison of its egoism and really surrenders itself unconditionally, love of neighbour is the event and factuality of justification.

At the same time of course (though it is not possible here) it ought to be shown that, if it reaches its own absoluteness and radicalness, such a love of neighbour includes within itself what are known in theological terms as faith and hope. In regard to this traditional teaching on the unity of love of God and love of neighbour in their mutual perichoresis, it ought also to be remembered that love of neighbour is not restricted here to a sphere merely of feeling or individual intimacy, that it may not be interpreted as a merely private affair; it is realized in deed and action, has a sociological dimension, must be realized in justice and the maintenance of a sphere of freedom for the others, must be seen in the light of a political theology. But then the connection between the one love of God and neighbour, between justification on the one hand and the Christian's world task on the other, is immediately visible, even though the concrete precepts for this world task in a particular historical and sociological situation cannot be deduced solely from that source, but must be found in some other way.

As such, the theological virtue of hope, too, which is a constituent element for justification, ought to be considered expressly with reference to its importance for the Christian's world task. For the theme of hope is now very topical among both Catholics and Protestants, even though less attention is usually paid to hope as a constituent factor of justification in the classical sense of this term. As a theological virtue, which is not to be understood simply in the light of the existential-ontological reflections of an Ernst Bloch or other present-day philosophers alone, it is first and last a hope of the absolute future, which is God in himself, a future given to man purely and simply as free grace and not simply and originally produced by man's own historical efforts and action: a hope for the absolute future which alone can liberate man wholly and finally from his self-alienation. But if in regard to this hope of the absolute future in immediacy to God himself we remember what was said earlier with reference to the whole triplicity of the theological virtues about the categorial (that is, intramundane) mediation to the immediacy of God, then of course this hope positively and negatively has a meaning for the hope in which man in his world task anticipates his continually new, historical, individual, and collective future which he creates himself. Such a hope and its objective are necessary mediations for the hope of the absolute future, which is God. Only in the realization of intramundane hope can man realize his hope in the absolute future in genuine freedom. And only if he aspires in this theological hope to his intramundane goals of his history, continually to be seized on creatively in hope, does he gain the right attitude to his desired intramundane goals and tasks. Since he has an absolute hope in which he reaches out to an absolute future, which is granted to him by God throughout victories *and* downfalls, he has the right relationship to his intramundane goals: he will deify neither his present nor his intramundane future, he can accept and endure utterly without fear his continual historical turbulence, he can live genuinely historically without simply being surrendered and subjected to his historicity. He can really live tranquilly; he will not flee from his historical task as something that is ultimately unreal, since it is the categorial and necessary mediation to immediacy toward the absolute future, and he does not cling either to a past or to a present or to a future intramundane future so absolutely as if he could not exist without it.

For the Christian the theological virtue of hope is the ground and liberation of his secular hope, even if he knows that this theological hope can be an event even outside institutional and verbalized Christianity. For him his world task and his salvific task do not simply coincide, but are mutually dependent. In its concrete realization justification may certainly demand the relinquishing of an intramundane value, if and when the realization of faith and hope in an absolute future means giving up some worldly idol; it can therefore imply asceticism, insofar as this is an anticipation in faith and hope of a death in the course of which the absolute future is grasped in all its purity; but it can never mean purely and simply a flight from the world, since escapism of this kind, seen in isolation as a means adopted by man to reach his absolute goal, would be a denial of the fact that the absolute future, which is God, must in the last resort be granted entirely for its own sake as free grace.

There is still a great deal that could be said in regard to our theme as a whole, but which can only be outlined here. For example, the Christian logic of existential decision might be discussed: the question, that is, of how a Christian really knows here and now in a concrete situation, precisely in his world task, that just one and not another intramundane goal as object of his choice is the mediation to God's immediacy required as binding here and now, the material, the bodily presence of his immediacy to God, that justifies him and brings him to salvation. For this knowledge cannot be acquired deductively solely from the universal norms of Christian morality; discovering the concrete will of God in a concrete situation is not merely the application of universal norms to a particular case; practice and freedom do not emerge merely as consequences of theory and universal reason. But how such a logic of existential decision in the light of grace, the 'discernment of spirits', the discovery of an individual decision as willed by God, is arrived at: this is a question that has not been at all adequately considered in the traditional textbook theology of justification and grace, but it cannot be pursued further here. A theology of sin and the cross might be brought to bear much more explicitly on our theme, since it is impossible without these two aspects to understand objectively and realistically either justification or the Christian's world task. If even in a Catholic doctrine of justification man can and must certainly be seen as *simul justus et peccator,* this implies that his 'state' as justified and his world task are always faced by the threat and the actual reality of what in Christian terms is known as 'sin'. In the last resort it remains a secret and must be left unconditionally to God's judgment whether the individual has grasped his justification, whether his world task has been objectively and personally fulfilled as the concreteness of his justification. At the same time (also with recourse to a rightly understood doctrine of original sin) it should be remembered that sin is not merely a private matter, an internal disposition, but is also objectified in historical and sociological institutions where there is also the mingling of righteousness and sin which is not completely separable from man. Our theme ought likewise to be confronted with a theology of the cross as the concreteness of both sin and salvation. From this standpoint the peculiar character of the Christian world interpretation and world task would have to be more precisely defined, since the Christian world task obviously shares the peculiar character of the existence of the justified person, who exists in this life before death in the transition between the death of Jesus and his resurrection.

16

LAW AND RIGHTEOUSNESS
IN THE CATHOLIC UNDERSTANDING

Given this theme and knowing that he has only a few pages in which to deal with it, the Catholic theologian cannot fail to have serious misgivings. Where is he to begin? Should he start with the New Testament? Begin with Paul and ask how his very wide-ranging teaching on the law and the righteousness granted us by grace and not by fulfilling the law, how this according to his own perhaps very problematical conception is related to the teaching of the Old Testament and to the Jewish theology of his time, and whether and how Paul's teaching can be incorporated into the teaching of the New Testament as a whole? Is this theologian to follow the history of this doctrine in its vicissitudes through all the periods of Christian theology? Are the contrasts and the compatibility between the teaching of the Reformers and the Catholic teaching on law and righteousness from the time of Luther and the Council of Trent to be discussed? Is this Catholic teaching, which is perhaps by no means as consistent as the theme implies, to be set in the context of a modern mentality in order to bring out clearly its peculiar character? These particular themes present the theologian who has to deal with the relationship between law and righteousness with an immense amount of material, requiring careful, objective, and historical differentiation. Is it surprising if he is discouraged, if he cannot see the forest for the trees and has no idea where to begin?

In this desperate situation I think I have the right to leave aside all learned exegesis, all expertise in the fields of history of dogma and history of ideas, and try to say simply what occurs to me as the quite normal Christian that I want to be, in the light of Christian life and not of theological scholarship, when I hear the terms 'law' and 'righteousness'. If at the same time a joint Christian (and not by any means specifically denominational) statement should emerge, I shall neither be surprised nor shocked. For I think (incidentally) that from Reformation times onward the theories on righteousness and law in Catholic and Protestant theology have been so clarified and more particularly further differentiated in each church that this theme no longer presents any reason for a schism between the churches. Of course, both Protestant and also Catholic theologians will discover in what I say defects and omissions, subjective emphases, etc., with which they certainly cannot simply agree. If the theme here requires the exposition of a *Catholic* understanding of the relationship between law and righteousness, this can mean from the very outset only that the author is persuaded with good reason that his understanding of this relationship is set within the framework of Catholic theology and the Church's proclamation, without claiming to be simply identified with these factors. I shall not venture at all to explain how what I have to say is related to a modern Jewish understanding of life. But, after these preliminary remarks, let us begin with the theme itself.

I hear the word 'law'. It rouses in me thousands of different and mutually contradictory ideas and emotions. I can think of hundreds of kinds of laws, norms, regulations, rules, customs, patterns of behavior, which demand my attention, require the homage of my freedom and my obedience. The origins of these innumerable laws with the most varied names are also very diverse. There are laws of what we call 'nature' and these punish disobedience with sickness, death, disruption of our lives, even when we infringe them in ignorance and inculpably. I try to obey them, even though they create the impression of visibly restricting me as subject of freedom, because I fear the sentence of death they pass upon me and, prior to all deeper considerations, in the last resort do not see much point in opposing, attractive as it may sometimes be, the sentence of death threatened by these laws.

There are laws, norms, and customs of the society in which I was born and in which I must live. Up to a point they appear to me as a kind of continuation and interpretation of the laws of nature already mentioned, as relatively meaningful, as useful and unavoidable, and I obey them more or less as I obey the laws of nature, as norms which there is not very much point in infringing. But up to a point also these norms and laws of society seem to me questionable, pointless restrictions on my freedom against which it is possible to protest, thrust on me purely from outside, without the opportunity of really internalizing them, making them my own, regarding them as laws given by my own freedom itself. Where these laws of society can be seriously regarded as *merely* such (and there are laws of this kind), the only question that arises is how far we must be prepared to adapt ourselves to them, since it is not worthwhile to infringe them in view of social sanctions, or whether we are shrewd enough to get out of them, since even from a Christian standpoint there is a legitimate demythologizing and 'de-tabooizing' of the binding authority with which a society is accustomed to clothe its norms of this kind in order to secure obedience to them. (The emancipation of early Christianity from the social and religious norms of its Jewish origin can certainly be interpreted primarily as a process of this kind. In the concrete case it is very often not easy to say whether such laws of society are of the first or the second kind; and most of the norms of society as they affect us are an amalgam of the two kinds that we distinguished and consequently are not as such completely homogeneous in their durability or their moral claim.

In addition to all these however, I am aware of laws of a different kind which cannot simply be derived from society or from nature in a physiological sense. In particular, the person who knows he is free (that is, who is not prepared to shift off responsibility for his actions to an anonymous 'it' behind his subjectivity) is faced with requirements which do not have their force from nature and are not objectifications of society alone, but impose themselves on freedom as such, acquit or condemn, rise out of a mysterious depth of the free subject itself, so that, if they are not observed, they bring the subject into a fatal conflict with itself. Truthfulness, love, loyalty, readiness to accept responsibility, the requirement of maintaining the dignity of our own existence and likewise that of other human beings: these and other 'laws', as far as the concrete substance of their claim is concerned here and now, may always have in themselves an element of historical and sociological relativity, but their real meaning and their real dignity are independent in the last resort of this relativity, are the expression of what man as free subject ought to be, have a dignity of absoluteness and unconditionality. Opinions diverge as to how they are to be further and more deeply interpreted in this absoluteness. But it is very doubtful that there are more or less normally developed human beings who have not come across such laws. For even someone who denies the fact of such absolute requirements will make this denial with an awareness, even though perhaps merely implicit, that he must cling to his conviction and not deny it at any price: he thus affirms the absolute binding force of his profession of truth. Nor, as we said, is the existence of such laws brought into question by the fact that their material content with which they make their appearance in particular periods, nations, cultures, societies, is very different, even materially contradictory. The Christian interprets the absolute authority of these laws, at least in their formal claim, as the will of God, as God's law. We shall not argue here for the accuracy of this interpretation, it can simply be assumed as a fact.

This is not a mistake or a feeble excuse, since we can certainly assume that knowledge of God and of his deliberate claim on us is not simply another piece of knowledge added from outside to our experience of absolute laws, with these two items of knowledge being subsequently linked; knowledge of God is nothing but the radical interpretation of the experience of absolute laws, of freedom and its responsibility. When we encounter the dignity of these laws in free obedience we have already learned what is meant by the word 'God', even if we do not know or understand how to use this explicitly theological vocabulary. But some observations must be made on law as God's will in order to gain an understanding of explicitly Christian theology on this theme.

At any rate in their widest extent (we shall have to speak later of other material) these laws, understood as God's holy will and insofar as they raise claims to concrete fulfillment, are related to finite, intramundane realities and values of man and his society, distinct from God: respect for a meaningful order of society, for the life and scope for freedom of one's neighbour, etc. But this involves a fundamental problem which, it seems to me, has not been considered clearly enough on the whole either by Jewish or by Christian or by 'Mohammedan' theology. How can an absolute claim be based on a finite value, however highly esteemed? Without appealing to God, this question seems to be *a priori* unanswerable. But if it is said that these values raise an absolute claim on our freedom (as Christian theology says) as the will of *God,* the question still remains open as to how God can meaningfully will such finite values as absolute, how he can regard them as more important than they really are (and as they appear in his own attitude to them), how we can perceive this absolute claim of these realities as derived from God. In face of this question, must a Christian have recourse to an ethic of secular realism, calling for rational objectivity, the infringement of which in the last resort leads man to evils that he cannot bring himself to admit are avoidable only hypothetically and conditionally? Are these laws God's will only insofar as we cannot think meaningfully of the God known from other sources except as the one who now wills the finite sum total of realities and values, because he willed them as Creator? But is the will of God as legislator then not simply identical with the will of God as Creator, who willed a very finite and relative world in which there can be nothing at all that is absolutely and unconditionally important?

At this point of course it is possible to refer to the fact that the real and express relationship of man to God, because God is its reference point, has such a dignity and absoluteness that our problem no longer arises in regard to this relationship, that the law of seeking God and being open toward his incomprehensibility, of worshiping him and (which is certainly possible) loving him, has in any case this absolute dignity which permits no doubts in regard to divine laws with an intramundane content. We can insist then that commandments with a finite material content might nevertheless have such an absolute character as law of *this* God to whom we have an absolutely binding relationship, even though their material content as such cannot confer it. But we are then involved in a new question: how is this relationship to God, which is supposed to sustain the absolute dignity of the moral law properly so-called, to be understood more precisely, so that this relationship can sustain that absoluteness of the law or (and this is still far from clear) even of itself curtail it and up to a point relativize it?

With this question we have reached a point at which we must make an entirely fresh start and at which we catch sight of the other term of our theme as a whole: righteousness. How this comes about will soon be made clear. Righteousness, or 'justice', in the sense understood by Christian theology is not a particular virtue within the sociological sphere, but means purely and simply the right relationship, the relationship that ought to exist, of man to God, bringing man to salvation; it means holiness, peace purely and simply, reconciliation with God, to mention at least a few other words of Scripture and tradition which in the last resort mean the same thing as righteousness, but get rid of the impression given by that term of a legal relationship between God and man, which is regulated by an authority superior to both parties and establishes the right relationship when both parties keep to this higher norm. It is clear that this is a form of righteousness that does not exist for the Christian.

This righteousness of the finite and sinful creature must be seen quite differently from the Christian standpoint. It is the unmerited gift decreed by God's supreme love; although it must be accepted in freedom, it is God's Holy Spirit himself (in a word, God himself) who gives himself with his most intimate divine life to the intellectual creature, so that God is not only the creative donor of a finite gift distinct from himself and perfecting man, but is as such the gift itself. It is impossible to explain more clearly here how this is to be understood and how man himself must be seen if he is to be able to be the recipient of such a gift, to be *capax infiniti*. But if the teaching of Christianity on the nature and definition of man, of his perfection and righteousness, is understood radically and we are not content with naive metaphors, there can be no doubt that the right relationship of man to God can be established only by God in his own free initiative, that it cannot really mean a 'between' between us and God, as something also different from God, but is God communicating himself, the Holy Spirit who is himself God. He himself gives himself as the innermost centre of our existence; for in this respect he does not really come upon us from outside as an additional reality, but is from the very outset what is most deeply rooted within us, because what we call the creation of the finite distinct from God occurs in the concrete order as a result of the fact that God as love wants to lavish and does lavish himself and thus at the same time creates the finite on which the miracle of this self-surrendering love of God can occur. Once more, it is not possible here to elucidate more closely what has been said or to make clear that it did not amount to a utopian speculation, of which there is no evidence in the real experience of everyday life.

What has just been said places us in an odd situation in regard to our question about the relationship of law and righteousness. The

term 'law' led us to an experience of a sacred unconditional requirement from the subject of freedom, to a law that had to be seen as
God's holy will and could only be understood in this way in its true
nature. But the term 'righteousness' did not lead us, as might have
been expected, to the idea of the status of the subject fulfilling the
law in freedom, but to a reality which at least in its initial stages has
nothing to do with law or the fulfillment of law, with morality, but is
infinitely above this moral sphere and consists in the miracle of love
in which God gives himself as innermost life to man. In this properly
biblical sense law and righteousness are primarily as remote from
each other as objective norms arising from the nature of finite realities are from the infinite God, as the fulfillment of norms reaching
man externally and which are up to a point 'external' (if they are
demands of the noumenal subject on concrete freedom) is from the
love in which God's love and that of the subject of freedom become
one: because in the radical freedom of such love the human subject
of freedom really becomes completely aware of itself and not merely
of a norm from outside; because in this love God gives himself and
does not merely authenticate a norm distinct in its content from
himself; and because in this self-communication of his he makes
possible our love for him, sustains it and so liberates it that it really
attains God himself and does not collapse into its own finiteness at
an infinite distance from him. For a Christian understanding law and
righteousness are in the first place quite disparate factors.

It can of course rightly be said that this God of infinite love imparting himself in this righteousness is in fact the one whose will requires
the observance of individual material moral norms, of 'law', so that
it is only conditionally on the fulfillment of the law that the miracle
occurs of the unity of God and man in righteousness, which is the
love between God and man from within. This, of course, is true. The
thesis according to which fulfillment of the law is made the precondition or the consequence (these two amount to the same thing) of
righteousness as unity of love in no way alters the radical distinction
between law and righteousness, which simply is not the fulfillment
of the law. It is possible, of course, though only by obscuring the
facts, to say that man has a 'commandment' to love God and thus
love of God can be subsumed under fulfillment of the law and made a
part or (if we want) the whole of the righteousness which is the
fulfilling of the law. This kind of language is not simply forbidden to

us by the New Testament, since it is in fact occasionally used there. But it we not only speak of the commandment of love of God, but go further and subsume this commandment under law in general, it is no longer clear that this love of God is not the fulfillment of a law which by its dignity, albeit finite, demands respect and worship for God's greatness, that it is not, in scholastic terms, *religio* rather than love of God; it is not clear that we are speaking of the most immediate closeness of God and man, where there can really be no talk of law, since the legislator outdoes himself by his self-communication and in man's personal love for God every external norm disappears or is surpassed. This love between God and man knows no commandment, is not law in the real sense, since it does not consist in respect for a moral requirement over and above what is materially commanded, since it is this love alone which itself gives content, meaning, and demand.

This dissociation between law and fulfillment of law on the one hand and righteousness as love on the other of course does not dispose of the problems of the relationship between these two ideas. But neither are they disposed of, as we saw, when fulfillment of the law is proclaimed to be the precondition or indispensable consequence of righteousness as unity of love between God and man, using 'precondition' in the sense of a logical and not chronological priority, although only in a certain respect. We then came up against the problem of how exactly the material content of a moral law can be seen to acquire an absolute character from the will of God. We can now state this question more precisely, although this may mean that the answer is thus made all the more difficult. We may ask: Does the absoluteness of particular moral laws consist in the fact that, over and above their objective (but up to a point hypothetical) significance, their fulfillment is a precondition and consequence of the love between God and man? If we commit ourselves to this assumption, if in other words we assume that individual commandments and laws acquire their absolute binding force by the very fact, and only in this sense, that they are the preconditions and consequences of the love between God and man and that without this connection they might express what is reasonable, appropriate, and preferable, but would not be purely and simply absolute, if we assume all this we would certainly make things easier for ourselves by interpreting the absoluteness of law as theonomy. But this would not dispose of the problem indicated earlier: the question, that is, of whether, why, and how God's holy will can endow finite values, which make up the material content of the law, with such a character of absoluteness if these values nevertheless are and remain finite. At least to modern man it is perhaps not so obvious that it is possible to love God only by respecting intramundane norms, when the values they protect seem very finite and consequently relative and to be continually in conflict with one another; when it also seems as if God did not attach too much importance to their realization through blind nature and its antagonisms. Do these finite values, which form the material content of the laws, acquire an absolute character from the will of God because this will as it refers to them is conveyed to us by a positive revelation of God and it is through, and only through, this revelation that these norms acquire their character of absoluteness which otherwise they would not have at all?

It might be possible perhaps to think in this way, even though such an idea of the unity between objective norms and the will of God can scarcely be reconciled with the traditional doctrine of natural law, since this doctrine ascribes to natural law an absolute binding force, independently of a properly supernatural revelation. But even if we thought we had overcome this difficulty, a great deal would still be far from clear. In the first place it is certainly not yet clear how an absolute will of God, even though now understood as expressly revealed, can be linked with finite values and material norms in such a way that the norms asserting these values become absolute commandments of God and an infringement of them becomes really an offence against God as such. The question would also arise as to how a revelation properly speaking can really be directly related to such material norms, which belong to the world as such, if we have a correct idea of supernatural revelation, which does not permit each and every thing that is objectively right to be made a possible object of an actual revelation (unless God *wanted* to reveal something of this kind). It is clear that a divine revelation can be and is related to God's self-communication in grace and the incarnation of the Logos to man's transcendentality and history, since this is what can be communicated only by God himself and not by setting up a finite creaturely reality, which is distinct from God. But, if their real nature is understood in the way indicated, it is not clear that intramundane norms can also be the object of such divine revelation.

It is easy to see that in the light of this understanding of revelation in the properly Christian sense the Old Testament history of revelation and the Old Testament itself as a book create a serious problem, since the essentially New Testament self-communication of God in Jesus, the Word made man and in the Holy Spirit as God himself, had not then occurred. An attempt might be made to overcome these dilemmas by assuming that actual divine revelation occurs *always and everywhere* by God's inward grace, offered to every human being always and everywhere, so that revelation properly speaking as God's self-communication is present unthematically, and in a sense anonymously of course, also in the sphere of the Old Testament, where it can convey the character of absoluteness to the old law and from that standpoint (that is, in the light of God's self-communication as grace and revelation offered to all always and everywhere, even apart from an explicit, thematic, and verbal revelation) the character of absoluteness of the law can be experienced. This would bring us once more to the basic problem of why and how God's holy will, now seen as God's gracious and revealing self-communication, is connected with finite values and thus gives them the character of an absolute obligation. I must admit that the answer to this question, which in fact is identical with the question of the connection between law and justification, is not clear.

Is this connection to be established directly in a general way by saying that the holy God, who imparts himself in his most intimate reality in justifying us, is identical with God the Creator who must demand respect for the structures of reality, since he himself willed them and therefore cannot enter into any loving union with the human subject of freedom if the latter does not respect this will of his? But against this explanation the objection might perhaps be raised: Is this will of God, as related to something finite and relative and often to what is antagonistic to other realities, so absolute that the absolute purely and simply (which is God in himself and in his self-communication) depends on respect for it? We might also be tempted to shift off the solution of the dilemma into a more subjective dimension by saying that in every human life there are constantly concrete situations in which a person knows that he cannot in practice and concretely synthesize the rejection of a particular intramundane finite value of a normative character with an absolute and unconditional openness to God himself, who wants to bestow on him his own reality. But it is still by no means clear in the concrete individual case why this discrepancy and incompatibility can exist and does exist between the rejection of a finite value and the acceptance of God's self-communication. But I think there is nothing to prevent the assumption of an individual revelation, not only making known this discrepancy but also setting it up, a revelation which need not be regarded as striking or miraculous, but would simply be part of the concreteness of God, who according to Christian belief imparts himself in any case at the heart of our existence. If this teaching is concerned, not with God abstractly, as being, but with a God of personal freedom approaching the individual as such on each occasion, the doctrine of an individual revelation making what is right in intramundane terms something absolutely willed by God here and now (that is, actually connected indissolubly with his self-communication) would not be more surprising or incredible than the doctrine of a general revelation.

We cannot pursue further here this problem of the relationship between law and justification as reconciliation with God himself. The distinction between the two factors (stressed by Protestant theology) and the connection between these two distinct factors (to which Catholic theology attaches more importance) are both facts which must be clearly seen and realized in Christian life. Human morality has something to do with our relationship to God, and this relationship of unifying love between God and man is something quite different from a man's moral worth which is recognized and rewarded by a Lord of the world.

It is time to point out, at least in a sentence, that we have not hitherto spoken about one aspect of our theme as a whole: namely, that justification in biblical and ecclesiastical usage implies also forgiveness of sin, granted to the sinner by God's free grace, while the initiative in this forgiveness lies exclusively with God and the renewed turning of the sinner to God itself the effect of this divine initiative. But although this aspect of forgiveness of sin would also help to elucidate the radical distinction between righteousness on the one hand and law and fulfillment of law as such on the other, it cannot be further considered here.

A more important consideration must be put forward in conclusion. Hitherto we treated this relationship of law and justification as if it were static, remaining invariably the same. But this is not so. This relationship itself has a history; the two factors involved do not always occupy the same existential place in a person's life and consequently their mutual relationship has a history. Before attempting to say something about this history, we might look at the general history of salvation and revelation. Paul at any rate (to put it cautiously) was acutely sensitive to the historicity of this relationship, to the dividing line drawn by the cross of Christ across this history. It marks a dividing line at least because on the cross the victory of the free grace of God bestowing righteousness over a mere fulfillment of the law took place and was declared irreversible. Nevertheless, this general history of the relationship between law and righteousness is also something that cannot be further considered here. But we may attempt to glance at the particular history of this relationship in the life of the individual.

In the life of the individual, too, there can and should occur this victory of God-given righteousness, of grace, over the sacred dignity of the law which summons and overtaxes man. In the history of his existence a person will normally begin with the experience of the sacred dignity and the claim of the law on him. Even this experience is of essential importance and turns man from an ingeniously selfish living being with knowledge and social training into a person who exercises his freedom responsibly; it is this in the first place that gives man his dignity and his inalienable responsibility. The experience of the moral subject with his moral autonomy, as it was made clear particularly in the ethos of the Enlightenment, is an experience which man cannot renounce and which even today he cannot shrug off by pointing to all the internal and external, psychological, depth-psychological, and sociological determinants to which he is exposed. But the experience of the moral subject (which of course varies greatly with individuals, with their very different opportunities and at different phases of life) is no more than the beginning of religious experience. The law that created and confirmed man's lofty dignity slowly becomes an oppressive burden, a law that makes excessive demands. Slowly we get the impression that we do not know exactly what is really required of us, the impression that the law's demands force us into insoluble dilemmas, the impression that it overtaxes us and thrusts us into sin, leaving man to sink again into the still undrained morass of his shortsightedness and his selfishness. We also feel increasingly that all the splendour of the morally good as man's achievement is very finite, very ambiguous, very selective (where there should be no selection, but complete righteousness), that it becomes pale, until eventually we do not really know if all this splendour of morality does not fade out in the unconsciousness of the history of nature.

In brief, man experiences the finiteness also of what is humanly moral, and this experience is not disposed of by saying that the decisive factor is not the formal dignity of the law as external norm, but that to which this formal normativity protectively points: beauty, love, fidelity to truth, etc. For even a law understood in this way and even under God's sanction remains a law of finite man, a law of finite goodness. But in man there is an experience of an infinite claim, even though he cannot authenticate this for himself, a claim that is not satisfied by the finite reality of his fulfillment of the moral law. But man thus comes slowly to experience the secret hope, almost in fear of itself, that, despite the finiteness of human morality and despite what for us is irremoveable guilt, there is a fulfillment of our own existence, an infinite fulfillment that we call God, a righteousness that does not come from us and does not suffer from our finiteness. If this experience continually grows, is increasingly radically accepted by freedom, is increasingly obviously spread over existence as a whole, then our relationship to the moral law is changed. The law is surpassed by this experience, the overtaxing and always overexacting obligation from outside is slowly dissolved into a want and capacity from within, into the inward law of love that the Holy Spirit writes in our hearts (as Ignatius of Loyola says), its fulfillment is turned from an achievement of respecting a holy law from outside into the utterance of a love which, since it possesses God himself, is not a law and lives in the freedom of God himself.

This transformation of course does not take place suddenly and all at once; it is completed only when man has left *everything* in the renunciation of death and in this emptiness receives without mediation the infinite mystery that is God. But, even though it is found at different stages with different individuals, this process of transformation of the holy law (that is not God himself) is following its course from the outset in every human being. The theoretical dialectic between law and righteousness and the history of the relationship between law and righteousness, as it happens and is documented in the wider religious history of humanity, in the history of revelation, in the books of the Old and the New Testament, is no more than a reflection of the history of this relationship as it occurs in the heart of every human being when he slowly turns from being a sinner and a doer of the law into a person justified by God himself, someone who beyond all legal justice receives the life, the holiness, the freedom of God, who is infinitely above all laws. When God, as promised in Jeremiah (31:33), plants his law *deep within* man, writes it in his *heart;* when, as Ezekiel promises (36:26), a new heart and a new spirit is given us instead of a heart of stone, when the law, as Paul says (2 Cor. 3:3) is not written on stone tablets, but by the Spirit of the living God on the tablets of our hearts themselves, then there is no problem between law and righteousness, then the law is fulfilled by a fulfillment that is no longer God's law, but God himself.

17

ON THE IMPORTANCE OF
THE NON-CHRISTIAN RELIGIONS
FOR SALVATION

The theme presented to me runs: The importance of the non-Christian religions for salvation.

Here, in this question (as distinct from *Nostra aetate* of the Second Vatican Council), the term 'non-Christian religions' must be understood as excluding the Jewish religion and Islam, since the Old Testament contains part of that divine revelation which Christianity regards as its own and Islam is related expressly at least to Christian revelation as a whole. In these reflections a systematic theologian can obviously speak only of what lies within his own field. Consequently he cannot incorporate into his reflections what the empirical sciences of religion, especially history of religion and phenomenology of religion, can contribute to this theme. What is to be said here must therefore inevitably remain very abstract and formal. In the last resort it amounts only to an inquiry in regard to these sciences as to whether they can really discover historically and concretely in the individual religions what the systematic theologian thinks he can find there at least partially and imperfectly. If the systematic theologian, the dogmatic theologian, puts this request to the historical sciences of religion, working with their *a posteriori* method, in order not to exceed the limits of his own competence, what he is doing is only analogous to what the dogmatic theologian expects from the fundamental theologian in the light of the Catholic understanding of the relationship between faith and human experience; his request therefore cannot be *a priori* rejected as impossible or unreasonable;

on the contrary, it gives the dogmatic theologian a better right and a better conscience to keep within the limits of his own competence.

For the dogmatic theologian *Nostra aetate* is on the one hand a precious guide and on the other hand leaves to him what is theologically the ultimate and essential question as a *quaestio disputata*. For a variety of reasons this declaration of the Second Vatican Council is an important aid for the dogmatic theologian. The declaration begins with an aspect that the Church had not presented with this clarity before Vatican II. There is a relationship of the Church to the non-Christian religions as such (that is, as concrete sociological realities with their doctrinal structures and their life as such) and not only a relationship to non-Christian individuals. Moreover, the declaration by no means presents its theme from the standpoint of how the Church in its own self-understanding is distinct as a unique force from all other religious communions. This customary apologetic-missionary aspect is deliberately omitted here. The motif of the declaration is taken, not from the missionary command, but from the Church's task 'of fostering unity and love among men, and even among nations'. The council does not for that reason raise doubts either about the Church's self-understanding as the presence of the fullness of revelation or about its pressing obligation to engage in missionary activity. But the council opens up a perspective of a greater tranquillity in its mission and in a missionary method which permits a patient and positive co-existence of the Church with the other religious communions and a dialogue with the latter as such. The council sees the basis for this relationship in the universal salvific will of the sovereign and benevolent God, the author of the universal history of salvation, lasting from the beginning to the final consummation and not abolished even by sin. The declaration recognizes what is 'true' and 'holy' in the different religions and that the concrete forms and doctrines of these religions are to be regarded with straightforward seriousness. The declaration sees the ultimate root of these religions in the quest for an answer to the unsolved riddle of human existence and in a certain perception and acknowledgment of that hidden power which is present in the course of the world and in the events of human life. In a word, the council invites us to take seriously the non-Christian religions as such.

In view of the limited scope of our theme *here,* the question can be left aside as to whether the far too brief descriptions of Hinduism

and Buddhism are beyond all doubt and whether too little attention
has been given to other religions among non-Christians, especially
among the culturally less developed peoples. On the other hand it
must be said (although this is not meant as a criticism of the declaration) that the essential problem for the theologian has been left open.
In the Constitution on the Church (no. 16), in the Decree on Missionary Activity (no. 7), in the Pastoral Constitution on the Church
in the Modern World (no. 22), it is said that even a person whom the
historical message of Christianity has not reached, even an atheist,
can be without fault and thus touched ('in ways known to God') by
God's redeeming grace, can have a salvific *faith* in the proper sense
of the term and so can gain salvation. Consequently it is really
obvious that effects of this inward possession, even in the 'heathen',
of the authentic content of salvation, acknowledged in a spirit of
vast optimism, must be found in the religions themselves in which
such a person concretely lives out his relationship to God. But this
conclusion from the premises of the council is not drawn by the
council in *Nostra aetate*. In this declaration the properly theological
quality of the non-Christian religions remains undefined. Are they
religious constructs which human beings themselves in virtue of
their 'naturally' religious inclinations, albeit under a certain salvific
providence of God, have created with all the limitations and debase-
ments which are attached to such human achievements?

Are they (as institutions and doctrines) merely 'religion' as opposed to 'faith'? If in these and other passages the council admits
that properly salvific faith is possible in principle even in pagans and
atheists, does this mean that it is achieved only outside the life of
these religions as such—for instance, fidelity in the dictates of conscience, in love of neighbour, etc.—so that acts within the sphere of
these non-Christian religions as such are not effective of salvation?
Or can such acts, achieved *within* the non-Christian religions *as
such*, perhaps be evaluated as salvific acts? Despite the depravities
occurring there, is it possible to regard the history of these non-
Christian religions as a part of the history of revelation properly so-
called? Is the contrast between revelation and faith from above on
the one hand and religion from below on the other hand terminologi-
cally correct, but only in the sense that the real religions from below
are always (although in very different ways and to a different extent)
also determined by revelation and faith from above? Understand-

ably, *Nostra aetate* gives us no information about these questions. But they are of the greatest importance for a theological appreciation and interpretation of the history of religion, of the right approach to missionary work. In more than a millennium of struggle theology has overcome Augustinian pessimism in regard to the salvation of the individual and reached the optimism of the Second Vatican Council, assuring supernatural salvation in the immediate possession of God to all those who do not freely reject it through their own personal fault; our question now must be whether theology can regard the non-Christian religions with the same optimism. In order to get further with this question, the systematic theologian must consider several things which admittedly are themselves disputed or disputable theologoumena and can be treated only very briefly here.

A doctrine of God's universal and supernatural salvific will and other reasons lead to a theory of the relationship of grace on the one hand and man, mankind, and its history on the other which sees this grace (if it is to be brought at all within the traditional systems) more as 'habitual' than as 'actual'. 'Habitual' of course does not mean here *that* state of grace in which grace is accepted by man's free consent. It means grace seen as present from the outset, as offered to freedom, as we generally think of it, for example, as 'habitual' in the baptized infant. When textbook theology considers supernatural grace (as possibility of faith, hope, and love), seen there also as possible even before baptism and outside an explicitly Christian situation, it always assumes that this occurs at isolated points of time, here and there in particular situations. But this grace need not be seen as 'actual' to that extent. Notwithstanding its supernaturality and unmeritedness, it can certainly be seen as a permanent existential of man, of mankind and its history, always and everywhere present, as permanently present possibility of a salvific relationship of freedom to God, as innermost entelechy of the history of the individual and of mankind as a whole, in which the unmerited gracious self-communication of God to the world is the ultimate finality and dynamism of the world and world history, whether the human freedom of any particular individual accepts this innermost entelechy or closes itself up against it.

This endowment of the world and its history with grace, thus understood as 'habitual' by the very nature of grace as supernatural finality of the transcendentality of mind-in-world, is always also the most fundamental event of revelation, since it opens up this transcendentality toward the immediacy of God, whether this is made explicit and objectified or not. Because of this the history of supernatural revelation and the history of supernatural salvation are necessarily co-extensive and co-existent. What we generally call history of revelation and history of faith is therefore the history of the *acceptance* and *objectification* of this innermost deification of the world offered to freedom, which is also an offer of salvation and revelation and a permanent existential of humanity and its history. This 'habitual' existential is nothing other than the reality of God's universal salvific will, which should not be seen as a mere intention of God existing 'inwardly' in him, which is objectified as 'actual' grace only here and there in the world. All that has just been said ought of course as such to be more clearly developed and substantiated. But for the moment this must suffice. Even where it is really present, history of revelation is not *a priori* immune from the possibility of not being fully objectified in objectification and deed by man's reflective knowledge and his freedom, and of being debased in a way contrary to its innermost nature. It is only the history of salvation and revelation in and after Jesus Christ as the eschatological and unsurpassable Word of God, by which God has irreversibly promised himself to the world in *historical* tangibility, that excludes and renders obsolete an ultimate denial by human freedom of the grace-given existentiality of history.

The thesis of the imperfection or even the possible failure of a genuine history of revelation is implied for Christian theology by its teaching on the failure of the Old Covenant and the rejection of the Messiah by the institutional religion of ancient Israel. It is also evident from the whole history of the Old Covenant, in which the incompatibility between the people of God as they actually were with their religious institutions on the one hand and the claim of God represented by the prophets on the other hand was continually present. But this Old Testament history of revelation in particular *before* the coming of the salvation-bringer in Jesus Christ shows that a concrete, verbalized, and institutionalized religion cannot be regarded *a priori* and in principle as either *pure* objectification of the grace and revelation of God, or as the absolute rejection of this offer by God of himself, or as merely a religion 'from below'. The history of the Old Testament shows that an institutionalized religion as objectification of divine revelation in social life can in the last resort appear to human eyes to be no more than an indissoluble mixture of both divine revelation with its sociological institutionalization and also blockages of further development and debasement of this revelation and its history. At the same time it must be remembered that, if we Christians today regard and apply the Old Testament canon as an unambiguous norm for what God willed in the Old Covenant and what was contrary to his will, we are using a criterion which the people of the Old Covenant simply did not possess completely and as clearly defined before Jesus Christ and were thus faced with a question that they could by no means answer adequately and with certainty. For these people the origin of their religion from God was a factor that was no easier to determine than it was for people of other religions. They could neither simply accept the actual reality of Old Testament history as entirely caused by God nor could they reject it outright, nor had they an institutionally established criterion of a permanent character in the light of which they could distinguish with certainty between what came from God in the Old Covenant and what was merely a transient phenomenon or a debasement of what God had effected. But if that is true even of the Old Covenant, then it may be regarded as true particularly of non-Christian religious objectifications and institutions. These are not to be regarded either entirely as objectification of divine revelation and grace or merely as a human invention from below or purely and simply as an evil perversion of divine revelation.

A third point must be made. If, according to Vatican II, an opportunity of supernatural salvation and the opportunity of a real faith in revelation is offered always and everywhere to every human being at all times; if revelation properly so-called is not possible without faith in the strict sense and must be offered always and everywhere (and in this connection it is not possible after Vatican II to have recourse to a *fides virtualis* as substitute for actual revelation and faith), then such a revelation and such a faith, whose intrinsic possibilities in the subject we cannot explain at greater length here, occur *concretely* and *on the whole* only by the mediation of those categorial, institutional, and verbal realities which we know as non-Christian religions. In man, his transcendental, mental, and supernatural relationship to God is always mediated by categorial realities of his life, and in the last resort the most sublime and formless mysticism is no exception to this. This categorial mediation of the transcendental relationship of man to God—that is, of the acceptance of the openness of the mind to God in freedom radicalized by faith, an openness we know as faith, hope, and love—can certainly occur also through categorial objectivities (as far as the individual act of this kind is concerned) which are not explicitly religious. For Vatican II, accordingly, there are circumstances where such a mediation exists (for example, an atheist who is faithful to his conscience) which is certainly not thematicized in an explicitly religious way. But since the view cannot be maintained that explicit, verbalized, and institutional religiousness can be irrelevant to man's relationship to God in human life as a whole, this verbalized and institutionalized explicit religious factor certainly cannot be denied this categorial mediatory role for the totality of human life and of mankind. At any rate, a person to whom such a religious factor (of whatever kind) is actually offered in his life and accepted by him in freedom can obviously apply and will in fact apply that factor as a categorial mediation of his relationship to God, unless it is absolutely contrary to the latter. Catholic moral theology, however, admits that an objectivity objectively and as such opposed to God's will can nevertheless mediate a positive moral act; it must consequently be recognized that such objectivities may in principle be ways of mediating positive religious acts, even though objectively and implicitly they are in a certain sense opposed to God. It is, for example, quite possible for a polytheist to act positively in regard to the true, absolute God, for whom in his objective, verbalized consciousness he finds a name from his polytheistic pantheon. In their institutions and theoretical objectifications non-Christian religions can be categorial mediations of genuine salvific acts, both because they always retain some truth (at least the postulate of a transcendentality of man beyond the field of his immediate experience) and also because even false and debased religious objectivity can be a way of mediating a genuine and grace-given transcendentality of man.

Non-Christian religions then, even though incomplete, rudimentary, and partially debased, can be realities *within* a *positive* history of salvation and revelation. They are able admittedly to overcome their ambivalence (between objectification of God's first and last self-communication to the world as grace and revelation on the one hand

and the incompleteness and debasement of this objectification to the point of an absolute existential rejection of God's self-communication on the other hand) and to reach a final discernment of spirits only in the light of Jesus Christ as eschatological Word of God. But this is true also of the Old Testament and, to a lesser extent which cannot be precisely defined here, can be true of non-Christian religions, to which as such therefore a positive salvific function cannot be *a priori* and entirely denied.

Here the systematic theologian must stop and hand over the question to the historian of religion working on experience. At this point the systematic theologian can at most draw the attention of the historian of religion (if the latter wants to work not simply historically, but also up to a point in terms of 'fundamental theology') to certain aspects from which he might consider this history of religion and which might perhaps otherwise escape him. The systematic theologian might, for example, ask the historian of religion if he cannot discover in a concrete and religious form those 'sacraments of nature' which the dogmatic theologian postulates in the abstract and acknowledges as important for salvation. He could offer the empiricist fundamental insights perhaps revealing in and under an apparently solid polytheism a genuine relationship to the absolute God. He could show him that it is not *a priori* forbidden to discover genuine supernatural mysticism in the 'mysticism' of religions of higher cultures, even when this extra-Christian 'mysticism' is not itself by any means thematicized in an explicitly religious form. In a word (and this has largely not happened and is not possible here) the systematic theologian could offer viewpoints and a framework to the historian of religion which would make it easier for the latter, even in all the diversity and sometimes terrible debasement of extra-Christian religions, to discover that God's grace is always and everywhere active for man's salvation and its salvific power, although obscurely and imperfectly, also manifested in the non-Christian religions, making them ways of salvation by which human beings approach God and his Christ.

LIST OF SOURCES

YESTERDAY'S HISTORY OF DOGMA AND THEOLOGY FOR TOMORROW
Published in *Zeitschrift für katholische Theologie* 99 (1977), pp. 1–24, under the title 'Dogmen- und Theologiegeschichte—gestern und morgen'.

PSEUDO-PROBLEMS IN ECUMENICAL DISCUSSION
Lecture on 27 August 1977 at the Seventh Ecumenical Congress of Jesuits, 24–27 August 1977, in Frankfurt/Main.

MAGISTERIUM AND THEOLOGY
Lecture on 10 March 1977 in West Berlin at the Catholic Academy of Berlin.

ON BAD ARGUMENTS IN MORAL THEOLOGY
Published in the Festschrift for Bernhard Häring: *In Libertatem vocati estis: Miscellanea Bernhard Häring,* Studia Moralia SV, ed. H. Boelaars and R. Tremblay (Academia Alfonsiana, Rome 1977), pp. 245–57.

THE HUMAN QUESTION OF MEANING IN FACE OF THE ABSOLUTE MYSTERY OF GOD
Lecture on 20 November 1977 at the University of Bamberg, published in *Geist und Leben* 50 (1977), pp. 436–50.

ONENESS AND THREEFOLDNESS OF GOD IN DISCUSSION WITH ISLAM
Lecture on 31 May 1977 in St Gabriel's, Mödling bei Wien.

DIALOGUE WITH GOD?
Published as a contribution to the Festschrift for Johannes B. Lotz, SJ, on the occasion of his seventieth birthday, 2 August 1973: *Der Mensch vor dem Anspruch der Wahrheit und der Freiheit,* ed. J. de Vries and W. Brugger (Frankfurt/Main 1973), pp. 229–38; also in K. Rahner, *Wagnis des Christen* (Freiburg 1974), pp. 84–95.

THE DEATH OF JESUS AND THE CLOSURE OF REVELATION
Lecture at the International Congress of Passionists in Rome, 15–18 October 1975.

WHAT DOES IT MEAN TODAY TO BELIEVE IN JESUS CHRIST?
Lecture on 18 May 1976 in Innsbruck for the Katholisches Bildungswerk, Tyrol.

FOLLOWING THE CRUCIFIED
Lecture on 14 March 1978 in the Cathedral of Mainz.

EXPERIENCE OF TRANSCENDENCE FROM THE STANDPOINT OF
   CHRISTIAN DOGMATICS
Lecture on 11 February 1977 in Vienna at a symposium on the experience of tran-
scendence, published in *Transzendenzerfahrung, Vollzugshorizont des Heils. Das
Problem in indischer und christlicher Tradition. Arbeitsdokumentation eines Sympo-
siums*, ed. G. Oberhammer (Vienna 1978), pp. 137–49.

EXPERIENCE OF THE HOLY SPIRIT
This meditation was given on Pentecost, 26 May 1976, in the Catholic Academy of
Bavaria; publication followed under the title *Erfahrung des Geistes* (Freiburg 1977),
pp. 9–63.

FAITH AS COURAGE
Lecture on 19 September 1975 in Berne, published under the same title in the series
Theologische Meditationen, ed. H. Kung (Zurich 1976).

CHRISTIAN DYING
Published in *Mysterium Salutis, Grundriss heilsgeschichtlicher Dogmatik, Zwischen-
zeit und Vollendung der Heilsgeschichte*, Volume 5, ed. J. Feiner and M. Löhrer
(Zurich 1976), pp. 463–92.

JUSTIFICATION AND WORLD DEVELOPMENT FROM A CATHOLIC
   VIEWPOINT
Lecture on 20 April 1977 in Mainz in a series on the theme of 'Justification', arranged
by the Department of the History of Western Religion of the Institute for European
History, 1976/1977, published in the Festschrift for Peter Meinhold: *Die Einheit der
Kirche*, ed. L. Hein (Wiesbaden 1977), pp. 445–56.

LAW AND RIGHTEOUSNESS IN THE CATHOLIC UNDERSTANDING
Lecture on 7 March 1978 in Munich for the Society for Christian-Jewish Collabora-
tion.

ON THE IMPORTANCE OF THE NON-CHRISTIAN RELIGIONS FOR
   SALVATION
Lecture at the International Congress of Missiology, 5–12 October 1975, in Rome.
The general theme of the congress was 'Evangelization and Culture.'

INDEX OF PERSONS

INDEX OF SUBJECTS